SIR JOHN PLUMB

The Hidden Life of a Great Historian

SIR JOHN PLUMB

The Hidden Life of a Great Historian

A Personal Memoir by Neil McKendrick

EER
Edward Everett Root Publishers, 2019

EER
Edward Everett Root, Publishers, Co. Ltd.,
30 New Road, Brighton, Sussex, BN1 1BN, England.

Details of our overseas distributors and how to order our books can be seen on our website.
www.eerpublishing.com
edwardeverettroot@yahoo.co.uk

Sir John Plumb. The Hidden Life of a Great Historian. A Personal Memoir
By Neil McKendrick.
First published in Great Britain in 2019.
© Neil McKendrick 2019.
This edition © Edward Everett Root Publishers 2019
ISBN 978-1-911454-83-0 Hardback
ISBN 978-1-911454-86-1 ebook

Cover and Production by Head & Heart Book Design.

This memoir is dedicated to my wife, Melveena McKendrick,
and to our daughters, Olivia and Cornelia, who all
witnessed at first hand and for many years
the Marmite character and
personality
of
Sir John Plumb.

CONTENTS

ILLUSTRATIONS

* Illustrations can be found between pages 132 and 133

1. INTRODUCTION

This book is a very personal attempt to delineate in some detail the life and career of Sir John Plumb. It tells the story of a fascinating and controversial individual who believed in living both his multi-faceted career and his bisexual life to the full. It attempts to shed new light (much of it very surprising and known only to his closest friends) on a man who lived a life often shrouded in secrecy and often embellished and improved upon by his fertile and creative imagination.

It was a life that, in fact, needed little embellishment to make it unusually interesting. His character was sufficiently beguiling and sufficiently intriguing to attract the attention of four novelists. It has been claimed that, between them, they left six vivid fictional versions of him. They are, to say the least, not all unambiguously flattering. They depict him as ruthlessly ambitious, engagingly self-aggrandising, and successfully upwardly mobile. They also depict him as a highly intelligent, highly entertaining, life-enhancing, multi-talented individual and as an endearingly self-congratulatory lover, of both sexes. One of them even bizarrely portrays him as an academic fraud and a murderer planning further murders.

Jack Plumb's life began on one of the lowest rungs of the social ladder and ended being spent among those on the highest. It started in a humble red brick two-up-two-down terrace house in the back streets of Leicester where his father was a "clicker" in a local shoe factory and where he was (most unusually) wet-nursed by a friend of his mother. It ended amongst the smart set of London and New York and as a friend of the English aristocracy and a familiar of the Royal family – invited to stay as a guest of the Queen at Sandringham, invited as a guest to the Prince Charles and Diana wedding and frequently invited to spend holidays on the beach with Princess Margaret on the Caribbean island of Mustique.

An equally remarkable rise up his career ladder began with a humiliating rejection by Cambridge, after turning up for his interview at St John's misguidedly wearing a bowler hat (the headgear of the un-amused college porters), and ended up as Master of Christ's College with a knighthood, a Cambridge professorship, a Fellowship of the British Academy, a Litt.D. and seven Honorary degrees amongst many other accolades.

His financial situation started as that of a poor working-class boy, unable to afford the place reluctantly offered to him at Cambridge when he failed to get the scholarship he needed, and progressed to a life as a young don so hard-up as to need to ask for windfall apples from his mother's garden to be sent up to Cambridge. Yet he finished his career as a multi-millionaire, able to give away millions as a result of the huge royalties earned by his writing.

His political sympathies changed as dramatically as his financial fortunes. In the 1930s, he was an ardent Communist sympathiser (some say that he was a card-carrying member of the Party); in the 1960s he was an almost besotted supporter of Harold Wilson and the Labour Party; by the 1980s he had moved so far to the Right that he often criticised his new heroes, Thatcher and Tebbitt, as being "timid pinkoes". When confronted with the appalled reactions of his old liberal friends, he smugly replied, "there's no rage like the rage of the convert".

His teaching career in Cambridge started as someone not thought grand or distinguished enough to teach Christ's undergraduates and finished as the acclaimed mentor of probably the most remarkable stable of successful students and colleagues from any single college in either Oxford or Cambridge. Many of them went on to follow his path to academic eminence and popular acclaim. They included Sir Simon Schama, Roy Porter, Quentin Skinner, John Vincent, John Burrow, Joachim Whaley, Norman Stone, Geoffrey Parker, Jonathan Steinberg, David Reynolds, Niall Ferguson, Sir David Cannadine, Linda Colley and many others.

His war-service, spent in code-breaking secrecy at Bletchley in Hut 4 and Hut 6, started in a scruffy anonymous wartime lodging, and ended up (as a result of his gallant and explosive response to a snide anti-Semitic comment about Yvonne de Rothschild) as the only, and much indulged, lodger of the Rothschilds, spending his evenings drinking their finest first growth clarets.

His writing career was so delayed that he was nearly forty when he produced his first significant book but so productive that over the next twenty-five years he published forty-four books bearing his name either as editor or sole author. He was at the same time a hugely prolific journalist in both Britain and the United States. By then he had earned the reputation of being one of the most widely-read living historians.

His first efforts at publication were rejected, first a novel and then a learned article. His PhD dissertation was also regarded as not worth publishing and his early research was dismissed as very disappointing. Yet the prose in his later work was to earn the praise of novelists of the calibre of Grahame Greene, C. P. Snow and Angus Wilson, and its influence was regarded as so pervasive in the States that, on the direct order of the President and a unanimous vote in Congress, the Union flag was flown over the American Capitol in his honour to mark his 80th birthday and to recognise a man whose writing had taught the American people so much.

It was not only as a teacher and a writer that he excelled. It must have been a pleasing irony to him in his mature years that the aspiring writer, who had had his first literary efforts rejected by editors and publishers alike, should eventually come to control a dazzling portfolio of editorial appointments himself. Those appointments led to a huge array of significant publications with an impressive cast of distinguished authors and distinguished publishers. The list of books he commissioned and promoted arguably ultimately exceeded his own writings. They also helped to boost his enviable income level, as did his prolific and well-paid international journalism.

As a result, even in years of stratospheric tax levels (83% on earned income and 98% on unearned income, at their peak) he was able to enjoy a munificent lifestyle far beyond that of the average don. These were the years when he enjoyed a pleasure-loving lifestyle, as well as a hugely productive one and a much acclaimed one. These were the days of ever more expensive fast cars, and ever more expensive and expansive foreign holidays in Provence, the Algarve and the Caribbean for himself and his friends.

These were the prosperous years when he also bought in profusion: eighteenth-century English silver; seventeenth-century Dutch paintings; and in particular fine wine, which led him to amass the finest private cellar in Cambridge; and, perhaps most notably of all, fine porcelain, which became a finer collection of Vincennes and Sèvres than that in the Fitzwilliam museum.

These were the heady years when he aspired to become Regius Professor of History in Cambridge, President of the British Academy, and ultimately a peer of the realm.

These were the upbeat years when Sir David Cannadine has described him as being "at his Balzacian best" when "he radiated warmth, buoyancy, optimism and hope".

These were the years when he was at his exuberant and inspiring best, attracting and helping to promote his remarkable and unparalleled phalanx of brilliant pupils.

From these dizzying peaks of achievement and acclaim, and even more dizzying peaks of aspiration, there were to follow the years of disappointment and decline and ambitions not achieved. These were the darker years of rage, resentment and recrimination, which saw him in what Cannadine has described as "his more Dostoyevskian mode" when "he was consumed by doubt, loneliness and disappointment".

In old age his private life seemed to offer few compensations. He had always claimed that he had based his life on serial friendships with both sexes. He had always derided marriage. He claimed to have had a daughter but he never recognized her. Without children or grandchildren or a permanent partner to comfort him in his later decades, he began to think that he might have made the wrong choices in his personal life.

The end was the darkest episode of all – a lonely and embittered old age, when, echoing the closing words of his great work on Walpole, "the future would bring the death of friends, the decline of powers, age, sickness and defeat".

Perhaps the grimmest moment of all was the manner of his lonely death, and the even lonelier manner of his burial. At his insistence he was buried without friends or mourners or music, without elegies or eulogies, without even a coffin. For a man who wrote so many elegant words it seems especially stark that no words should mark his passing from this world. For a man who promoted the careers of so many pupils it seems especially sad that he left orders that none should attend.

This book is an attempt to explore the reasons for these dramatic changes of fortune, and to examine the significance of his lasting literary and historical legacy. It also attempts to explain how the man who inspired and charmed so many, infuriated and offended so many others, and why, in consequence, that legacy is as controversial and questionable to some as it is considerable and undeniable to others.

The isolated headstone, which marks his unattended burial spot in its neglected country churchyard, may symbolize his lonely and miserable end, but in the libraries of the world his work lives on in his still sparkling and memorable prose. And many have judged that his ultimate legacy lives on in the form of the many other books alongside his own, written by his many flourishing pupils, some of whom have gone on to match or perhaps even surpass his remarkable achievements as a communicator and populariser of serious academic history.

*** *** *** ***

This book is not a conventional biography of Jack Plumb. Even less is it an academic critique of Plumb's publications. His books are all freely available in the libraries of the world. They can largely be left to speak for themselves. Their author, however, has mainly remained hidden from public scrutiny and this book is designed to lift the veil on an extraordinary character who lived an extraordinary life. It is a very personal memoir and personal memoirs are by definition a collection of memories recorded by one individual from their knowledge of another.

This memoir is inevitably based to a large extent on my own memories, although the story it tells is reinforced by those of many of my friends and colleagues. I make no apology, therefore, if my part of the story seems to some to be disproportionately large. In consequence it can be read in some senses simply as the story of the changing nature of a close friendship between two Cambridge academics that lasted over fifty years.

Its main intention is to do for Plumb what George Otto Trevelyan did for that earlier great historian Macaulay when he wrote "there must be tens of thousands whose interest in history and literature he has awakened and informed by his pen, and who would gladly know what manner of man has done them so great a service". In identifying and describing "what manner of man" Jack Plumb was, it also attempts to put into perspective his academic rivalries, his personal ambitions, his prolific publications, his major role as a editor, his inspiring role as teacher, his role as a promoter of his remarkable school of famous pupils, his role as a war-time code breaker and his achievement as a Master of a Cambridge college.

Most of all it attempts to paint a portrait of a remarkable individual who did so much to change the nature and direction of travel of popular academic history, and seeks to explain why he provoked so much interest and so much controversy amongst novelists, portrait painters, fellow historians and Cambridge colleagues. It depicts a man who climbed very high from very lowly beginnings, but also alas a man who ended his life as a sad, lonely and embittered individual.

2. J.H.PLUMB'S CURRICULUM VITAE

B.A. (London), M.A., Ph.D., Litt.D. (Cambridge), FRHistS., FBA., FSA., FRSL., Hon. Litt.D. (Leicester, East Anglia, Bowdoin College, Southern California, Westminster College, Washington University, St. Louis, Bard College, New York), Honorary Foreign Member of the American Academy of Arts and Sciences, Honorary Member of the Society of American Historians, Honorary Member of American Historical Association.

Education:

Alderman Newton's Boys School, 1923-30

University College Leicester, 1930-33

B.A. (London) 1st Class Honours in History 1933
Cambridge University 1934-2001
Ph.D. (Cambridge) 1936
Litt.D. (Cambridge) 1957

College Career:

Christ's College, Cambridge, matriculated October 1934
Ehrmann Research Fellow, King's College, Cambridge, 1939-46
Christ's College, Cambridge, 1946-2001
Fellow, 1946-2001
Steward, 1948-50
Director of Studies 1949-66
Tutor, 1950-59
Vice-Master, 1964-68
Master, 1978-82

University Career:

University Lecturer in History, 1946-62
Reader in Modern English History, 1962-66
Chairman of the History Faculty, 1966-68
Professor of Modern English History, 1966-74

War-time Career:

Foreign Office, Bletchley 1940-45

Honours and Appointments:

Honorary Foreign Member of the American Academy of Arts and Sciences, 1970
Honorary Member of the Society of American History, 1976
Honorary Member of American Historical Association, 1981
Trustee of the National Portrait Gallery, 1961-82
Syndic of the Fitzwilliam Museum, 1960-77
Trustee of the Fitzwilliam Museum, 1985-92
Member of the Wine Standards Board, 1973-75
Elector of the Wolfson Prize for History, 1974-86
Fellow of the British Academy, 1968-2001
Member of the Council of the British Academy, 1977-80
Chairman of the Centre of East Anglian Studies, 1979-82
Fellow of the Royal Historical Society, 1969
Fellow of the Society of Antiquaries, 1969
Fellow of the Royal Society of Literature, 1969
Visiting Professor at Columbia University, New York, 1960
Distinguished Visiting Professor NYC University, 1971-72
Distinguished Visiting Professor NYC University, 1976
Charles & Ida Green Honours Chair, Texas Christian University, 1974
Distinguished Visiting Professor, Washington University, 1977
Knighthood, 1982

Lectures:

Ford Lectures, University of Oxford, 1965-66
Saposnekov Lectures City College, New York, 1968
Guy Stanton Ford Lecture, University of Minnesota, 1966
The Stenton Lecture, University of Reading, 1977
George Rogers Clark Lecture, Society of Cincinnati, 1977

Honorary Degrees:

Hon. D.Litt. University of Leicester 1968
Hon. D.Litt. University of East Anglia 1977
Hon. D.Litt. Bowdoin College, U.S.A. 1974
Hon. D.Litt. University of Southern California 1978
Hon. D.Litt. Westminster College, U.S.A. 1983
Hon. D.Litt. Washington University, St. Louis 1983
Hon. D.Litt. Bard College, New York 1988

Editing:

Editor of the History of Human Society, 1957-1978
Editor of the Fontana History of Europe, 1957-1997
Senior Editor of American Heritage, 1957-1982
Historical Advisor, Penguin Books, 1960-91
Editor of Pelican Social History of Britain, 1982-91
Editor of the Library of World Biography for Little Brown of Boston, 1972
Editing work for British Museum Publications

Festschrift:

Historical Perspectives: Studies in English Thought and Society in Honour of J. H. Plumb, edited and introduced by Neil McKendrick (1974)

3. PREFACE
JACK PLUMB: A PERSONAL
MEMOIR FROM 1949 TO 2001

"When we encounter a natural style we are always astonished and delighted, for we expected to see an author and found a man."

- Pascal

This is an informal and very personal, and necessarily incomplete biographical memoir of Sir John Plumb. Professor Sir David Cannadine has already offered the best critical summing up of his importance to English historiography in *History Today* and has added further important insights in his formal assessment in *The Proceedings of the British Academy*. Professor Sir Simon Schema has produced the most affectionate appreciation of his role in keeping alive the traditions of history as literature in *The Independent*, and Professor Niall Ferguson has written a formal assessment of his work as an introduction to a new edition of Plumb's *The Death of the Past*. This offering is an attempt to record some more personal insights about his life and work and character.

I have known Jack Plumb since I was thirteen. I first met him when I sailed as a cabin boy with the Green Wyvern Yacht Club in Easter 1949 – even then he was clearly very different from the other sailors. He was more interesting, more entertaining and much more demanding. He was a Cambridge don, an as yet largely unpublished historian, an exceptional cook, and a frantically competitive sailor who made up for any technical deficiencies in his sailing skills by picking and later buying the fastest boat, choosing the best crew and making sure that they were up early enough to leave before everyone else – arguing persuasively that this would ensure us the choice of the best mooring for the night and the longest period of drinking in the pub. In those days, bitter beer was his chosen tipple (a taste largely abandoned in the late 1960s), cigarettes his drug of choice (a habit given up in the 1950s) and serious wine drinking was still mainly preserved for his more sophisticated friends. The sailing club was a school and university-based society. It sailed as a flotilla of yachts, each of which housed often highly competitive crews of about five or six schoolboys, Old Boys, schoolmasters and an assortment of guests, the most memorable in my time being Pat Moynihan (later U.S. Secretary of Labour Moynihan, Ambassador Moynihan and Senator Moynihan) who effortlessly drank everyone under the table.

Being chosen to crew for Jack was a mixed blessing – his boats were chosen or bought for speed rather than comfort, but everything that money could buy was employed to make the week's sailing a memorable experience. His fastest boat, *Sabrina*, was dismissively nick-named "The Gilded Canoe" by those sailing in the larger, heavier, sturdier boats which trailed more sluggishly in its wake; his food was disdained as the product of the "Garlic Galley"; and his fellow sailors were pitied as the galley slaves in Plumb's forced labour crew. I felt that the cooking and the speed and the conversation more than made up for the shouting and the cursing and the incessant insistence on maintaining our competitive edge. It was a good introduction to Jack's teaching methods in Cambridge – on board his yacht, as in supervisions in Christ's, he saw his role as part teacher, part father-figure and part tyrant.

Having known him for over fifty years and having seen him within hours of his death I feel that I have gained some insights into the man.

Having observed the full curve of his adult career, I can claim to know him pretty well.

I came from a very similar background. I lived in the same Leicester street that he did, went to the same grammar school, was even taught by the same two history masters there some quarter of a century after he was. He taught me and directed my studies for three years in Christ's. He was even – very briefly – my tutor. I shared a staircase with him in the First Court for five years (three as an undergraduate, one and half as a graduate student, and half as a Research Fellow). I can, I feel, fairly be described as both a product of the Plumb school of history and a product of the history school which produced Plumb.

My family and I also shared a house with him in Suffolk for over thirty years. I wrote a book with him. I edited his *festschrift*, worked on "Plumb's century" and discussed his work with him on a daily basis during the most productive years of his life. I have been asked to give innumerable speeches in his honour and he, in return, spoke as the best man at my wedding. My family and I took holidays with him for at least thirty-five of the last fifty years of his life and I have dined with him more times than either I can or care to remember. I knew almost all of his friends, many of his male lovers, some of his mistresses and most of his professional rivals.

When I wrote his obituary for *The Guardian*, I was generously offered 2000 words in which to do so. But since he died on a Sunday and my obituary appeared on the Monday morning little more than twenty-four hours after his death, I obviously did not have the time or the space to say all that I would have wished to say. He was a complicated man, and so I welcome this opportunity to expand my obituary and to expatiate a little more on some of the complexities that made him such a fascinating and maddening friend and colleague. If nothing else it will contain quite a lot of information about his life that few others will know about and even fewer might wish to record. It is very far from all that I could say but the time is not yet ripe for the publication of all the rich details of an exceptionally full life. His archive was purchased by the Cambridge University Library (for the surprising sum of £60,000 several decades ago when that sum would have bought a pretty substantial house) and will provide rich biographical pickings when it is free from its fifty-year embargo. Some sections of it are even embargoed until the death of the last surviving grandchild of the current monarch.

On the Sunday of his death when I was writing his obituary, my younger daughter said, "Forget about the black years and concentrate on the good Jack". That is what I tried to do. But one cannot deny that the last years of his life were often very black indeed. To try to explain what happened to Jack in his later years I have added "A Postscript on the Black Years". It was difficult to write and the contrast between the man it portrays and the ebullient, inspiring and uninhibitedly generous man about whom I wrote in a "Valedictory Tribute" when he retired from the Faculty in 1974 is painful to contemplate. Without it, however, this personal memoir would be incomplete and the portrait of Jack would be cosmetically distorted by excessive censorship and excessive kindness – he would have disapproved of the former and despised the latter. In his old age, he rarely practiced either.

I make no apology for this portrait being presented very much from my point of view. Others doubtless have different perspectives on Jack's life and character. Doubtless some will disagree with my version and my judgements. Doubtless other portraits will appear. All I can say is that this is how I saw him and this is how I remember his distinctive personality. I have enjoyed casting my mind back to the exhilarating early years of our friendship and have found it curiously therapeutic to try to explain and to understand the later darker years.

He always used to divide people into those who enhanced life and those who detracted from it. We should never forget that for most of his life he was without question one of the great life-enhancers – someone who raised the temperature of life just by being there. But there is more of interest to him than that. Perhaps this memoir will offer more evidence and some greater insight into what kind man was the Sir John Plumb who awakened so many people's interest in history and literature in the late twentieth century.

I hope that this memoir will be read as an affectionate if un-illusion piece. I hope that it will be seen as genuinely admiring and compassionate in tone and content, if not uncritical in spirit and analysis. I have tried to include some of the more revealing and more characteristic episodes in his career and I have concentrated on those aspects of his life of which I had the most direct experience. So, above all, it is how I remember my old teacher and friend. I owe him a great debt of gratitude – indeed, apart from my wife and my daughters, he unquestionably had more influence on my life than any other individual. If history is, in one sense, the record of memory, then perhaps these memories and very personal recollections can be regarded as my modest contribution to the first draft of a history of a fascinating if ultimately much troubled life.

It was clear in 2001 that, with his death, Cambridge had lost one of its most influential historians of the late twentieth century. It had also lost one of its most memorable characters.

He was one of a remarkable group of dynamic and charismatic scholars (including Sir Moses Finley, Sir Geoffrey Elton, Sir Harry Hensley, (Sir) Owen Chadwick, Sir Denis Brogan, Sir Herbert Butterfield, Dom David Knowles, Mania (Sir Michael) Postman, Philip Grierson, Walter Ullmann, Peter Laslett and Denis Mack Smith) who made the Cambridge History Faculty such an exciting place to be in the 1960s and 1970s. When one recalls that Joseph Needham and E.H. Carr were then at the height of their powers in Cambridge, that exciting young scholars, such as John (later Sir John) Elliott, Quentin Skinner, Christopher Andrew and Norman Stone, had already joined the Faculty, and that ambitious youngsters such as Richard Overy, Geoffrey Parker, Roy Porter, Simon (later Sir Simon) Schama, John Brewer, Keith Wrightson, David (later Sir David) Cannadine, Chris (later Sir Christopher) Clark and Chris (later Sir Christopher) Bayly were beginning their research careers here, it is little wonder that one looks back on it now as a Golden Age which has not been equalled since. It was (as Roy Porter once memorably said of the eighteenth century) "a tonic time to be alive".

Few if any could claim to have played a more central role in that golden era than Dr. J. H. Plumb as he was then known. As a hugely influential teacher, the most popular lecturer and the most prolific writer, and as an unforgettably colourful character, Plumb dominated Christ's and Cambridge History during much of this period. In the final years of his life it gave him great pleasure that he had outlived almost all of his contemporaries, and he reacted to the death of particularly fierce rivals, such as Lord Todd in Christ's and Sir Geoffrey Elton in the History Faculty, with undisguised glee.

4. PLUMB IN LEICESTER: FAMILY UPBRINGING AND SCHOOLING

Jack Plumb did not enjoy the effortless rise to the top that so many of his colleagues did. He often complained – probably justifiably – that the scales of social justice were stacked against his succeeding in life.

Certainly he was not blessed with a privileged or wealthy background. He was the product of a working-class family in Leicester and of the local grammar school, Alderman Newton's. His father toiled away on the shop floor of a local boot and shoe factory and Jack spent his childhood in a humble red brick terrace house typical of nineteenth-century workers' housing. It can still be seen at 65 Walton Street, leading off Narborough Road, Leicester. His family later moved to suburbia – a modest semi-detached house near the corner of Dumbleton Avenue and Somerville Road (both of which also lead off Narborough Road), which he felt signalled his parents' success in joining the lower middle classes. I briefly lived in the same street in 1939, and I was much surprised and mildly amused to learn how much it irritated Jack that my family lived in one of the large three story Edwardian houses at the town end of Somerville Road whilst his family lived in an undistinguished inter-war semi at the other end. I was even more amused to hear Jack's adult efforts to re-write a more romantic background for himself. On the slender basis of six silver teaspoons carrying the arms of a family in whose service his grandmother had worked, he wove a fantasy of himself as a by-blow of an aristocratic English family. He even claimed to be able to trace a family resemblance. When he later confided this suspicion to one of his aristocratic friends and offered the decisive evidence of his mother's possession of the silver teaspoons, he was quite crushed when she replied, "But Jack darling, the servants always steal the tea-spoons!"

What was always obvious was that he had no intention of staying any longer than he had to in the social milieu into which he felt an unkind fate had so very undeservedly tipped him. His schoolboy diaries make it abundantly clear that he yearned to explore a wider world and that he had the energy and drive and intelligence to ensure that he would succeed in doing so. Even as a schoolboy he was active in persuading and if necessary bullying his friends – and even his schoolmasters – into accompanying him on cycling trips to explore ancient Welsh castles, historic sites and any available country houses.

These he felt would provide his fertile historical imagination with the scope that the humble back streets of Leicester lacked.

The first surviving diary in his archive, which describes one such trip, is the work of several hands (including his first history master, Mr Joels, who later taught me) but it is dominated by Plumb, as he was called by his school friends and, more surprisingly, by his father. It is always Plumb doing the planning, Plumb dominating the talking, and Plumb whose experiences are being recorded. Even the fact that "Plumb's poor little snub-nose" suffered the worst sunburn was faithfully recorded for posterity. This diary (neatly typed out and decorated with photographs of the travelling party) offers some revealing insights into the young Plumb, as do the postcards he sent home. Some surprising clues to his early self- image and his relations with his parents come from one such postcard signed (surely rather remarkably) with the words "from your only handsome son". It also contains a rather snide reference to his handicapped elder brother (described as "the Loved one") who he always felt enjoyed an excessive amount of parental attention, which could more deservedly have been directed to him.

He always felt that he had been starved of affection in infancy because Sid, the elder of his two brothers (the other was called Bert), had had to undergo major brain surgery just when Jack was born. Not surprisingly his mother was distracted by the joint arrival of a very demanding new baby and another son suddenly reduced to total dependence on her. As a result Jack was that very rare twentieth-century infant who was breast-fed not by his own mother but by a friend of hers who volunteered to act as a wet-nurse. Seeing Louie Moodie (the wet-nurse in question) and Mrs. Plumb together I always felt that it looked as if Jack had sucked far more than simple nourishment from the ample breasts of Mrs. Moodie. Where Sarah Plumb was small and bony and bird-like, Louie Moodie was stocky and muscular and mesomorphic. Where Jack's mother was reticent and discreet, his wet-nurse was boldly outspoken. Where the birth mother seemed indecisive and lacking in energy and drive, the surrogate mother exuded physical stamina and the self-confidence that came from her certainty that she was always in the right. She was born to take charge and she ruled her family with Napoleonic decisiveness. Even on her deathbed when her relatives were trying to tempt her to eat by offering to open a precious wartime tin of salmon, she barked with Plumb-like ferocity, "You leave that alone. I want that kept for the guests at my funeral". One always felt that there was a lot of Louie Moodie in Jack. He quickly assumed power over the other members of his family (many of whom, again rather remarkably, also always called him "Plumb"). He, too, was never reluctant to take decisions on their behalf. He, too, expected his extended family to heed his wishes, obey his instructions and "do what I bloody well tell them to do!" Like a cuckoo in the nest, he came to occupy a disproportionate part of the house, and take up a disproportionate part of his parent's attention. His mother always took him morning tea in bed and his father always polished his shoes.

More importantly he always planned ahead – whether for his life, his death or for his future education.

His first school was Narborough Road Primary School, but winning a scholarship to Alderman Newton's Grammar School was his first significant step on the educational ladder. Known as the Green Coat School because of its distinctive green blazer, it was the oldest grammar school in Leicester (having been founded in 1784) but was by no means ranked as the best.

The history of the school is scarcely mistily nostalgic about its building or its setting. It opens with the words "Alderman Newton's is not an impressive building. Its Victorian drabness is not improved by the scars inflicted on it by a modern industrial city. Its position scarcely serves as an inspiration to a scholar. The thunder of traffic produces an atmosphere even less conducive to academic work."

One has to concede that its position in the centre of Leicester was very far from the pastoral ideal of the many schools that consist of distinguished architecture set in arcadian surroundings. The only grass to be seen at Newton's was not the rolling acres of playing fields but the thin strips surrounding the gravestones that we overlooked from the playground. Newton's was closely hemmed in by the cathedral cemetery, a large municipal bus depot, a huge hosiery factory, and, on the fourth side, a building works called, to all small boys' delight, "British Erections Ltd" which operated on Peacock Lane.

I much prefer to recall William Cooper's description of Plumb's and my old school in the opening words of his brilliant first novel *Scenes from Provincial Life* (1950), which was published when I was there in the VIth form:

"The school at which I was a science-master was desirably situated, right in the centre of the town. By walking only a few yards the masters and the boys could find themselves in a cafe or a public house.

"I used to frequent a cafe in the market place. It was on the first floor, and underneath was a shop where coffee was roasted. A delicious aroma drifted through the maze of market-stalls, mingling with the smell of celery, apples and chrysanthemums: you could pick it up in the middle of the place and follow it to the source, where, in the shop-window, a magnificent roasting-machine turned with a flash of red enamel and chromium plate – persistently reminding you that coffee smelt nicer than it tasted."

That was the cafe – called Bruccianis, which opened in in 1937 and is still operating in Leicester to this day — in which historians from Newton's spent many hours of their schooldays educating themselves in seemingly endless debates and successive cups of coffee. It was a bit like the common rooms I later encountered in Cambridge colleges, panelled in oak and restricted to "gentlemen only". If my schooldays evoke nostalgic reminiscence, it is the aroma of coffee and the memories of robust argument at Bruccianis that flood back not the grim Victorian pile opposite the bus station. It was our common room and debating society all rolled into one. Its significance was that we were allowed to use it in school hours, indeed we were strongly encouraged by the charismatic history master H.E. Howard to do so. It was symptomatic of his teaching methods which launched so many historians (including Plumb and myself) on their route to Cambridge.

Plumb was one of the first of many that Howard set on this path even if his launch was initially to prove abortive and embarrassing, This was all the more disappointing because Howard had quickly recognised that with Plumb he had a candidate of exceptional promise with a very clear idea of what he wanted to do. When asked by Roy Plumley on *Desert Island Discs* what his earliest ambitions had been, Plumb replied promptly "To write", adding that he had initially wanted to teach ("What bright little boy doesn't want to teach"), but by the age of fourteen or fifteen he had decided on a writing career. By the age of 15 he had mapped out a whole series of Mercian novels after the model of Hardy's Wessex series, but admitted that they never got beyond a list of titles. He was, he said, a boy of "infinite curiosity", and history seemed likely to offer him endless possibilities on which to exercise it.

So his education was always his first priority and there was never much doubt that he would seek it initially as an historian. Even as a schoolboy he claimed that he was engaged in critical assessments of historical sources – carefully comparing the accounts of the fates of Charles I, Strafford and Cromwell as recorded by Clarendon, Gardiner and Carlyle. Such an intuitive critical response to history boded well for his future. His teachers' assessment of his abilities boded even better. So urged on by his remarkable schoolmaster, H.E. (Bert) Howard (later immortalized by C.P. Snow as George Passant in his *Strangers and Brothers* series of novels), who had such a profound influence on him at Newton's, the goal was ambitiously agreed on – to get him to Cambridge to read History.

Howard's teaching methods, as I learned from first-hand experience in the 1940s and 1950s, were robust and relaxed and relatively free from normal schoolmasterly formality. At times they were so relaxed and so free as to excite much head-masterly disapproval. He smoked in class and he drank heavily out of class. He encouraged his pupils to do the same – meeting the sixth formers in raffish pubs near the school at the end of school hours, to argue about history and life and politics. The sessions could be long and combative and could end in angry confrontation – it was an instructive precursor for those of his pupils who got to be taught by Plumb in Cambridge.

His methods of instruction were equally un-conventional. Rather than feeding his pupils with well-prepared lists of 'essential points' to be made in answer to major historical questions, he encouraged us to do the work for ourselves. Rather than insisting on our turning up to school for his lessons, he would give us significant historical problems to work on and then advise us to go off to work in the local Reference Library in the town centre. Instead of giving us prepared bibliographies of recommended reading he told us to read as widely as possible and to seek out our own sources. Having completed our research on say the Reformation or the English Civil War or the Industrial Revolution, we would be required to give a lecture on the subject to the whole class whilst he sat at the back smoking his pipe and delivering withering criticism on anything he thought inadequately researched, poorly explained or sloppily delivered. Work, which he approved of, would receive fulsome praise. It was a pattern of praise and blame that Plumb was to copy in his supervisions at Christ's.

Howard never stuck to any formal syllabus. We were encouraged to read widely and to pursue any subject that we found interesting. We were encouraged to argue and debate amongst ourselves and the fact that we all met up for coffee in the town centre to do so, rather than clocking in at school, was perfectly fine as far as he was concerned. It gave him more free time in which to write his own novels and publish his own history books, or to travel down to London to appear on the BBC's Brains Trust.

The result of these methods was that we were encouraged to be independent, encouraged to pursue our own research, encouraged to choose our own subjects and reach our own conclusions with as little schoolmasterly intervention as possible. Standing up in class to deliver one's findings (to our fellow pupils as well as to him) encouraged us to be well prepared and to be as entertaining as possible. If one could come up with some original and provocative arguments so much the better. The results were in time to prove to be dazzlingly successful in getting his pupils into Cambridge. For thirty years he attracted almost all of the brightest pupils in the school (much to the irritation of other subject masters) and (much to the ill-concealed envy of those colleagues) collected scholarship after scholarship at Cambridge. It was always Cambridge.

Many have described his methods, and the relaxed informal atmosphere in which we were prepared for our assault on the Cambridge Scholarship examinations, as uncannily similar to those which Alan Bennett portrayed so brilliantly in *The History Boys*. Indeed some, such as Asa Briggs, have told me that they were convinced that Bennett's play must owe something to tales of

Howard's methods and his legendary success becoming well known throughout Oxbridge. I have no direct confirmation of this, but the resemblance was very strong. Bennett's charismatic Hector (with his scatter-gun approach to imparting information and his belief that learning must be respected for its own sake) was very reminiscent of Howard's unstructured teaching methods. But like Bennett's contrasting character, Irwin, Howard was also dedicated to achieving success for his pupils. Indeed he was reminiscent of Bennett's Hector, Irwin and Mrs Lintott all rolled into one. He completely dominated our pursuit of a place at Cambridge, and he set the tone of what life was like for the "seventh term sixth formers". When Alan Bennett wrote: "Teachers need to feel they are trusted. They must be allowed some leeway to use their imagination; otherwise teaching loses all sense of wonder and excitement", he might well have been quoting Howard.

Even the relaxed tolerance of the sixth-formers in *The History Boys* towards what they regarded as the harmless homoeroticism of their history master was a striking echo of our relaxed attitude to Howard's affectionate (but in our eyes, at this stage of his life, pretty asexual) interest in his pupils.

It has to be conceded that in today's moral climate, some of Howard's teaching methods, which produced so many Cambridge historians (including Jack Plumb and Rupert Hall as long term Fellows of Christ's, Arthur Hibbert as a long term Fellow of King's and myself as a long term Fellow of Caius, and many others), would probably not now be tolerated.

His method began by picking the six brightest first year boys at Newton's, based on their scores in the entrance Scholarship examination, to form Howard's club. These six eleven year olds would then be regularly invited to Howard's bachelor home to play simple educational games, which allowed him to assess in detail their individual academic potential. The games were carefully designed to test their knowledge, their memory, their intellectual curiosity, their reasoning skills, their verbal agility, their competitiveness, their sheer need to win. Having assessed their potential, Howard could then do his best to steer those he thought would excel in his own subject to concentrate on History. In a sense we were groomed, but in a very positive sense, not in the pejorative sense that grooming has come to indicate. At least I never heard any hint or rumour of inappropriate grooming in my day, but one has to admit that this process all ended very badly – indeed it ended disastrously for Howard. Many years after I had left the school an adolescent boy accused him of inappropriate behaviour and Howard was forced to resign. To avoid public disgrace he left his job and left the country. He fled to Amsterdam were he happily reverted to his previous love of prostitutes.

When a few years later he died there, he was buried in an unmarked grave. His brother Cecil Howard had opted for the cheapest choice of burial spot which allowed the authorities to plough it up and re-use it after only a very few years of "occupation". There could be very few more anonymous endings. It was an appalling conclusion to nearly forty years of spectacularly successful teaching. Many us feared that the steady flow of scholarships to Cambridge would come to a sudden end, and so it proved.

After his death, I was asked to write a tribute to his achievements for the school magazine. Having rehearsed the remarkable record of his successes, I ended my piece with the grim but prescient words: "new talent, like milk to a suicide's doorstep, will inevitably continue to be delivered to the school gates, let us hope that it will not be allowed to go sour, in the absence of the devoted attention to make the maximum use of it that Howard provided for so many decades". Alas my hopes largely proved to be illusory, the flow of successfully harnessed talent that had begun with Plumb dried up dramatically with Howard's departure. The occasional unstoppably bright pupil emerged (I admitted one outstanding Newtonian to read history at Caius) but they were pretty rare after Howard.

To be fair to the school the chances of finding a replacement of his calibre and his commitment were not great. His record was almost impossible to match, even if his initial efforts with what was to prove to be his most successful pupil was to end in abject failure when he prepared Plumb for his assault on Cambridge.

As the most charismatic member of the teaching staff, his influence on the young Plumb was predictably profound, but initially embarrassingly unsuccessful. With a First in History from London under his belt, and powerful literary ambitions as yet unfulfilled, Howard had just the kind of proven track record and promise for the future most likely to appeal to the aspirations of the schoolboy Plumb. Admission to Cambridge with a scholarship to provide the necessary financial support was the first thing he aspired to; with Howard's help, it must have seemed to be intoxicatingly within reach.

With the assistance of the then Dr. C. P. Snow (later Sir Charles Snow and later still Lord Snow), an Old Newtonian who had made it to Cambridge via the fledgling Leicester university college, and who had quickly recognized the exceptional qualities of the young Plumb, the plans were hatched with all the precision of a military campaign. The strategy included contingency plans that seem astonishing to those who knew the adult Plumb. Perhaps the greatest astonishment would come from the knowledge that the teenaged Jack was instructed to become a confirmed Anglican in case he did not make his first-choice college, St John's, and had to seek admission to Selwyn. Selwyn was in those days an altogether less glamorous and less desirable college than St. John's, but also a less demanding one in terms of the likely competition for admission. Selwyn was not even to achieve full collegiate status until 1958, and as long as Jack met its singular requirement – that undergraduates had to be communicant members of the Church of England – then surely, it was argued by the conspirators, Selwyn would take him if all else failed.

The youthful Plumb was as fierce an atheist then as he was to remain until the end of life. Nothing could better signal his determination to get into Cambridge than the fact that he was willing to be confirmed, willing to fake a set of beliefs he despised, if it could open the gates of a college which he was to regard with dismissive contempt in later life. He had the grace to appear somewhat shame-faced when confronted by this awkward revelation about how far he was willing to go to achieve his ambitions, but claimed that it was the Machiavellian Snow who prompted him to go to such lengths.

As it turned out all their carefully concocted plans were in vain, for his first attempt to get into Cambridge ended in a humiliating form of rejection.

He took the St John's Scholarship Examination in December 1929. According to his account (which he said was based on the Cambridge Group 3 Scholarship Examination Book which he studied many decades later when he himself was the Chairman of Examiners) he was well up amongst the scholars after the first round of marking, but after the second round of marking (in which the dons at St John's had a decisive say) he was demoted to tenth place in the list of Exhibitioners.

He actually came top amongst the potential Johnians placed in the Exhibition class and second amongst all the applicants for St John's. Colleges were obliged to offer Scholarships to those listed as scholars but they could, and very exceptionally did, reject an Exhibitioner. He was one of those very exceptional rejects. St John's offered Exhibitions to other applicants in spite of the fact that they came lower in the list than the young J.H. Plumb, and not even lowly Selwyn wanted him. The fact that St John's had turned down their top Exhibitioner must inevitably have sent out warning signals to other colleges still in the market for award-winners.

Jack went to his grave still resenting the injustice that he felt – not without some justification – he had been subjected to. It is true that he could have had a place at St John's if he could have afforded to accept it. He could not. As David Cannadine has put it "He was a scholarship boy without the scholarship!"

As he told the story (very memorably and very amusingly at his retirement dinner) much of the fault lay in his mother's advice on how he was to dress for his assault on St John's. First she advised him to wear his "funeral suit" for his interviews and then, quite fatally, suggested that he topped off this lugubrious outfit with a bowler hat to arrive in. One look at the languid public school boys in their tweed jackets and cavalry twill trousers quickly alerted Jack to his first sartorial error. One encounter with the formidable bowler-hatted Head

Porter of St John's immediately alerted him to his second even greater mistake. In despair he trudged to the Bridge of Sighs and (like an adolescent Odd-Job) hurled the offending bowler hat into the Cam, but by then the damage had been done. The story of the bowler-hatted young "funeral director" or "aspiring porter" from Leicester had already reached and entertained the dons. The confidence of the young Plumb had been deeply dented and he over-compensated in his efforts to impress what he regarded as his patronizing and disdainful interviewers. His excited parade of his current enthusiasm for Freud and Proust did not go down at all well. French homosexuality and the psycho-dynamics of everyday life were not much to the taste of Johnian historians in the late 1920s. He would have done far better at King's.

In the eyes of the dons of St John's (including apparently the distinguished Tudor historian J.R.Tanner), he must have seemed pretentious as well as provincial and sartorially embarrassing as well as proletarian. What was worse, instead of social *savoir-faire* he offered ardent socialism. Instead of uncontaminated historical scholarship he offered suspect literary tastes and an unhealthy interest in sexual psychology. Such offerings were to prove a fatal mixture. Doubtless the story of the bowler hat did not help.

Undeterred by this rejection Plumb wrote again next year (on his school notepaper on the 12 May 1930) asking for the entrance forms for a sizar-ship at St John's. This time he was aiming rather lower. Sizars were originally student servants who earned their keep by such duties as waiting in Hall on the other wealthier undergraduates, but by 1930 the title was given to poor but worthy students on the basis of an examination. It was rather like a poor man's scholarship or bursary. I do not know for certain whether or not he made use of the application forms but we do know that Plumb's name was not amongst the list of successful sizars at St John's published in *The Reporter* of the summer of 1930.

Whatever the motives of those involved in his first assault on Cambridge, the dons of St John's had not offered him the financial support he needed, and so he went to University College Leicester (later the University of Leicester) and became the first person ever to take a First in History as an external London degree from that modest university college. It cannot have been easy. He certainly did not get the kind of teaching he would have enjoyed at Cambridge. No one would claim that Leicester had a richly endowed or generously staffed university in 1930 – the residents numbered just eighty students and faculty members, and that number included "the hall porter who taught botany". For his first two years at Leicester, there was only one History member of the staff – a sad Oxford M.A. without ambition or hope – who taught everything: all six papers from Greek Political Thought to Nineteenth-Century European History.

As Plumb has recorded, in *The Making of an Historian*, by the age of 23 he had met only five professional historians – and two of them for only a few minutes. The one he remembered with most warmth and gratitude was Rosalind Hill, who in his last year arrived to her first teaching position with a First Class degree from St. Hilda's College, Oxford. She was a woman of exceptional warmth and kindness who was to go on to enjoy a distinguished career as a medieval historian. In recognition of her distinction and to show how much he had valued her presence at University College, Leicester in the early 1930s, he gave a celebratory lunch for her some sixty years later in Christ's on Friday, 10 February 1995.

At the lunch Professor Jonathan Riley-Smith, the leading Cambridge historian of the Crusades, was invited to join them in recognitions of Professor Hill's research on the Crusading movement. Less than two years later, as Chairman of the Faculty, he wrote to Plumb to tell him that Rosalind Hill had died. In his reply to Riley-Smith, Plumb wrote, "a wonderful woman to whose memory I will always be indebted".

The respect was mutual. She proudly named him as one of her first and most successful students and Plumb's name was the only pupil mentioned in her obituaries.

Grateful as he was for her early encouragement, it was nevertheless a very far cry from what he might have experienced if St John's had accepted him. To get a First with such very modest teaching was a very considerable achievement, and, perhaps understandably, he always took a sardonic pleasure in the fact that of the twelve historians St Johns had preferred to him for admission only one got a First in their Cambridge Finals and only three more managed even to get into the 2.1 class.

Perhaps it was his sense of burning injustice about his initial rejection at Cambridge, or perhaps it was his and Snow's addiction to organising other people's lives, but I know from my own experience that they could not resist what Snow called "a kind of personal imperialism". They both loved to give advice. They both loved to pontificate. They both loved to instruct. They both could not resist telling the uninitiated how the world worked. In spite of their spectacular failure to organise a successful assault on the Cambridge admissions system for Plumb, they had no hesitation in instructing me what I needed to do to gain admission.

They had heard from Bert Howard about what he regarded as my academic promise and about his frustration that he could not persuade me to read History. As a consequence, I was nearing the end of the second term of my first year in the Sixth Form taking Maths, Physics and Chemistry for "A" Level. Most would, at this stage, have given me up as a lost cause as an aspirant to read History at Cambridge, but convinced that the science teaching at Newton's would be insufficient to exploit my Cambridge potential, Howard arranged for me to meet Plumb and Snow and him one Saturday afternoon in the unlikely setting of the Grand Hotel in Leicester. I had reluctantly to miss a trial for the Leicester County Rugby Team to attend this improbable meeting, at which I was told that switching to History was the only way I stood a chance of getting into Cambridge. They pointed out Howard's remarkable long run of success in guiding Newtonians to admission, and contrasted it with the woeful record of the scientists.

When I impertinently pointed out that Snow's scientific career had been launched from Alderman Newton's, he forcefully pointed out that in order to do so he had to stay on at the school after his time in the Sixth Form to work for several years as a lowly lab assistant, and then had to take an external London degree at University College Leicester. If I thought I was the intellectual equal of Snow, and if I was willing to face the many years toiling away at school after taking my "A" levels, and if I would be content to remain in Leicester to take my degree, then perhaps I should stick with science. It was presented as a series of conditions that only a fool would accept.

My protestations that it was far too late to switch to a whole new set of "A" levels were brushed aside as weak-kneed; my protestations that I much preferred science and maths to History were brushed aside as self-indulgent; and my admission that I was not sure that I wanted to go to any university, much less Cambridge, were brushed aside as pathetically unambitious. It was, I was told in no uncertain terms by Plumb, one's duty to maximize one's potential.

Impressed by their dogmatic certainties and no doubt flattered by their attention, I agreed to change to three new Arts "A" levels and to concentrate on History. The decision meant that I had just over a year to master my new syllabus.

My mother was infuriated by my decision, and marched up to the school to demand an explanation. As a young war-widow with four children to bring up on her own, she was not surprisingly somewhat risk-averse. She was particularly suspicious of sudden ill-thought out decisions. This was very understandable given that my father (from a secure position in the Royal Armoured Corps after their successful North African Campaign against Rommel) had bravely but recklessly volunteered to join the SAS; and given that he had then volunteered to join the Special Boat Squadron, the most exclusive Special Forces unit in World War II; and given that he had then been sent to his almost certain death by Churchill's even more reckless decision (against almost universal advice not to do so) to invade the Dodecanese Islands in 1943. It proved to be the spectacularly incompetent, the comprehensively disastrous and the absurdly optimistically-named "Operation Accolade". It has rightly gone down in history as "Churchill's Folly".

The Special Boat Squadron may have been "highly trained, totally secretive and utterly ruthless" as Gavin Mortimer describes it in his history of *The SBS in World War II*. It may have gone "from island to island in the Mediterranean, landing in the dead of night in small fishing boats and launching savage hit and run raids on the Germans", but it never comprised more than 100 men and when sent to take the Dodecanese Islands with no air cover at all, they were sitting ducks for the German Stuka bombers who blew them to bits at their leisure.

So little wonder that my mother was so risk averse. Unhappily well-versed in such male folly (and, for her, their life changing outcomes), she was determined to prevent me from taking what she saw as an equally sudden and foolish change to the course of my future education.

My science teachers gave her a warm welcome, heartily agreeing with her that they thought that this was a ridiculous and reckless decision. It was particularly ill-advised they said because "Neil is the best mathematician we have ever had". Fortunately at this point my mother asked what successes they had ever had? How many had they sent up to Cambridge for instance? When they said "None", she decided that, on reflection, "perhaps my trio of advisors had a point".

When I tell this story, many people express surprise that I accepted my elders' advice, which in many ways went against my strong inclinations, but for a fatherless teenager, Howard, Plumb and Snow were a formidable trio to refuse.

Howard, after all, was a proven past master at preparing his pupils for the Cambridge scholarship examinations and was the most influential teacher at my school. Plumb and Snow were established academics who had both experienced major problems seeking to get themselves into Cambridge from our less than glamorous grammar school. All three had powerful personalities. All three were used to getting their own way. Their authoritative advice, when added to the magical effects of flattering encouragement, was difficult to resist.

Just how important such encouragement was, can be judged when compared to the attitude of the deputy Headmaster of my school who had assured me that it was a disgrace for me, and the three others who also decided to apply, to even consider applying to Cambridge. Such an application would "only bring shame and dishonour and humiliation on the school", he said. It was absurd to think that "boys like us" could hope to succeed at such a distinguished university. As we were the brightest boys in the school and I was Head Prefect, it showed the levels of discouragement that even the most promising received. When we all won open awards in the Scholarship Examination (I won a Scholarship and the other three got Exhibitions), he refused to change his mind and greeted us on our triumphant return to the school with the words: "Don't expect any congratulations from me. The standards at Cambridge have obviously fallen to an abysmally low level".

Such an attitude shows just how influential Howard's contrasting encouragement could be, and (in seeking the authoritative backing of Snow and Plumb to achieve his ends) also shows how far he was willing to go to guide his pupils to success. He and Snow may have failed with Plumb in the late 1920s but that setback had merely convinced him that better plans of attacks in the early 1950s would yield greater and greater success.

My experience demonstrates all too clearly the self-confident certainties that Plumb brought to advising and directing and encouraging the success of so many of his pupils at Cambridge. His own initial humiliating failure made him all the more determined to guide others to a smoother path to success. Many have told me similar stories of how they were flattered, bullied or generally browbeaten into taking his advice on the direction that their lives and careers should follow.

A typical example was the experience of Wallas Eaton, the actor. Eaton was taught by Howard at Alderman Newton's in the 1930s and also went up to Cambridge to read History and then English at Christ's. He told me that he was not only advised by Plumb and Snow on how to apply for admission to Cambridge, he was also then advised that he would never enjoy a successful acting career with the name he was christened with – namely Reg Eaton. In their customary authoritative way, Plumb and Snow decided that he needed a more distinctive theatrical first name. Unfortunately in the mid 1930's they recommended a new name, namely Wallis, which Mrs Simpson was just about to make the most unpopular name in the country. By then Eaton had started theatrical work with his new name and the best that he could do was to unobtrusively change the spelling to Wallas.

Plumb admitted that their choice of Wallis could have been better timed in light of Wallis Simpson and the abdication crisis, but still argued that Eaton would never have become either a major in the war or a household name as an actor after it, if he had stuck with Reg. Jack always boasted that Wallas Eaton would never have appeared on stage with Vivien Leigh or been cast by Joan Littlewood if he hadn't abandoned his distinctly down-market original first name. His new name, he argued, made him far more memorable in the ten years he starred in "Take It From Here" on the radio, not to mention making him sound more glamorous in the gay world he so enthusiastically lived in throughout his adult life.

This re-naming was typical of Plumb's complete certainty that he was always right and characteristic of his unshakable conviction that his friends and pupils should always heed his advice: whether it was to change subjects, change names, change colleges, change fiancés, change careers, change wives, change husbands, change their children's schooling, change homes, change political allegiance (nationally as well as collegiately) or even change sexual orientation – all of which he had been known to do or try to do.

All in all, I think I got off pretty lightly in taking his advice.

Much as I regretted abandoning my fledgling career as a scientist I cannot deny that his advice that I should switch to history was almost certainly right in the short-run. He certainly had no doubt that I owed my career to his advice and he was never slow to take full credit for it. Once again, who is to say that he wasn't right?

His initial painful rejection by St John's and the stuttering start to his career at Christ's convinced him of the need for more expert guidance than he had received himself, and, once he had achieved success, he was only too happy to pass his advice on and insist that it was followed. His startling success as a teacher (and as a promoter of the careers of those he taught) must surely justify his self-confident and at times dictatorial plans for his protégées.

5. PLUMB COMING TO TERMS WITH CAMBRIDGE

Armed with his First (one of only three awarded to external candidates for the London degree), he was awarded a London Post-Graduate Studentship worth £150 in May 1934 – one of only six available for all subjects, in science as well as the humanities. He was always very proud that R.H. Tawney was one of those who chose him for this. With this modest funding and with the backing of Snow, who was by then a Fellow of the college, he was eventually admitted to Christ's in October 1934. There he started his research (as one of G.M. Trevelyan's very rare research students) and so began a relationship with the college which was to last for sixty-seven years. Apart from a brief interlude as a Research Fellow at King's and his time at Bletchley during the war, he never left Christ's again. He became a Fellow in 1946 and for the next fifty-five years loyally devoted his life to the college. Such devotion and such loyalty are all the more to his credit because he was not offered easy access to Christ's High Table. There were other aspiring young Cambridge historians who stood much higher in the pecking order than Plumb – the provincial product of what Plumb himself described as "an almost unknown and certainly despised University College". Whilst what he called "the blue-eyed boys in command of the inside track" prospered, he had to scrape a living by supervising any undergraduates he could find.

Fortunately, coming from the Howard school of history at Newton's, Plumb passionately believed in the value of good teaching. He did not simply encourage his pupils to aim high, he insisted on them doing so. If they did so they could be sure of his full and undivided attention. Anyone exposed to the blinding glare of Plumb's curious mixture of high-octane teaching methods and persistent psychological probing will testify to its mesmeric, almost hypnotic, power. Few could resist such intense interest in them. Fixing them with his bulging exothalmic eyes (they protruded so much he swore that they got sunburned in summer) he asked the most personal questions. Whilst he listened so attentively and so sympathetically, he expertly extracted the intimate confessions that so interested him. According to him, it was all too easy. Since so many late adolescents are wonderfully self-obsessed and only too willing to talk about themselves, the inquisitive Plumb had a field day.

Little wonder that he started to prosper as a teacher. His supervisions offered his pupils not only a professional concern with their scholarship but also an almost obsessive fascination with their life histories – especially their sex lives, and, failing that, their emotional lives and their family relationships. Young women from Newnham and Girton proved to be especially responsive to these highly personal teaching methods. Few things appeal more irresistibly to the impressionable young than a powerful interest in them as people and a powerful interest in their work – especially their prose. So his pupils loved the fact that Plumb was as interested in their literary style as he was in their command of scholarship and the structure of their arguments. They loved the fact that he spent as much time in polishing their prose as he did in picking holes in their arguments. Pride of authorship is a powerful emotion. Telling undergraduates that they write well can have the most magical effect on their attention and their motivation. Jack recognized very early that flattering people into working hard and succeeding can be as effective as bullying them into doing so.

Since he was an expert flatterer and if necessary an accomplished bully, his results grew more and more impressive, and his reputation as a teacher grew with them.

They grew at Christ's much more slowly. Jack has recorded that in these years he was not thought to be grand enough to teach Christ's men. Indeed to use his own phrase, he first "cut his teeth on the Cambridge Supervision system on female students". In the mid-thirties there was a revolt amongst the undergraduate historians at Newnham. They demanded a new supervisor in English history and "through the good offices of Christopher Morris" (who directed studies at King's), "three girls, brilliant, beautiful and wilful, became my pupils". Through them his reputation as a stimulating and demanding supervisor soon spread and most of the tributes to his teaching in the thirties come from Newnhamites and Girtonians who gratefully recall his ability to make them strive to succeed and his sympathetic concern with their personal problems and preoccupations. A touching dedication in *The Hinge of History* (1996) to "Sir John Plumb, my kindly tutor and mentor for the History Tripos in those far off days of 1933-36" was from the octogenarian Charlotte Waterlow, M.B.E. of Newnham College, the only female First in either part of the Tripos in 1936. Sixty years after the event, Jack still talked fondly of her, and of Angela Gray from Girton who first sat at his feet in the mid-thirties. He spoke even more fondly, although alas anonymously, of "the beautiful Newnham girl from Much Hadham, whose house was full of paintings from the Scottish colourist school and who was a leading light of the Newnham anti-virgin club". What a sweet description, and what a touching reminder of a lost innocence and a past era.

Acceptance in Cambridge in terms of a tenured job grew even more slowly.

He knew that his early research was felt to be disappointing and he knew equally well that his Ph.D. which he was awarded in 1936 (having been examined by Sir Keith Feiling and Harold Temperley) was not the key which would immediately open any career doors for him. He knew that the local stars, such as Herbert Butterfield, who had been elected into a Fellowship immediately on graduation, would never think of taking a Ph.D. Indeed, as David Cannadine so elegantly put it, Plumb's doctorate was felt, by him as well as by his starrier contemporaries, to be more "a badge of inferiority" than "a passport to preferment".

One of the reasons why he would not let me submit my research for a Ph.D. was that he thought once one had been elected early into a Fellowship the best way to advertise that status was to retain the title of Mr. And, of course, at that time he was right. When I was elected into first a research Fellowship at Christ's and then a full Fellowship at Caius in 1958 within two years of graduating, the last thing my advisors wanted me to do was to take a lowly Ph.D. My supervisor Charles Wilson had never had to take one, the historians in Caius such as Philip Grierson and Guy Griffith had never had to take one and all of them urged me not to do so. The Master of Caius, the Nobel-winning physicist Sir James Chadwick, had taken one to try to make it respectable, but it had little effect on Cambridge historians at that time. It was thought by most of the leading people in the History Faculty to be an unnecessary Germanic fad.

I took the same attitude towards my outstanding pupils and urged those such as Quentin Skinner and Norman Stone not to bother with a Ph.D, in the early 1960s. Jack continued to do the same, which is doubtless why Simon Schama never took one.

It was only when ambitious young historians started to seek work in the States that we all had to change our views and insist that they must have a doctorate to gain employment in an American university.

Back in 1936, the title Dr J.H. Plumb cut little ice either academically or socially in Cambridge. So at this period of his life he tended to return to Leicester for much of his social life. There he was a "star" who had made it to Cambridge. There he could join his old friends in heavy drinking sessions (invariably beer) in his favourite pubs. There he could indulge his radical left-wing political opinions without fear of offending his listeners. In Cambridge he had learned that his openly expressed atheism and his ardent socialism could earn him very powerful enemies. Sir Herbert Butterfield and his powerful right-wing and Christian allies never fully forgave him for either. He felt that they did much to block his promotion in Cambridge and his public recognition outside it.

Those who knew Jack Plumb only in his mature years would be very surprised to learn how much of his early life was spent drinking beer in distinctly down-market pubs. In later life his drinking was dominated by claret and champagne, and his standard social habitat was by then a mixture of college common rooms and London club-land and aristocratic drawing rooms. In his youth things were very different. Even as late as the mid-1960s he still held very informal seminars for young Cambridge historians in the rather seedy setting of the Red Lion in Petty Cury.

Copious amounts of Worthington "E" and Greene King bitter beer were drunk. Reputations were cheerfully shredded. The world – especially the narrow world of Cambridge history – was enthusiastically put to rights. Simon Schama has well described these lively weekly "gatherings of the like-minded" under the tutelage of the dominant figure of Plumb: "Monday evenings in the *Red Lion* in Petty Cury, there since Macaulay's day, but long since reduced to a state of scrofulous decrepitude, flakes of plaster dropping into the Greene King, saw Plumb, Kenyon, McKendrick, Burrow, Skinner and the undergraduate Schama (in descending order of being able to hold their drink) batting gossip, academic and political, back and forth". The ability to hold one's drink was subjected to a pretty demanding test because the prevailing rule was that everyone paid for a round of drinks and each round was a pint of bitter. Thank God the party was usually restricted to about half a dozen or so.

Jack's devotion to his Monday evenings in the *Red Lion* culminated in a memorable evening dedicated to mourning its closing down. The mourning proved to be about as sober as an Irish wake. The old pub, condemned in a piece of sixties' vandalism to be demolished to make way for a very undistinguished shopping centre, was given a stirring send-off. Bill Noblett, who was then an undergraduate in his first term at Christ's in October 1968, has vividly recalled the attempt of a party (consisting amongst others of the future Professor Sir John Plumb, the future Professor Sir Simon Schama, the future Professor David Nokes, the future Professor David Blackbourn and the future Dr Peter Musgrave) "to drink the place dry before it finally closed". How well they succeeded in their attempt can be judged from the evidence of Jack tearing down the brass Final Orders Bell as they left and making off with it back to Christ's. The, by now, well-liquored party marched triumphantly down Petty Cury with Jack at their head waving the bell to ring out the demise of one of his favourite drinking haunts. We found the bell at the back of one of his cupboards when he died. It sold at auction at Jack's own "closing down" sale for £90. The auctioneer allowed himself the wry comment that "this bell was apparently stolen from the *Red Lion* in Petty Cury. It was torn from the wall by Sir John Plumb, an act that casts an unusual light on how distinguished Cambridge academics once conducted themselves!" After a thoughtful pause, he added, "Sir

John seems to have been rather a lively chap". Apparently the bell now decorates the bar of the *Queen's Head* at Newton.

Beer drinking had also set the tone in yet earlier days when Jack Plumb spent every Easter vacation sailing with the Green Wyvern Yacht Club. On these expeditions all life revolved around the pub. Craig Barlow, another historian schoolmaster, described the "electrifying effect of the arrival of Jack in these beer and sawdust surroundings" and these long drinking sessions certainly allowed Jack to give full expression to his dominant personality – tongues were loosened by beer, inhibitions were cast to the winds and things could be said which would have been unacceptable in the cold light of day. It was a situation made for Jack to say the un-sayable, ask the un-askable and argue the indefensible – just the situation he enjoyed most. In these tumultuous debates senior figures in the Green Wyvern hierarchy, such as the Howard brothers and Gordon Winterton (the three schoolmasters who had originally set up the club) gave as good as they got; occasional imposing visitors like Pat Moynihan and Frank Fenton (with his double First in Greats at Oxford, and later Vice-President of US Steel) put up stout resistance; and youngsters like myself occasionally tried our hand at challenging the dominant voice, but an alcohol-fuelled Plumb relished the arguments and rarely gave ground and never gave in. They could be turbulent times.

Not everyone was an admirer. The odious toad-like mother of Bert and Cecil Howard declared Plumb to be "a sunket" – a Norfolk insult I never fully understood but which I was assured was about as low as one would ever want to be. Since Plumb had seduced and then promptly dumped her only daughter perhaps one can understand and forgive Mrs Howard's less than flattering description. And I have to admit that Mrs. Howard had an enviable way of pinning people down with her nicknames – Jack came to be known as "**the** Sunket of all sunkets" (the defining example of this despicable creature); Gordon Winterton's wife, Valerie Winterton, who looked like a young and sexier Felicity Kendal, was nicknamed "all bum and pockets", which exactly caught the impression made by her tight fitting jeans; and I was called "the long-haired Lothario" for reasons which I could never understand and, alas, certainly did not deserve.

In these years Jack had a taste for even less salubrious dives. In those days London did not mean St James's Street, much less St James's Palace. It could mean East End Pubs on the Isle of Dogs – hardly the haunt of the respectable professional middle class that Jack then aspired to join, but good places to let down one's hair in relative anonymity. I recall one such evening that came close to disaster. Having dragged a group of rather doubtful friends out East on the grounds that the jazz was exceptionally good in the smoky, noisy interior of the very crowded pub we finished up in, Jack caught the eye of a very pretty young woman across the room. Having made eye contact, Jack stared intently at her.

Given his bulging eyes and concentrated attention, just looking at her might have been interpreted as having lascivious intent, but he then very deliberately licked his lips. Just what this act denoted in the East End one can only guess at, but suddenly we were surrounded by a threatening group of heavies convinced that one of their women had been publicly insulted. The situation looked quite ugly but was dramatically transformed when Jack's right hand shot inside his jacket. In an instant the circle took a collective step backwards and, against a gasp of "This one's tooled up", there was a chorus of "No guns, there's no need for that". Jack left his hand inside his jacket, put on what he called his 'Peter Lorre look', and the circle retreated further. The less brave of us thought that this was a good moment for a strategic retreat and quietly withdrew, firmly taking Jack (hand still inside his jacket) with us.

To this day I am convinced that Jack reached instinctively for his wallet in the hope that (by buying a round of drinks for everybody) he could buy his way out of trouble, but, in the story as he told it, he had saved us all from a beating by his own quick thinking. In claiming to have saved us all from the heavy mob, he conveniently forgot that we were not being threatened, he was. And he had created the offence in the first place. We were guilty only by association. But he remained triumphant. It just showed, he argued, that he knew exactly how to face down a threatening mob! "Meet force with force" was his characteristic advice. Fortunately the other side, the much tougher looking East Enders, were of an altogether more conciliatory disposition.

Many of his old friends have equally arresting stories of Jack's youthful enjoyment of a Bohemian lifestyle in the thirties and forties – stories of heavy drinking sessions in Paris pavement cafés which grew so uproarious that Jack would summon taxis to drive the whole party less than ten yards to the café next door; stories of excessively amorous farewells with most unsuitable partners being watched disapprovingly by more up-tight academics and their outraged wives; and many other stories of a free-wheeling lifestyle and abandoned behaviour, none of which would have greatly advanced his prospects in Cambridge.

Later in life, when he perhaps felt that his status and success would protect him, he continued to behave in what he called his "unbuttoned style". After one uninhibited occasion in Caius, it took a very long time before the College staff stopped saying (with heavy irony) "We know how much your friends enjoy themselves when they dine here, Sir", whenever I booked another dinner in college. Their comments were the entirely justifiable consequence of Jack's behaviour after Gordon Winterton's 50th birthday, which I had foolishly agreed to host in Caius. Jack, in his cups, had paraded round the dining room extravagantly kissing every compliant woman in sight and within reach. He did this to the accompaniment of extravagant declarations of unbridled lust, and, if allowed, embarrassing public manifestations of it. In a pitiful attempt to rescue my reputation I led the party back to my rooms in Caius Court where my wife and I thought his drunken antics might at least be more discreetly hidden. All that happened was that he twined himself around Selina, the first wife of his old friend Dante Campailla, with such enthusiasm that their combined weight completely destroyed a charming Victorian buttoned-back nursing chair. The chair was a much-cherished favourite of my wife's. Its sad wreckage was a reminder of the (admittedly only occasional) hazards of entertaining Jack Plumb in his cups.

On a later occasion in New York his behaviour with Selina led to his whole party being asked to leave the Rainbow Room. After a very good dinner, Jack and Selina had taken to the floor under the watchful if indulgent gaze of her husband Dante. According to Dante's account at Jack's memorial dinner they danced with impressive expertise. Carried away with his own prowess Jack asked his partner to kick off her shoes the better to respond to his dancing skills (and, I expect, the better to balance their heights). Having done so she then removed her stockings (the better to retain her balance on the polished dance floor). Whether it was the public shedding of her clothes, which led to the request that they leave or, as Dante claimed, the extravagant eroticism of Jack's dancing, we shall never know. As usual, when faced with such problems, Jack's solution was to order more expensive wine. An order of a couple of magnums of their best champagne apparently appeased the outraged American staff and led those in charge of the Rainbow Room to change their minds and let his party stay.

Such enthusiastic partying in such expensive surroundings was very much for the future. His behaviour may not have changed as much as his friends would have liked over the years but the locations went steadily up market. New York nightclubs and super smart restaurants were all a far cry from the beer and sawdust of his youthful drinking haunts. He was a master of successful social disguise and a master of social adaptation. The man and the methods remained the same, but he quickly learned how to make himself acceptable (sometimes only just acceptable) wherever he finally pitched up. The journey from the working class two-up two-down of his birth via the petit bourgeois semi-detached and seedy pub life to a royal palace and plutocratic pleasure domes was one he greatly enjoyed. When he first stayed the night at Sandringham as a guest of the Queen he used the headed notepaper in his bedroom to write to his friends, saying simply "Made it!"

He loved learning the new rules that prevailed in these heady social circles and loved imparting them to a succession of what he called his "more un-travelled pupils", even if his own behaviour did not offer an ideal role model.

He first learned the arcane skills of successful social adaptation in Cambridge. He believed not only in watching and learning by example. He also believed in reading and learning by rote. He was the only person I have ever met who knew *Debrett's Correct Form* off by heart. If you wanted to know how to address an archbishop, an archdeacon or an ambassador Jack was your man. If you wanted to know the proper way formally to address a letter to the vice-Chancellor of Cambridge, as against the vice-Chancellor of Oxford (not as simple as one might think), Jack was a quick and authoritative source. As for the aristocracy no cadet title was too minor for Jack not to know its place in the social hierarchy. Perhaps – given his chosen research topic – all this information really was necessary. The important thing was that the young Plumb really believed that it was. He was pained beyond belief by my insouciant unconcern with such social trivia. To him a detailed knowledge of the niceties of English etiquette was vitally important. If he was to succeed in his chosen profession, he felt that he must learn to conduct himself as a gentleman, or at least as someone who could from time to time pass himself off as one. He was certainly very well informed on how to behave – however badly he often put that knowledge to use. As the distinguished economic historian, Munya (later Sir Mchael) Postan, once said to me, "How extraordinary it is that the man from the back-streets of Leicester should be better informed about the rules of social precedence and protocol than my wife who was the daughter of an earl". He then pointedly added, "And how even more extraordinary it is that the man with such an insistence on the rules of social behaviour should also be the rudest man in Cambridge".

He even riled those senior professorial colleagues who, having received a knighthood, proudly listed themselves as "Professor Sir", by pointing out that according to *Debrett's Correct Form* it was a dreadful solecism to use any title ahead of one bestowed by Her Majesty the Queen. Understandably few of them were willing to stop using their hard-earned academic titles, but to do him justice when Plumb was knighted he always presented himself as Sir John Plumb, dropping *Professor* because court etiquette expected nothing less, and dropping *Jack* "because the Queen does not like nicknames". Such advice did not go down well with colleagues such as my colleague Professor Sir Sam Edwards at their moment of career triumph.

From all accounts the young Plumb was at first more cautious about what he said and did in Cambridge. He knew he had to make himself socially acceptable. And even more importantly he had to make himself professionally employable. Making unnecessary enemies would simply make his ambitions more difficult to achieve. He checked his tongue and learned to listen and to flatter.

The uninhibited street-wise habitué of East End pubs was not the image the young Plumb was trying to project in Cambridge and in the academic world at large. There, he was learning the tricky arts of pleasing such disparate and demanding potential academic patrons as L.B. (later Sir Lewis) Namier, Herbert (later Sir Herbert) Butterfield and George Macaulay Trevelyan (later to be awarded the Order of Merit). The least demanding and in the long run the most influential (on history in general as well as on Plumb in particular) was the great G.M. Trevelyan.

All Trevelyan seemed to demand was that Jack kept up with him on his thirty mile walks and that he be allowed the pleasure of polishing Plumb's apprentice prose.

The other two were much more complicated personalities. Both wanted disciples, both wanted complete devotion to themselves, both wanted uncritical acceptance of their historical methods. Each loathed the other. Even the subtle and quick-witted and sure-footed Plumb would eventually have found it impossible to serve two such masters. Fortunately he decided to serve neither.

The decision made him two powerful enemies – but by refusing to join Namier in the *History of Parliament* project he gave himself the freedom to write the kind of books he wanted to write, and by breaking with Butterfield he created the freedom to attract pupils who shared his vision of what history should be. Both were brave decisions for a young eighteenth-century historian with his way to make. Both were the right decisions.

There was no way that he could have maintained for long a workable relationship with the teetotal, Methodist, right-wing Butterfield. Initially they were much drawn to each other. Plumb found Butterfield "brilliant, exasperating, devastating, mischievous, mixing in equal quantities malice and generosity". They argued until the early hours of the morning. "He dragged his principles before my blood-shot eyes", wrote Plumb, "with the skill of a matador. He forced me to reconsider every idea that I had; I got better at defending myself, and through Butterfield I gradually knew that I would never truly belong to the profession of history. I loved yet distrusted Butterfield's impish qualities, his almost electric versatility at times daunted me but his major principles – his deep belief in the role of Providence (Christian of course) in human history – left me, in the end, bored as well as disbelieving. We disagreed too on the function of history. I believed then as I believe now that history must serve a social purpose no matter how limited – to try to teach wisdom about the past and so, perhaps, no more than perhaps, about ourselves and our times. Butterfield thought historians should suspend all judgment about history". So Jack decided to disengage himself. To judge from reports from those who have worked on the Butterfield archive, Sir Herbert never fully forgave him. The love-hate relationship was a long-lasting one, but it was a relationship doomed to fail.

There was no way either that Plumb could have become one of Namier's long-term disciples. Here the barrier was historical methodology and historical interpretation as much as incompatible personalities and religious beliefs. Namier was convinced that the keys to understanding politics, and therefore to understanding political history, were to be found in greed and self-interest. Realist as he always was, and cynic that he often was, Jack nevertheless found this view a depressingly reductionist interpretation of politics. As he said, even if one accepted such a view one still had to recognize the very different ideological routes that one could choose in pursuit of one's self-interest and self-promotion. Such choices could control an individual's career, dictate the outcome of historical events and determine a country's future. History without such dimensions would be an arid and incomplete record. It was not a form of history that could have much long-term appeal for Plumb.

Quite apart from the methodological gap between them, Plumb was increasingly drawn to a view of history that was poles apart from that of Namier's bleak technical vision. He wanted to write history that was read outside the modest limits of academia. He was increasingly drawn to the view that Trevelyan was a better guide to that ambition. He was increasingly convinced by Trevelyan's view that "history's power was essentially poetic rather than scientific". If he had to choose between the classic narratives of Gibbon, Macaulay and Trevelyan and the so-called "technical" history as espoused by Namier and later by Elton, then what Simon Schama has called "the lumbering Goliaths of technical history" had no chance of enlisting his support.

It is no accident that the only historian Plumb felt the need to organize a *Festschrift* for was Trevelyan. It was no accident that the piece he quoted from him in his introduction was about "the poetry of history". Trevelyan had written that "the poetry of history lies in the quasi-miraculous fact that once, on this earth, once, on this familiar plot of ground, walked other men and women, as actual as we are today, thinking their own thoughts, swayed by their own passions, but now all gone, one generation vanishing after another, gone as utterly as we ourselves shall shortly be gone like ghosts at cock-crow". It was Trevelyan's conviction that "There is nothing that more divides civilized from semi-civilized men than to be conscious of our forefathers as they really were, and bit by bit to reconstruct the mosaic of the long forgotten past". It was increasingly Plumb's conviction that "hundreds of thousands of men and women read history [out of] curiosity mixed with a desire to escape into another world". It was increasingly his hope to satisfy those desires. It was a hope that would have excited dismissive contempt and derision from Namier and his followers.

Much of this debate about historical method was for the future. In his twenties and thirties, his main need was to secure a permanent position. He could not afford to offend any possible patron and his correspondence shows him skilfully keeping contact with all of them without making any firm commitment to any of them.

Eventually his patience was rewarded and Cambridge doors started to open up for him. With the perspective of hindsight he always used to reassure the brilliant young who were impatiently waiting for recognition that "all things come to those who wait". To people like Simon Schama and my wife who both suffered shameful delays in getting the university jobs they deserved he always insisted that ability could be slowed down but very rarely blocked altogether. Their experiences (and, of course, his own) gloriously proved him right, but for a young man of Plumb's impatient nature it must have been very galling to see lesser men effortlessly achieve what he pined for. It may surprise those who knew Plumb only in the years of his high success to learn that in 1938 he applied unsuccessfully for an Assistant Lectureship at Exeter.

Needless to say he did not tell many people about what he would later have regarded as a humiliating rejection.

It took him six years in Cambridge to get a Research Fellowship at King's and it was twelve years (admittedly including the war years) since he came up as a graduate student and sixteen years since he started at Leicester before he achieved a permanent job in Cambridge. Even then he had to swallow his pride when King's told him that there would be no permanent position for him there. So, when Christ's offered him a teaching Fellowship in 1946, he gratefully accepted what the Fellows of Kings rather cruelly called "going back to the suburbs" and devoted himself to making an unambiguous success of his position there. No job was too humble for the young Plumb to take on – his formidable energies and his undoubted stamina allowed him to thrive on over-work. He rapidly made himself indispensable.

So, unlike many academic "stars", Plumb dedicated himself to becoming "a good college man". Anyone who used that phrase in a disparaging way in his presence could expect an exocet-like rebuke. Not for him the uninterrupted research time that many academic prima donnas now demand. He was in turn an Official Fellow, College Lecturer and Director of Studies in History, Tutor, Steward, Wine Steward, Vice-Master and Master. He once even unsuccessfully stood for Bursar – he failed by a single vote. Greater love for his college has no man than the Fellow willing to take on such burdens whilst at the same time producing a stream of original research.

Of those who take on such college burdens, few pour as much energy (some would say as much interference) into them as Jack Plumb did. Many of these college posts had no exact terms of reference but Plumb interpreted them as a licence to take over the college, to energize his more torpid colleagues and to organize everything from a royal visit to a new building along the lines that he saw fit. When as a young don he was made Steward he assumed a Napoleonic interpretation of the range of his duties and generously took on responsibility for the kitchens, the gardeners, the porters, the bed-makers, the buildings, the allocation of rooms and the organisation of college entertainments. His correspondence with C.P. Snow in the late 1940s is full of gleeful descriptions of the absurdities of his colleagues and his even more gleeful accounts of how he made them do his bidding.

A classic example is his description of his role in the arrangements for entertaining Queen Elizabeth (later the Queen Mother) when she visited Christ's in 1948, as the first woman formally to take a Cambridge degree in person. According to Jack's account, the collegiate response was frenzied. In a letter to Snow, which opens with the words, "Never entertain a Queen", Jack vividly described the anxious delight with which the Fellowship prepared for the royal presence. Everything from the danger of rain falling on the royal head to suitable provision for royal comfort stops was anxiously debated. According to the Plumb correspondence, the whereabouts of the royal hat occupied two whole college meetings. Where it was to be removed before she donned the doctoral bonnet, how it was to be conveyed from the Senate House back to Christ's, where it was to be safely kept until it was returned to the royal head – all such details were exhaustively debated and meticulously planned for. The decision that an undergraduate runner should convey the royal hat across Cambridge led inevitably to the further delicate decision as to who the undergraduate should be and who would have the authority to choose him. Such matters went far beyond the revelations of Snow about the treacherous intrigues of college politics. It was *Microcosmographia Academica* at its richest and ripest. P.G. Wodehouse could not have imagined it. Tom Sharpe could not have bettered it.

In the photographs of the royal visit, the round, already-balding head of Plumb can clearly be seen. As befitted his comparative youth and junior position in the Fellowship, he was quite properly bringing up the rear of the party, but to judge from his letters it was Plumb who was in control, in command and in charge. It was where he always preferred to be.

The fact that he thought that his colleagues' reactions to such matters were profoundly comic did not stop him taking them very seriously himself. If there was an event he liked to run it. If there was a problem he liked to solve it. If there was an election he liked to win it. He was a natural college politician and he gave a huge amount of his time to plotting, persuading, bullying or flattering his colleagues into agreeing with his plans. One of his favourite maxims for running the College was "always have a candidate".

When it came to Mastership elections, he was in his element and he certainly always had a candidate. I remember how hard he worked to set up Sir Oliver Wright as his successor and how dashed he was when he failed. He had got the necessary support from the Fellowship to elect him and he had extracted an agreement from Sir Oliver that he would accept. All was set fair when one Sunday morning in his Suffolk home the telephone rang and Sir Oliver said that he had received an offer he could not refuse from Mrs Thatcher. It amounted to a royal command that he should take the British Ambassadorship at Washington. He would have to decline the Mastership. Jack was nothing if not a realist. He knew at once that he was defeated. But although he was completely out-gunned by the Thatcher initiative, he immediately switched to plan B and started to mobilize support that afternoon for his pupil, Professor Barry Supple. He was determined to stop Professor Hans Kornberg being elected but he failed by one vote. Supple and Kornberg were tied at 22 votes each. When the tie was broken, the decisive vote, to Jack's not inconsiderable fury, moved the other way.

Little wonder then that at the next election when Kornberg was to be replaced, Jack insisted on coming out of hospital in a wheelchair so that he could cast his vote for Dr Alan Munro, the biochemist and immunologist who was to prove such a success as Master, especially in establishing the college's fund raising campaign. I tried to persuade him not to take risks with his health. "Surely", I said, "you can agree to pair with one from the other side". "I wouldn't trust any of the buggers", he growled. "Anyway", he said, "there isn't really another side. Alan Munro is the only candidate still in the race, but the mean-minded buggers cannot be cajoled into producing the majority he needs. They would rather abstain than vote for him". For a man of Plumb's decisive nature, abstaining was for wimps. So out he came by ambulance, cast his decisive vote, and then returned, triumphant in his wheelchair, back to Addenbrooke's.

To do justice to Jack Plumb's role in college politics would require a lengthy biographical memoir devoted to that alone. Even from my own correspondence with him, which admittedly stretches over fifty years, I could produce several richly evidenced chapters. But college politics are an acquired taste and one that most people sensibly never acquire. I will, perhaps, write something elsewhere on the political manoeuvrings of the Fellows in Christ's and try to explain the use Snow made of them in *The Masters*. Sir David Cannadine has recently had a passing look at this in his sparkling, beautifully crafted Lady Margaret lecture on "Snow, Plumb and Todd". It might be worth saying here (given the merriment he evoked in his audience at the endless round of drinking that, according to Snow's fictional account, the Fellows of Christ's seemed to indulge in) that this was much closer to the truth than he might imagine. I am amazed and not a little embarrassed to read in my correspondence from the 'fifties and 'sixties just how much life seemed to revolve around drink. Cannadine's audience rocked with laughter as he quoted from Snow's novels his accounts of how dons would ask one to join them for a glass of Chablis at 10.30 in the morning or a glass of Madeira at coffee time or a whiskey before dinner and a bottle of claret with it and a bottle of port after it and "perhaps a brandy as a nightcap". Alas, on the evidence of my letters, this seems very close to the truth. Old "Daddy" Grose, the Senior Fellow at Christ's, really did say things like "We find it rather fortifying" as he asked one to join him for a glass of Madeira in the morning or "a really rather decent bottle of claret" in the evening. Young historians forget that in those pretty enclosed, all male societies, (without the distractions of television or young women or much money or power), there seemed much more time for petty college politics.

Drink was the almost universal solvent which loosened tongues, encouraged indiscretions and allowed perceptive interrogators like Plumb and Snow to prise open secret ambitions and ancient animosities. Much of the time the SCR at Christ's was run like a miniature Whips Office in the House of Commons – consumed by a need to get the votes out. Soliciting support, spiking the opposition's plans, judging who could be "turned" and which Fellow always bore the imprint of the last person to sit on him, all this was part of everyday college life. One was sucked into it from the moment one joined the Fellowship. There are colleges well known to me that still operate like this today. There are many fellows equally well known to me who are still "exalted by wine" many nights in the week.

Politics and drinking still go hand in hand. Most academics have little power and less money. So scoring points and plotting minor coups have greater appeal than in many other spheres of life. It is like office politics with the difference that many of the plotters do not have a home to go to. They live and work, eat and drink, plot and plan all in the same small college world – when Plumb was elected to a Fellowship at Christ's, the whole fellowship amounted to only eighteen Fellows.

And in some colleges they never have to retire – continuing to plot and plan and vote as Life Fellows until death finally releases them from addictive college politics. Little wonder that the politics sometimes fester. Little wonder that malice and bitterness sometimes thrive. When one of my colleagues boasted that he was going to give up malice for Lent, there was a great shout of alarm. "Oh please don't", his colleagues cried in unison "What would poor malice do without you?" Alas the petty feuding and minuscule animosities do not translate well to paper. They mostly seem irremediably trivial. But that does not mean that they were not ferociously fought over. Henry Kissinger was only too accurate when (having been asked why academic politics were so vicious), he replied, "Because the stakes are so small".

Perhaps if I quote from a single letter written by John Kenyon, a distinguished historian of the seventeenth century and a Jack-supporting Fellow of Christ's, it might give some flavour of my old college in the mid-1950s. It powerfully evokes the intense emotions that Jack aroused. It also incidentally gives a little hint of the way dons in those days tried to sublimate their sexual needs by burying themselves in work and politics. The letter is from Kenyon to Dante Campailla, a former schoolmate of his in Sheffield who had read Law at King's. It describes a tiny part of the internecine battles over the election of a new Bursar in Christ's.

Jack, ever eager for any form of power and influence, very much wanted the job. He saw it as a stepping-stone to the Mastership. In fairness to him he would have done it very well in terms of driving the College forward financially and in fairness to his enemies he might well have done it pretty badly by stirring up enmity in the Fellowship. Fortunately for him (and probably for them) he did not get it.

Jack was too ambitious, too creative, too dynamic a personality to have been a safe, boring Bursar. He would have been a decisive, even a risk-taking, Bursar. Most colleges are not comfortable with Bursars who take risks. I have known colleges that could be scandalized by Bursars who took even the smallest decisions without lengthy prior discussions. I know of one Cambridge college in which a General Meeting recently listened to a thirty minute tirade seeking to "turn back the tide of Bursarial tyranny" when a newly elected Senior Bursar took it on himself to replace a water-ruined television set with a new one without seeking the Fellows' permission. With Jack Plumb it would have been a building he bought without permission, not a T.V. set. So perhaps it is just as well that the economist Arthur Prest got the job. He was not as charismatic or exciting as Plumb would have been (Plumb used to say, very unkindly, that he could have bored for England) but I can confirm that he was a decent chap and a safe pair of hands; and as an academic economist he was thought to be likely to be a good investor – a very common mistake in Cambridge colleges who rapidly learn that not all economists are as effective as Maynard Keynes. The point was that Christ's ultimately preferred the promise of a quiet life with Prest to the fear and excitement of a turbulent one with Plumb. And who is to say that they were wrong. Prest liked the banality of the tried and trusted, Plumb liked to trust his judgement on the new and exciting. Prest was a War Bonds man, Plumb was an Equities man. Prest liked safe agricultural land. Plumb liked the hope-value of development land. But above all Christ's could rely on Prest seeking consensus. They feared that they would be bullied and bulldozed by Plumb into accepting his decisions. So, not so very surprisingly, they chose Prest, but not without a battle royal, not without a typical bout of bitter Cambridge college politics.

If the seemingly uneventful outcome was that Christ's got a perfectly competent, if un-exciting Bursar, the politics that led to that outcome were not at all uneventful and were far from boring for those involved – as John Kenyon's letter to Dante Campailla reveals.

"Christ's College,
Cambridge
13 January 1955

About Jack (confidential).

My Dear Dante,

I met him on Sunday, when he calculated the odds at 13:7 in his favour, with two doubtful. We had reckoned without the Midianites, otherwise the Three Murderers. Pratt, Davies and Kempton. Hating Jack like poison, they pushed the claims of Arthur Prest, the economist; far too nice a chap to be associated with them.

When we met on Monday at 10 it was soon clear that the Midianites had won over the two doubtfuls: Yale, the lawyer, who genuinely preferred Prest, and Sir Alexander Todd, who likes Jack but fears his competition later on for the Mastership. {That made it 13:9 in Plumb's favour} But the boat was really torpedoed when two of Jack's most loyal allies revealed that they had been brainwashed: Raven, a treacherous old swine, from whom nobody ever expects much, and Hamilton. Jack has a very high regard for Hamilton, and likes him very much – I think his defection hurt him more than anything. (I should add, of course, that Jack and Prest had left the meeting.) Kempton put up a strong case for Prest, arguing very temperately, and at about 11 a vote was taken – a dead heat 11:11.

By this time the Master had come out in Jack's favour, and voted for him. We sat about for some time; several futile suggestions were made; and another vote was taken at 11.10 a.m. with the same result. We then adjourned for half an hour for coffee, until 11.45; after much caballing and false bonhomie, but not much result.

The fun started when we re-assembled. Pratt and Davies began to pull Jack to pieces, saying he had a gift for alienating people, that he was disliked by many people in the University, and that the servants hated him when he was Steward: in short, he wasn't tactful enough to make a good Bursar. Since the late Wyatt was hardly the most tactful of men, there was also a lot of shit thrown at him in passing, as it were. Much of what they said of Jack, I feel, entre nous, to be quite true, but irrelevant; and doubly so since it was quite evident that nobody was going to freely change his mind at this stage. Some of the Opposition were clearly embarrassed at the tactics of their campaign managers.

But unless somebody did change his mind, we would have to go outside the College, which was unthinkable with two first class men available. After about ten minutes' futile bickering in conditions of mounting tension the Vice Master (Steen) announced that he was going to abstain. Prest was then elected 11:10.

The tension of all this was quite unbelievable. I had to have a bath and lie down for most of the afternoon, and I wasn't the only one.

Jack, as I've said took it philosophically, even puckishly. ("Shall I terrorise the servants", he enquired blandly after dinner, "if I ask for the candles to be lit?"). Also the Midianites are somewhat ashamed of themselves, and are making no objection to Rupert Hall's Official Fellowship. The Master is sure to appoint a sound man to succeed Prest as Tutor, so Jack will be able to consolidate his Empire. Prest himself is rather in the position of Eisenhower, a very clean man elected by dirty tactics and dirty men – which way he'll swing is anybody's guess. Everybody is now very nice to everybody else.

Thinking it over, it is clear that in some respects Jack has himself to blame. I am reminded of Wellington's remark on being told that Parliament had refused to increase the personal allowances of the Princes of the Blood: – "By God!" he said, "They have insulted – personally insulted – two thirds of the gentlemen of England, and how can it be wondered at that they take their revenge upon them in the House of Commons?"

This letter is wonderfully revealing about Christ's College politics. It highlights the bitter intensity and unforgiving rivalry that so often convulsed the college; and it highlights, too, the need in such a small claustrophobic community to return as soon as possible to some semblance of civilised behaviour in order to keep the place running.

Kenyon's postscript to this letter is equally revealing about how much less time was spent discussing their personal lives. Sex and women all too often get confined to the footnotes. To judge from John Kenyon's description of his recent girlfriend they were not always treated or discussed with any great sensitivity. Of this un-named mistress, he wrote: *"The affair of Black Bitch is not so strange as you suppose. She insisted that I take her to some stupid dance instead of returning to Cambridge to write my lectures. On the other hand, I don't want to feel obliged to stay in Sheffield or even go there very often – this Christmas, for instance, I only wanted to stay ten days, but because of her I had to make it three weeks. But I admired her very much (she was a girl of real character and spirit) and I was genuinely sorry to see her go. As you say the solution would be an occasional girlfriend (not prostitute) in London. However I can't really afford the time or the money, and my work effectively sublimates all unruly desires".*

It was quite clear that work and ambition ranked well ahead of sex, and love hardly came into it. One feels that "Black Bitch" is a very revealing name for his mistress. He might well have been talking about an old gun dog he admired but had had regretfully to put down when she ceased to fit in with his career plans and work needs.

As Kenyon said in his final sentences *"Of course, I approve highly of Molly (or*

Lena) – I am never polite in such matters, I'm afraid." Here he was speaking of Molly Randle who later became Selina Campailla when she married Dante, but such matters were granted about one twentieth of the time he spent describing Jack's failure to get the Bursarship. College politics were serious, time-consuming preoccupations. They required detailed concentrated attention. Sexual needs and future life-partners got half a sentence each. Emotional needs got even less. What could more vividly display what really interested the dons of Christ's than that letter? What could better illustrate how rapidly the high drama of college politics fades over time?

For that last reason alone college politics are best treated with the lofty disdain they deserve. The Fellows of Christ's may have been infuriated by the way in which Snow depicted them in *The Masters*, but, in truth, he rather flattered them. He gave a dignity and a strong narrative power to college politics that they very rarely deserve.

Jack, however, was an addict. He may have learned the sycophantic arts of seeking favour with the English aristocracy in later life, but in the early decades of his life at Christ's he sought power and influence in college through full-scale frontal attack after tireless plotting.

He was involved in long running battles with Canon Charles Raven, Master of Christ's from 1938-1950, and Alex Todd (later Lord Todd) Master from 1963-1978. He was also centrally involved in a poisonous campaign against Lucan Pratt, the Senior Tutor whom he forced out of office in 1961. In the battle with Pratt he made many enemies, but he felt wholly justified in forcing him to resign from his central role in college admissions. Pratt had become notorious throughout Cambridge for his success in attracting brilliant sportsmen to Christ's – so successful that it was not uncommon for an overwhelming majority of almost all university teams to be Christ's men. Pratt became so obsessed with his success that he would sit in the Junior Combination Room to pick up tips about promising sporting talent from undergraduates. He became notorious in admission interviews for tossing a cricket ball or a rugger ball at aspiring candidates and judging them by the skill with which they caught them. I can confirm from my own experience that, when in my admission interview he read from my school reference that I had represented my school for both cricket and rugger and represented my county for the latter, he threw both balls at me simultaneously and, when I casually caught both of them, said "You're in". In my own defence, I should add that I also won an open scholarship, and when I saw the super-charged quality of the college teams, I never played a game of any sport again.

Plumb was infuriated, not by the standard of the Christ's sports teams, but by the fact that Pratt allowed the college's academic standards to be damagingly lowered in order to let in any promising sportsman. He was determined to attack Pratt's admissions plans root and branch, and Pratt played into his hands by failing to rein back on his tireless pursuit of sporting excellence at the cost of academic standards. The lists of brilliant sportsmen grew and grew, the lists of brilliant Firsts in the Tripos went down and down. It reached a stage when Plumb was gathering more and more support for his anti-Pratt campaign, and finally Pratt had to resign. But the fact that Plumb had academic virtue on his side in this campaign made little difference to those who thought that Pratt had been hard done by. He had many friends and admirers amongst the Fellowship and amongst the alumni, and inevitably Plumb harvested an impressive crop of new enemies as a result of his campaign.

This seemed to matter little to him. He was exultant. He had defended academic standards in the admissions procedures. He had defeated a sworn enemy. He had demonstrated his mastery of college politics.

For someone as addicted as he was to such parochial matters triumphing in such arcane skills really mattered. Even in old age he could not kick the habit.

So suffice it here to say that even in his late eighties, he was still deeply involved in manipulating the college to do his will in electing new Research Fellows of his choice, or spending its money as he chose. Inevitably he still had a couple of candidates for the 2002 Master-ship election and was furious when they would not stand. Putting one's research interests before the interests of the College cut little ice with Plumb. "Do they not realise that the College will be here long after their research has been superseded?" he ranted. "Anyone of an age to be a Master will be past his research best, and anyone worthy to be a Master will have done quite enough research already. What matters is the academic leadership to ensure that the College survives and prospers as it has done for the last five hundred years". Jack was by no means consistent in his views on such matters, but no one can doubt that he more than did his bit to ensure the future for Christ's.

For over fifty years as a Fellow and four years as Master he worked tirelessly to promote its image, raise its profile, maintain and enhance its standards, and raise funds for its future.

For all his undoubted commitment to Christ's, he did not skimp on his university duties either, being, amongst many other things, a notably brisk and efficient Chairman of the History Faculty Board in 1966-68, and a controversial Syndic of the Fitzwilliam Museum.

When many faculty boards regularly meet for five hours at a time, the History Faculty Board under Plumb's chairmanship rarely lasted an hour. Those who arrived three minutes late were likely to be also three items on the agenda late; and I recall Professor Ullmann once leaving the Board Room almost reluctantly at 2.45 having entered only half an hour earlier, and recalling the days under more expansive and more deliberate chairmen when he would not expect to have left before the sun had set below the horizon.

Plumb's passion for speed and efficiency was evident in most of the things he did; from writing a review to writing a reference he rarely dallied, which was one of the reasons why he was able to do so many jobs at the same time. Where some academics agonize for days over an important and lengthy testimonial, Plumb usually wrote a single paragraph with an unambiguous verdict, and got promptly back to his current research.

Being an efficient administrator did not mean that he was an enthusiast for all committee work. When he served on the Council of the Senate, he described it as the most boring thing he had ever done in his life. Watching paint dry would surely be orgasmically exciting, he said, compared with sitting on the Council of the Senate in Cambridge. He cheerfully dismissed his colleagues on this powerful central body as "a mournful mixture of meddlers, nodders and nit-pickers – the very worst kind of academic under-achievers, blessed with only their profound sense of their own self-importance to sustain them". He used to say that as children they must have aspired to be not engine drivers but merely passengers on the train – and complaining passengers at that. He said that Balfour was being flattering when he described the "abominable system" of Cambridge central government as "an ingenious contrivance for making the work of ten wise men appear as if it were inferior to the work of one fool". The experience had its minor value, he claimed, only in giving him some insight into the mentality of the self-elected oligarchies of the eighteenth century.

What he did give his unstinted attention to were his university lectures. When I arrived in Cambridge in 1953 he had established himself as a star lecturer. He was one of the very few lecturers who created a real buzz of excited anticipation before he turned up to perform in the old Mill Lane lecture rooms. He was also one of the relatively few who kept their audiences throughout the year.

Cambridge undergraduate audiences can be a tough test of a lecturer's powers to inform, to instruct and to entertain. I well recall Harry Hinsley starting at the beginning of Term with an audience of over two hundred in Room 3 in Mill Lane and having to watch it dwindle down to two (I was one of the final two). Peter Laslett was another distinguished historian who singularly failed to keep his audience. Many others kept going with very modest audiences indeed.

Star performers, such as Moses Finley in Cambridge or A.J.P. Taylor in Oxford, were in the minority but Plumb was very much one of them. He had waited too long to get his faculty job to waste it and he put himself through agonies of preparation (regularly throwing up before each lecture) to achieve the popularity he sought. His lectures were fluent, witty and irreverent. The ingredients for public success, which allowed him to make so much money on lecture tours in the States later in his career, were already very apparent. He was not as compellingly authoritative as Hugh Trevor-Roper was at his best, he was not as elegantly eloquent and smoothly articulate as future stars such as Quentin Skinner or Sir Keith Thomas, he was not as playful or as vivid a wordsmith as Sir Christopher Ricks, he was not as good or as versatile a radio broadcaster as Sir David Cannadine or Lisa Jardine or Mary Beard or Linda Colley or David Reynolds, he was not as consistently politically polemical as Eric Hobsbawn, and he could not match the exuberant charm and enthusiasm of Simon Schama, but he could energize and enliven a traditional academic lecture in a way that very few of his generation could.

His pupils often fondly recall what Geoffrey Parker called "his genius as a lecturer" and compete with examples of his quick wit and natural showmanship to show how he appealed to the appreciative undergraduate audiences which gathered in such large numbers to hear him. "I remember to this day", recalled Parker "a moment in one of the austere Mill Lane Lecture rooms, during his course on English Constitutional History. He started off 'Charles II and James II: two of the worst monarchs in English history....' Only to stop when two men at the back got up and walked out. It happened that they passed in front of his podium, and we watched Jack speak briefly to them before announcing: 'Ha! Wrong lecture! Thought they were Jacobites!' From that day to this I have longed for a similar impromptu triumph while lecturing".

Those who so admired his relaxed self-confident lecturing manner would have been amazed to have seen the agonies of self-doubt that preceded them. He took enormous trouble to prepare himself for each performance, and treated the most mundane routine undergraduate lecture as if it was an address to his most demanding and critical peers. The energy he poured into them paid off in terms of his large and enthusiastic audiences who stayed faithful to him, but they were a significant drain on him for many years.

6. PLUMB'S EARLY RESEARCH AND HIS LATER PUBLICATIONS

Jack was well aware, however, that (for the successful international career he sought) he would need a solid foundation in published research. Always only too well aware of what he called "the wasted years" of the war and his delayed acceptance in Cambridge, and aware too of the disappointment of his early research in the 1930s and the distractions of his flirtation with fiction, he was determined to make up for lost ground. What he had done before the war had done very little to mark him out as a serious contender to be regarded as a significant scholar.

As a result, he was always happier, in the fifties and sixties at least, in eagerly pursuing his research interests. I was lucky enough to be invited as an undergraduate to accompany him on research trips to Houghton Hall and to see what research conducted in ideal circumstances could be like. Sybil, the Marchioness of Cholmondeley, who lived in the great Norfolk house built by Sir Robert Walpole, represented the platonic ideal of the perfect hostess to preside over such an enterprise. She was striking to look at, fascinating to talk to (with wonderful stories of Lloyd George's amorous activities on country house weekends), highly interested in the research itself, and hugely generous to her guests. She may well have been amused to have two humbly-born historians to entertain, but she certainly did so with verve, elegance and style. I was summoned to her side on a Kent sofa, with a Holbein on an easel at her elbow, while she explained the beauty and provenance of the contents of the house. She showed off with wonderful assurance and flawless scholarship the portraits of her by John Singer Sargent, the superb still life by Oudry, the fabulous baroque pearls fashioned into priceless jewels by Cellini, the magnificent ceramics, the superb bronzes and the world famous furniture made for the house when Sir Robert Walpole had it built and furnished.

Not surprisingly I felt deliciously indulged. I was allowed to choose what we should eat off from a china room stacked with priceless porcelain and I boldly chose Sèvres. I was given a magnificent bedroom complete with a roaring fire – even my bathroom had its own fire, especially lit for my bath. I tried to convince myself that the long hours spent in the archives justified such indulgence. We had after all been so thorough that we had discovered a book borrowed by Colonel Robert Walpole (Sir Robert Walpole's father) from Sidney Sussex College library in 1669 and not returned for 288 years! (The Guinness Book of records cites it as the most overdue book in British library history but I am happy to confirm that no fine was exacted by the magnanimous Fellows of Sidney Sussex). We certainly did not skimp in our scholarly duties but nevertheless I still felt over-generously rewarded for my efforts.

Some of the cosseting was admittedly less than entirely welcome. I have to admit that I was taken aback to discover that my very modest suitcase and its even more modest contents had been unpacked by unseen hands and carefully laid out for my use – I was aghast to find that my ancient socks had been given the hotel napkin treatment and turned into elegantly convoluted shapes so that one had only to insert the one's foot into an invitingly prepared space and then draw them effortlessly upwards. Such embarrassments soon dwindled as, in more than ample compensation, I was taken on a comprehensive tour of the Stone Hall and all the magnificent staterooms. Even the Library in which Jack and I worked was stupendous. As I sat surrounded by Walpole's sumptuously gold tooled calf bound books and gazed out at the herds of white deer roaming the Houghton estate, I (perhaps rather cynically) thought that I could see why Jack was so attracted to research in the great aristocratic houses of the eighteenth century.

He was certainly completely at home at Houghton. He had earned the respect, admiration and trust of the Cholmondeleys. He had also earned a friendship that survived unbroken into great old age. Sybil Cholmondeley always remembered his birthdays, and Jack always showed off with pride the charming gifts of Georgian silver or Lalique glass or a haunch of venison or such like, which she sent from Houghton.

Some of the other archives he worked in would not support the ungenerous view that it was luxury and indulgence that drew him there. Those who think that it was simply Jack's love of an apolaustic life-style that dictated his research interests might have thought that his research work at Blenheim Palace would provide further confirmation of his self-indulgent tastes. If so they would have been much surprised by the reality. I went as a humble research assistant on such a visit and the contrast with research at Houghton could not have been more marked. No aristocratic welcome and certainly no superlative food and wine were on offer from the Duke of Marlborough. On the contrary we entered the house by the tradesmen's entrance, we even paid an entrance fee, and we were then ushered into a white-tiled cellar, which passed as an archive room. It was unbelievably cold. So incensed was Jack at this welcome and this environment – or merely so cold – that he spent several freezing January days there wrapped in the royal standard for warmth, discontentedly but efficiently working his way through the evidence of the behaviour of the Cabinet under Queen Anne. When I, encouraged by his boldness, reached for some lesser ducal pennant to wrap myself in, I was sharply told to desist. My job was to keep copying the documents, not his behaviour. "Youth will keep you warm, McKendrick" was the cold comfort I received. Fortunately the research was productive and Plumb made some exciting discoveries about the working of Queen Anne's cabinet. And listening to the gossip of the Blenheim staff as they chattered about the behaviour of their employer had its lighter moments. Hearing a voice (slightly off stage, as it were, from our research in the Muniment room) ask rather wearily "You know, I really don't understand why his Grace needs a second footman when he dines alone" was worth the entrance fee. But such entertainment was very intermittent, and it was almost unbearably cold.

Little wonder then that, on this occasion, he was very happy to speed back to Christ's and all the college jobs he had to do there. He never skimped on these however pressing the call of his scholarly interests, which make his research output all the more remarkable. Fortunately he had the phenomenal energy and the huge reserves of stamina to make up for his very slow start in research and publications.

When I first met Jack Plumb he had published very little. His first publication had been a ninety-four page booklet on his father's factory entitled *Fifty Years of "Equity" Shoemaking: A History of the Leicester Co-operative Boot and Shoe Manufacturing Society Limited*, which was privately printed in 1936.

This was an act of filial piety, which he knew would earn at best a patronising response from his Cambridge contemporaries. He was the first to admit that much of the firm's archive made for "dull if pleasant reading", so he used it as a chance to showcase his political sympathies – eulogising the workers and condemning the capitalists. "The Equity", he wrote, "is an outstanding example of what the workers can do when power is in their hands. It refutes the often-repeated doctrine that there is a natural selectivity at work in the world which leads to a situation where some must be exploited and some exploit…. Contrasted with English industry as a whole, the "Equity" is a tiny haven of refuge, a foretaste of socialist method, in a capitalist world….The workers at the "Equity"…ought not to forget that many of their brother workers are forced into lives of misery and distress in the system of production for profit, which is the general rule of British industry".

There is much more in the same vein. It amounts to a hymn of praise of the workers' co-operative movement, and a sustained condemnation of capitalism: "the rights of workers are threatened on all sides…the forces of capitalism are so deeply entrenched as to be irremovable by coalitions of workers in production. Capitalism can only be overthrown by political means; only when that has happened will the vast mass of workers enjoy the security and the good wages and treatment which the workers at the "Equity" now enjoy".

This first publication was not then simply a work of filial piety, it was also a work of powerful left-wing piety. Given his dramatic swing to the right in his mature years, he was probably grateful that it was privately printed in very modest numbers and is now very difficult to find. Even in the 1930s it was pretty obscure. Its soft cardboard cover does not even carry the author's name. He must have known that this was not the kind of publication to win him a permanent position in Cambridge. Fortunately for the career he longed for, his later publications were neither obscure nor difficult to find. Once his Penguin history appeared and sold in serious numbers his career took off.

His more significant publications had started very slowly partly because of his frustrated dalliance with novel-writing; partly because of his distractingly anguished love life of the 1930s; partly because of what he always called "the wasted war years"; and partly because, when he finished his Penguin history of the eighteenth century in early 1948, there was such a chronic post-war paper shortage that it was not published until 1950.

After those initial delays, there was an explosion of publications. For in spite of all his college commitments, Jack proved to be a most productive researcher and a hugely prolific publisher.

By the time of my undergraduate days in Cambridge he had had a hand in eight separate publications. Books, articles and reviews had started to pour from his pen. When he supervised me in the mid-1950s he was mainly preoccupied with his forthcoming first volume on Walpole and rightly so because it was that project which established him as a significant scholar. He gave it to me to read in page proof, saying "this has already been checked in galleys and in page proofs by experts", but said that it might be a salutary experience for me to realise how meticulous one has to be in preparing a major history book for publication. It did teach me one important lesson: errors are far more likely to slip through the net in the most unlikely places. When I handed back the final page proofs just before they were to be sent to the printers, I was able to tell him that his title page announced the publication of "Sir Robert Wallope". My last minute contribution may have been very tiny but I used to boast that it saved him from a lot of gleeful mockery from reviewers.

It was good to be reminded of the amount of meticulous attention to detail that was involved in those years of prolific publication. All his work for the next quarter of a century was written in long hand, then typed, then corrected and re-typed, then corrected in galleys, and then corrected in page proofs. It makes it all the more impressive that between 1950 and 1973, he produced twenty-three books and that does not include the twenty-one books that he edited – the nine volumes he edited and introduced for *The History of Human Society* or the four volumes he edited and introduced for *Signet Classics* or the eight volumes of the Fontana *History of Europe* that he edited in those years. These were the decades when he was at the height of his powers and this was the period when he published his two great volumes on *Sir Robert Walpole: The Making of a Statesman* (1956), *Sir Robert Walpole: The King's Minister* (1960), his *Penguin History of England in the Eighteenth Century* (1950), his life of *Chatham* (1953), his study of *The First Four Georges* (1956), his Ford Lectures on *The Growth of Political Stability 1675-1725* (1967) and *The Death of the Past* (1969). These are the books that made his scholarly reputation, but Plumb wanted to be more than simply a scholar. He wrote to be read, and hungered to reach a large audience and it was with *The Renaissance* (1961) and in particular with *Royal Heritage* (1977), which sold 250,000 copies in its first edition, that he did so. These two books sold in massive numbers and together with his collected essays – *Men and Places* (1963), *In the Light of History* (1972), *The Making of a Historian* (1988) and *The American Experience* (1989) – established him as one of the few English historians to reach a wider public.

He must surely be the only British historian for whom the American flag was flown from the flagpole of the American Capitol by express request of the President of the United States after a unanimous vote in Congress on 20th of August 1991. It was flown to mark his 80th birthday. It was a remarkable tribute to an English historian's ability to carry the lessons of history to a wide American public and, in doing so, to do so much to foster Anglo-American relations.

He loved the freedom his American journalism offered him. It gave him the opportunity to expatiate on whatever topic took his fancy and the fact that he chose to pontificate on many of his rivals' chosen territory only added to their fury and resentment. The idea of this widely read, highly literate historian musing interestingly on a great range of centuries, societies and subjects was not popular in the world of narrow academic professionalism in England. So Plumb writing on China or India or Africa, or sounding off on slavery and the American Constitution, or speculating on sex and childhood and the family, or cheerfully propounding the virtues of Fanny Hill and Lucretius, all proved intolerably provocative to many of his more narrowly gifted colleagues back in Cambridge.

It did not help that he was only too happy to discuss their manifold shortcomings in print. He seemed delighted to do so. Where a critic such as Cyril Connolly managed to sound elegantly regretful when he described reviewing books as "the thankless task of drowning other people's kittens", Jack gleefully described the task as "the noble and necessary duty to slaughter other people's sacred cows". Since he did so in memorable prose, his words of condemnation and mockery were much and lovingly quoted – most especially, of course, to those who had been most mercilessly mocked.

He opened his review of *UNESCO's "History of Mankind"* with the following words: "*I don't often wish I were as rich as Paul Getty. Today I do. I want to buy time on every commercial radio and TV from Patagonia to the North Cape, to hire sky-writing planes in all the world's capitals, to take pages of advertising in all the world's press, just to say how awful, how idiotic is this second volume of UNESCO's projected six-volume 'History of Mankind'*".

Of the editor of what he called "this appalling volume", he wrote "*Luigi Pareti seems to have been a scholar of monumental incompetence*" with "*a mind of startling silliness*". Of the illustrations he wrote, "*The illustrations are as bad as the book; ill-chosen, ill-arranged and ill-produced, they would have been shameful 50 years ago*". Of the book as a whole he wrote, "*What is so infuriating is not the vast waste of money and time but that such a signal failure should be possible in a history of one of the most exciting dramatic and important epochs in the life of man. This is neither history nor encyclopaedia, but an incoherent stream of detritus, hacked out of a score of pedestrian textbooks*". There was much more in the same vein about the three-quarter of a million words composed at huge expense by an international team of scholars overseen by "*ancient and learned men*" such as Joseph Needham, Bertrand Russell and the deceased Ernest Barker who "*tottered at the world's expense, to Mexico City or New Delhi to sit in solemn conclave in proliferating committees to plan the un-plannable or comment on the unreadable*". In a single review, Jack must have managed to enrage a tidy proportion of the world's leading scholars. They were dismissed with near contempt. Even less palatably, they were memorably mocked as being boring, hugely incompetent and profoundly silly.

And there were plenty more reviews of the same ilk and the same ire from the same intrepid reviewer. It did not make for universal popularity.

It did, however, make for a certain welcome notoriety. It did not do his editorial ambitions any harm comprehensively to clear the field of most of his eminent rivals. It did not do his ambition to become an academic guru any harm to denounce the grand old men of the profession as superannuated incompetents completely out of touch with current scholarship and research. So Jack was increasingly in demand to pontificate on the nature of history and he was only too eager to do so. He wished to spread his wings and to explore new areas of historical interest.

He did much to encourage those willing to engage in exciting new historical disciplines.

Plumb's major long-term scholarly standing will surely rest securely on his work as a political historian of "the long eighteenth century". His great biography of Walpole has already stood the test of nearly fifty years' scrutiny and has still not been bettered; his Penguin history survived as the best general introduction to eighteenth-century England for forty years until it was finally surpassed by the work of Roy Porter (Plumb perceptively chose Porter to be his last supervision pupil whilst he was still formally in charge of History at

Christ's); and his Ford lectures have permanently changed our attitudes to late Stuart and early Georgian England.

But Plumb recognised very early in his career that other historical disciplines were increasingly coming to the fore. He wrote in *Studies in Social History* (which he edited in 1955) that "*social history, in the fullest and deepest sense of the term, is now a field of study of incomparable richness and the one in which the greatest discoveries will be made in this generation. Its purpose has long ceased to be merely evocativ*e". His prediction has long since been borne out, and he increasingly followed the dictates of his own prophecy – first in an editorial capacity but increasingly in his own writing and research which moved more and more into the sphere of social and cultural history. It was a decision that fuelled and exacerbated the strong antipathies between the Plumb and the Elton schools of historiography in Cambridge and beyond.

7. PLUMB, ELTON AND CHADWICK AND THE REGIUS CHAIR

The personal antipathy between Elton and Plumb was very real and very powerful.

Superficially they were not dissimilar. They were both short, bald and rather plain men (Elton was once memorably described as looking like "a moustachioed grape"); both were muscular and mesomorphic; both were thickset and bespectacled; both were driven by powerful ambition; both were enormously gifted; both gathered about them an impressive number of able pupils; both were massively productive; both were effective communicators; both were bullies who believed in the adversarial approach to life and to scholarship; both seemed to generate genuine affection and passionate dislike in roughly equal proportions; both were outsiders who were determined to achieve insider status; and both, of course, began their professional careers as political historians.

Fundamentally, however, they were very different and they actively revelled in those differences.

One was a product of the provincial English working class, the other (Gottfried Ehrenberg before he became Geoffrey Rudolph Elton) was a Jewish refugee from Prague; one flaunted his (then) left wing opinions, the other trumpeted his right wing views; one loved claret, the other loved whiskey; one cherished the English tradition of History as Literature, the other believed passionately in the Germanic tradition of History as a professional technique; one was a bachelor, the other was married; one made no attempt to hide his hedonistic lifestyle, the other made something of a parade of the simple unostentatious life in the Cambridge suburbs; one had held almost every college post and built his life around his college; the other was a Faculty man with apparently few collegiate ambitions; one believed passionately in the value of undergraduate teaching, the other was only really interested in graduates.

I think that it is also quite revealing that the hobbies of the humbly-born Plumb were claret, antique porcelain, old Master paintings and Georgian silver whilst the hobbies of the rather better connected Elton (son of one distinguished scholar and brother of another) were, as his first "Who's Who" entry proudly proclaimed, "squash racquets, joinery and beer". The self-images they wished to promote were strikingly different. According to their own accounts, one was bisexual, the other was straight. Also according to their own accounts, one lived a pretty promiscuous life style, the other was faithful to his wife of long standing.

They also heartily disliked each other. Both of them saw the other as a dangerous professional rival. Both dished the dirt with unbecoming relish. For my wife and myself, who could recognise the gifts of both of them, and who could also sympathise with their obvious shortcomings, and who were regular guests at both of their tables, it was difficult not be both amused and yet appalled by the blatant point-scoring in which they both over-indulged. Any disobliging rumour was grist to their respective mills. They sneered at each other's habits, they sneered at each other's favourite drinks, they sneered at each other's work, and they did their best to do down each other's pupils.

Their at times obsessive preoccupation with each other was much commented on by their contemporary academic colleagues. John Brewer, for example, recalled "a strange experience some time in the mid-70s, when I attended in the course of a week one of Jack's brilliant dinner parties and a more plodding affair chez Elton (both were well lubricated, but as you can imagine the quality of drink was higher in Christ's). What was odd was that both said the same thing to me, and asked me the same question. Each expressed a begrudging admiration for the other, and each asked me if I didn't think that the other was a rather sad person. Elton saw Jack as a frustrated bachelor surrounded by riches, and Jack saw Elton as chained to a shrewish and unattractive wife."

Whilst they obsessed about each other and continually clashed like two alpha males seeking dominance in their chosen territory, perhaps it is little wonder that Owen Chadwick (with enormous charm, perfect manners, remarkable good looks and excellent Establishment connections – none of which advantages were shared by either Plumb or Elton) should effortlessly out-perform them in collecting the world's prizes that they both so coveted. Chadwick's list of honours included a Mastership of a Cambridge college achieved whilst still in his thirties, a named Cambridge Chair, the Cambridge Vice-Chancellorship, the Chancellorship of the University of East Anglia, the Chairmanship of the National Portrait Gallery, the Regius Chair of History at Cambridge, a Knighthood (the title of which, to his great irritation, as a clergyman, he could not use, but which his wife insisting on advertising by using the title of Lady Chadwick), the Presidency of the British Academy, and the Order of Merit – not to mention a Cambridge Blue, a charming and attractive wife and four children. Of that baker's dozen of achievements, Plumb and Elton could manage only two each.

Chadwick also won in the competition for the quality of his honorary degrees. His rivals must have found it very galling. Indeed I know that they did. But neither of them recognised how much they each contributed to the frustration of their own ambitions by their own character defects. Impartiality and magnanimity were not the first words to leap to everyone's mind when trying to describe either of them. When contrasted with Owen Chadwick, they seemed to be dangerously combative and excessively committed to their own prejudices and their own pupils. Chadwick's academic achievements were very real, and he continued to produce excellent work long after his rivals, but, in addition, he was also almost universally liked and greatly admired for his personal qualities. Perhaps even more importantly, it was felt that he could be trusted not to misuse his power and patronage. He could be relied on, it was felt by those who mattered, to use the influence of office fairly. His judgement would be "sound".

Chadwick's worldly success must also surely have benefited from his charm of manner. As a young man he was almost impossibly glamorous – not only ridiculously good looking with a lovely wife and a double First in History and then Theology, and a record of a triple Blue in Rugby, who captained Cambridge in his third year and went on to play for England, the Barbarians and the British Lions. He was also ordained in the Church of England and elected to the Mastership of a Cambridge college before the age of forty and into a Cambridge chair very soon afterwards. Little wonder that he was offered two Bishoprics and was seriously considered as a possible Archbishop of Canterbury. When it came to the battle for the Regius chair in Cambridge, his success benefited even more from the absence of any of the glaring shortcomings that so many have detected in the characters of Elton and Plumb. The defects in their personalities did them far more harm than any defects (both real and imaginary) in their research. In many people's eyes, they were so bitterly opposed to each other and had so divided the Faculty that they had rendered themselves almost unelectable. In so doing, they left the path open for Chadwick to glide seemingly effortlessly to success.

If Chadwick had comparable defects they remained securely hidden – well masked by his courteous charm of manner and effectively disguised by the characteristic discretion of his conduct. There are certainly those (such as the Cambridge historians Harry Porter, Edward Norman and William Frend) who felt that their careers had suffered as a result of Chadwick's enmity but his smiling face and easy social manner seemed to disarm most criticism. He was certainly much harder to demonise than his two main Cambridge rivals.

Lord Annan diplomatically summed up the Establishment view of the battle for the Regius in 1968 in his book, *The Dons: Mentors, Eccentrics and Geniuses* published in 1999: "It was an appointment by the Crown which was resented by a number of aspirants who had excellent claims; but Chadwick's exceptional character, so devoid of partisan spirit, and his steady publication of books that arose from patient archival research on controversial themes handled without rancour or bias were qualities that not all the other candidates could match". He did not need to spell out that it was felt by the powers that be that Elton and Plumb most certainly could not match those qualities.

Their mutual dislike drove them to exaggerate the differences in their work. But if academic rivalry and personal antipathy intensified the divide, the differences remained very real. In the 1960s they appeared to be of major significance in deciding the future of modern English History in Cambridge. Whilst Owen Chadwick moved serenely and seemingly unstoppably onwards and upwards, gathering in his remarkable collection of positions of power and influence, and yet remaining seemingly above the battle, rival hostile camps gathered around Elton and Plumb. Those who changed sides (as John Kenyon was felt by Plumb to have done and as David Starkey was felt by Elton to have done) were rare, and never wholly forgiven.

Elton espoused ever more strongly the pre-eminent claims of constitutional history, Plumb moved ever more decisively towards the history of social realism. To those who thought that "true" history was to be found only in the archives of Church and State, such an approach was anathema, and Elton was very ready to lead the battle against it.

Elton might be said to have won the battle (after all he did eventually become Regius Professor), but Plumb has surely won the war. The study of history has marched irresistibly in the direction he predicted and led.

Others have used the same metaphor when describing the Plumb-Elton feud. Peter Richards wrote to the Cambridge alumni "Plumb ultimately lost the battle with Elton, retreating – not without rancour – to his elegant rooms in Christ's, where he became Master in 1978. But he won the bigger war for hearts and minds. Over the last twenty years history has become a broader church than ever before, acknowledging the dangers that flow from professionals knowing more and more about less and less".

One must not overstress the levels of personal enmity. They heartily disliked each other but there were limits to their mutual antagonism. Behind the parade of everyday animosity there lurked a basic respect for each other's professional skills and achievements. When Chadwick got the Regius Chair, Elton said openly that, for all their well-known rivalry, he would much rather that Plumb had been given it. That, he thought, would have been a much fairer outcome. It would more properly reflect the quality and importance of their published work. Cynics, on hearing this magnanimous judgment, reflected that such an appointment would also have left a longer period for Elton to inherit after Plumb's retirement.

Plumb showed a similar qualified respect for his old rival when asked by the Patronage Secretary for his recommendation for who should succeed Chadwick. Plumb had no doubt that the obvious internal candidate was Geoffrey Elton and said so.

There were, however, limits to his magnanimity because his first choice was the "external", the Cambridge educated John Elliott then at Oxford, to whom Margaret Thatcher offered the post. Indeed she spent a surprisingly long time trying to persuade him to take it. When Elliott declined, Thatcher reluctantly offered it to Plumb's second choice – Elton.

By then, in 1983, Plumb was increasingly detached from the Cambridge History Faculty. He had in every sense moved on. It had been a very different matter fifteen years earlier when Chadwick was appointed in 1968. Then Plumb knew that he was a very serious contender. Then he had what many of his colleagues thought was a very strong chance of being elected. Then he had high hopes of succeeding. Then, when those hopes were dashed from such an unexpected quarter, the defeat was very painful.

Interestingly, the Cambridge Junior Historians (Faculty historians under the age of forty) had met before the result was announced and drawn up their own shortlist. It was confidently expected that it would be an internal appointment, and Plumb and Elton were thought to be the clear front-runners chosen from a very strong Cambridge field of contenders including Harry Hinsley, Walter Ullmann and Moses Finley (in spite of the fact that the latter was hardly eligible for a Chair in Modern History). If it were to go "outside" then Asa Briggs was regarded as the strongest threat to Elton and Plumb, with Denis Mack Smith regarded as a youthful "dark horse". Chadwick did not even make the top ten. His only backer was Dr Margaret Bowker who presciently said that the junior historians were all completely wrong and that Owen Chadwick would certainly be chosen.

When we incredulously asked "Why?", she replied, "Partly because the Patronage Secretary has already offered him two Bishoprics and, by turning them down, he has impressed the powers that be that he is a dedicated scholar; partly because he was thought to be a far safer bet than either Elton or Plumb; partly because, although Plumb and Elton had far more devoted pupils supporting their claims, that would cut no ice with the Patronage Secretary who talked only to the great and good. Their powerful and influential voices would be far more inclined to support Chadwick". She turned out to be absolutely right, the Junior Historians were proved to be wildly inaccurate in their predictions, and Plumb was left to realise that one of his most cherished ambitions was forever beyond his reach.

It was probably the single career setback he found most difficult to accept. It especially riled him because he recognised all too well how the workings of the patronage system were likely to favour Chadwick over an outsider like himself. Chadwick's father was a wealthy barrister who could afford to send his eldest son to Eton and his other sons to almost equally expensive public schools; one of Chadwick's brothers was a diplomat; his other brother, Henry, was the first person in four centuries to become Head of House in colleges in both Oxford and Cambridge – he was first Regius professor of Divinity in Oxford and Dean of Christchurch, and subsequently Regius professor of Divinity in Cambridge and Master of Peterhouse.

Plumb's humble background as the third son of a lowly factory worker with a seriously disabled elder brother had none of the powerful social, financial, educational and family advantages that Chadwick enjoyed. As a result Plumb felt that Chadwick was forgiven for behaviour that Plumb was sure would have been fatal for him.

The charming, good-looking and well-connected Chadwick seemed to an envious Plumb to get away with murder. He liked to list alleged blots on the Chadwick escutcheon. In his first year in Cambridge, Plumb claimed (quite correctly) that Chadwick had taken a miserable third class in Classics; he loved to point out that in his final year when captain of the university rugby team Chadwick had trashed a railway carriage in a bout of drunken violence and vandalism; and he liked to remind people that (when as a result he was rusticated to Germany) Chadwick, in Professor John Morrill's words, demonstrated "lenient feelings" towards the Nazis and warm "support for appeasement". Any one of these blots on his record would in Plumb's eyes have been fatal for his own chances of future success in Cambridge, but Chadwick sailed serenely on to seemingly uninterrupted and unblemished and unchallenged success.

To be fair to him (which Plumb rarely was), when Chadwick died in his hundredth year the full curve of his career rightly earned him very well justified praise. His published work had been awarded the Wolfson Prize for a lifetime's achievement, and his obituaries spoke of his being "one of the most remarkable man of letters of the twentieth century". It particularly riled Plumb that Chadwick won the most prestigious *Prize for History Writing* (only the second historian to be awarded the Wolfson "Oeuvre Prize" in 1981), along with such stars as Sir Steven Runciman in 1982 and Asa Briggs in 2000. If only he had not fallen out so acrimoniously with Lord Wolfson, Plumb might well have justifiably received that prestigious award himself. He certainly thought he deserved such recognition but he never admitted that his own behaviour had probably effectively ruled him out.

Back in 1968, when they were competing for the Regius chair, Plumb was still confident that his professional reputation and his public recognition comfortably outshone Chadwick's – his published work was more distinguished, his public profile was better recognised, his international reputation was significantly higher and his achievements as a teacher were light years ahead of Chadwick's. Chadwick was not a great teacher, he had very few graduate students and he left no impressive legacy of brilliant students to burnish his future reputation.

In the light of these comparisons, Plumb's anguish and sense of unfairness are easy to understand and easy to sympathize with.

By most standards, however, his career was still pretty successful. The ample signs of recognition that he had received over the years would have satisfied all but the most ambitious and most driven of academics. I am sometimes much amused to hear young historians complacently write him off as a failure. Well, at the most stratospheric level perhaps, (and most careers end in some kind of failure) but very few of those dismissive youngsters will finish their careers having achieved a Cambridge Chair, a Cambridge Headship, a Cambridge Litt.D., an F.B.A., a raft of Honorary Degrees and a Knighthood; few of them will also have given the Ford Lectures at Oxford; and even fewer will have reached an audience measured in millions or had their achievements publicly recognised by the President of the United States.

He would have been both pleased and enraged by the response to his death and the career assessments that emerged after it. He would have expected the hidden assassins to reveal their hands but I suspect that he would have been pleasantly surprised by some of the extraordinarily generous overviews of his work.

Even the most demanding historian would surely have been pleased when the Cambridge alumni were informed by their official magazine that "the more all-embracing literary tradition that flows from Macaulay through Trevelyan to Plumb is now in the ascendant, thanks not just to Schama but to the work, within Cambridge and without, of the impressive roster of historians Plumb taught (or chose for Christ's): among them, David Cannadine and Linda Colley, Roy Porter, Geoffrey Parker, Norman Stone and Niall Ferguson". The fact that he did not actually teach four out of those six rather diminishes the impact of that sentence, but he certainly helped to promote the careers of all of them. Few of them would deny his influence.

Even the most ambitious promoter of history as literature would surely have been pleased by the judgment that "History is news, and Cambridge has done much to make it so. Not just through Starkey and Schama, but in pre-television days through a long line of Cambridge historians committed to writing for a broad public. Literary stylists all, they have tackled big subjects, revelled in colourful characters, grand perspectives and telling anecdotes, and ignored the sniffs of stuffier colleagues who dismiss such enterprise as journalistic. Few have received the highest academic acclaim in Cambridge, but the best achieve triumphantly the ultimate aim of history: to educate, enlighten and entertain."

He would surely have been pleased too, not only to hear Cambridge history summed up as "From Macaulay to Plumb", but also to have this justified on the grounds that Macaulay's aim had been to do what Plumb accomplished – namely "to call up our ancestors before us with all their peculiarities of language, manner and garb, to show us over their houses, to seat us at their tables, to rummage in their wardrobes, to explain the uses of their ponderous furniture". In short, "to reclaim those materials which the novelist has appropriated".

Such plaudits would have been especially consoling to Plumb, when they were favourably compared with the modest achievements of many who had held the post of Regius professor since 1724, when it was instituted in the reign of George I. Of the bizarre list of Cambridge Regius Professors since that time, Plumb always said that he would have been most comfortable in the company of the poet Thomas Gray, the novelist Charles Kingsley, and those eloquent historians who tackled big subjects and aimed at large audiences such as Macaulay and Trevelyan and Knowles and even Seeley. The fact that many of them were often denounced for their personal shortcomings as well as their work might also have brought him some comfort. The book by Seeley which earned him the Regius Chair in 1865 was described by one critic as "the most pestilential book ever vomited from the jaws of hell", whilst Elton generously described the work of his great predecessor G. M. Trevelyan as "sentimental, ignorant and an insult to the intelligence". Clearly Plumb's capacity for insulting put-downs was not unique. Nor, it would seem, were his personal failings: one early Regius "met his end by falling off a horse drunk on the way to chapel"; of another it was said that "he walks as if he had fouled his small clothes, and looks as if he smelt it"; of another it was said that he spent his undergraduate days in Cambridge "playing cards, rowing and frequenting a Barnwell brothel"; and of another it was said that "he was melancholy, dependent on opium and hen-pecked". Yet in spite of their many human failings, many of them could more than match Plumb in their self-confident certainty of their own superiority: of one of them, it was said by Lord Melbourne "I wish I was as cock-sure about anything as Tom Macaulay is about everything".

Many of these past historical giants were no more heroic in appearance than Elton and Plumb. Macaulay was once described as being short, obese, rough featured, coarse complexioned, with lank hair and small grey eyes", whilst Trevelyan was described by his colleague Kitson Clark as looking like a "dilapidated bird of prey" who was renowned for "baggy-kneed suits and his erratic shaving".

Even Plumb's early rejection by a Cambridge college was not unique amongst great Cambridge historians – Acton was turned down by Magdalene College for admission as an undergraduate. Like Plumb, he took ample revenge. When he was appointed to the Regius Professorship in 1895 he wrote dismissively "There is, I think, no great school of history there, and not much studious curiosity about it".

What might have pleased Plumb most of all about these posthumous judgments was that not only was he adjudged to have eventually won his war with Elton but also that there was no mention of Chadwick, Collinson or even Skinner in an article circulated to a quarter of a million Cambridge alumni. They had all climbed to the top of Cambridge History's academic "greasy pole" by being appointed to the Regius chair, but they had not attracted the huge popular audience that Plumb and his most successful pupils had sought and won.

In spite of some of his deeply felt disappointments, it is important that one acknowledges that his stature as a scholar did not go un-acknowledged. During the twenty-five years when his career was at its peak, he received a steady stream of honours. He took a Litt.D. at Cambridge in 1957, was promoted to a Readership in 1962 and to a personal Chair in 1966, he was invited to give the Ford Lectures at Oxford in 1965 and was elected to a Fellowship of the British Academy in 1968. He was elected to the Mastership of his college in 1978 and was knighted in 1982. Seven honorary degrees (five in America) testified to his international reputation as a scholar, but in many ways he still felt frustrated by the prizes that had eluded him. He was many people's favourite for both the Chair of Modern History and the Regius Chair in Cambridge and for the Presidency of the British Academy, but all three of these prized positions eluded him

He was also on Wilson's infamous resignation Honours list for a peerage but was dropped in the furore that followed its "leak" to the press. As a result of the controversy, Wilson decided to keep his cronies on the list and drop Jack Plumb and Asa Briggs, on the reported grounds (from an insider at Number 10) that they were "good enough to get peerages by themselves in the future". Asa, of course, did; Jack, alas for him, did not.

Those, who make much of the fact that he did not achieve his ambition to join the House of Lords, should perhaps make more of the fact that the lowly-born Plumb had succeeded in emerging from the scrutiny of the Patronage Secretary and his like to appear on the penultimate list of those to be honoured. That his ascent to the peerage should be thwarted at the very last step could reasonably be put down to extremely bad luck and a Prime Minister's insistence on looking after his own highly controversial nominees. Had it not been for the leak-inspired press controversy, Lord

Plumb of Leicester might well have triumphantly emerged in recognition of his achievements as a leading historian of his time. His name is certainly down in the list of those proposed for peerages on the famous "Lavender list" which has recently been offered for sale by Lady Falkender. This list, in Lady Falkender's handwriting, of Wilson's proposed retirement Honours also has a scribbled additional note by the name Professor J.H. Plumb. Written in red ink (and said by some to be in Wilson's own handwriting) it reads "? K" which suggests that an alternative honour to a peerage for Plumb was still under active discussion before the final list, with his name deleted, was announced to the public.

All these "near misses" continued to irritate him and he often mused on the mystery of why so many less gifted men seemed to glide so easily to the top. He was honest enough to admit the effects of charm. He was too good an historian to deny the subtle workings of connections and nepotism, but he felt the need to formulate some new theories to explain the effortless success of the dull and the humdrum. His theories had the advantage that they took note of his impatience with the pompous, the ponderous and those puffed up with self-importance. The first was Plumb's *Theory of Face Acreage*, which runs – "Given any two men of equal ability, the one with the larger face will go further". The second was Plumb's *Voice Velocity Theory*, which runs "Given any two men of equal ability, the one who speaks the more slowly will go further". The third was Plumb's *Profundity Principle* or *The Importance of Being Profound* which claimed that "Given any two men of equal ability the one who used the word "profound" the more often would go further".

When he expounded these theories to large-faced, slow-speaking men who repeatedly claimed the profound importance of their views, it is not surprising that he did not achieve unimpeded promotion or universal popularity. He would have done well to take heed of the advice of Gore Vidal's grandmother to her waspish grandson – "Don't stir up more snakes than you can kill". Alas, Jack made enemies almost as easily as he made friends – and having made them, they tended to stay made.

Many of the quarrels, which punctuated his life and hindered his career, came from his inability to hide his irritation with those who tried to thwart him and his even greater irritation with those he thought were second rate. If they had managed to prosper in spite of their lack of talent or if they misused the power they had merely inherited, then the chances of a serious falling-out rapidly multiplied.

His role as an elector for the Wolfson Prize for History was a case in point. He greatly approved of Leonard Wolfson as long as Lord Wolfson took his advice and let him have his own way, but, as Asa Briggs has written, "Wolfson was a testy character, and made it difficult for me or for Jack before me and with me to take decisions which had been delegated to us. Jack and I had delightful lunches or dinners together (they were fun) before meetings to co-ordinate strategy. He could not stand Alan Bullock. He thought him a second-rate historian as I did." The combination of what he regarded as the meddlesome Lord Wolfson and the mediocre Lord Bullock stopping Jack from choosing the prize-winners that he wanted could have only one outcome. After some acrimonious interchanges, he left. Having to leave the field to the sanctimonious Bullock infuriated him. The fact that Jack was later replaced on the committee by Owen Chadwick only added to his fury. The committee may well have been less stressful after he had gone, but many thought it was also the poorer for his going – the poorer in entertainment value as well as in historical judgement. As Asa Briggs generously wrote "When Jack left the Wolfson Committee much of the fun went out of it".

Those who think that Plumb misused his power on the Wolfson Prize Electors to promote his own friends and protégées point to the fact that between 1974 and 1986, Moses Finley 1974, Norman Stone 1976, Simon Schama 1977, Quentin Skinner 1979, John Burrow 1981 and John Elliott 1986 were awarded the prize, but there would be very few who could convincingly argue that they did not amply deserve it. After Plumb left the electoral panel, a further five of his pupils or protégées (Linda Colley 1993, John Brewer 1998, Roy Porter 2001, David Reynolds 2005 and Dominic Lieven 2010) all won the prize, which would suggest that his pupils continued to prosper without his influence. Since eleven historians taught by me (eight of them Caians) won the prize between 1976 and 2007, I find theories based on well-deserved merit much more persuasive than conspiracy theories based on undue influence.

There can be little doubt that the significant quarrels that punctuated his career (and there were many of them) did little to ease his way to the honours he so coveted. That he minded so much not getting certain honours (the Regius chair, the peerage, the British Academy Presidency, even the Honorary Fellowship that astonishingly he was never offered by King's) gives some clue to the nature of Jack's ambition. Probably he would not have achieved so much if he had not been so driven to succeed. Having succeeded, he needed the gongs and the titles to prove it. He could not understand my blithe indifference to the standard marks that are used in the academic world to chronicle one's progress. He was furious with me when I turned down a professorship in New York in 1972 and even crosser when I turned down a Vice-Chancellor-ship in England some ten years later, mainly because these jobs did not suit my family situation. "The trouble with you", he used to rail, "is that you have no ambition. You're competitive but not ambitious. You lack nothing in wanting and competing for the best degree, the most successful pupils, the most attractive and intelligent wife, the best children, the best garden, the best wine, the best furniture, the best Faculty, the best college – or whatever else you are attached to or involved with. But where is your personal ambition? Why are you not planning for the future, plotting the best route to recognition, preparing the necessary contacts to deliver the world's prizes? You will never maximize your abilities without driving ambition". That denunciation of me tells one a lot about what made Jack tick.

Burning ambition was something he never lacked himself. But the deeper his ambition burned, the more it hurt if the longed-for objectives eluded him. Some, such as the Mastership of Christ's, were achieved but they were achieved too late to give him any real satisfaction. Blocked by the massive presence of Lord Todd, the prize eluded him until he was in his late sixties. Having been turned down for the Bursarship and delayed in his pursuit of the Mastership, he never felt that he got the recognition he deserved from his own college. He even claimed that taking on the Mastership when he did was a mistake. He blamed it for draining him of his declining energies, he blamed it for preventing him from completing some of his most treasured projects, he strongly advised me never to make the same mistake and could never understand that being the Master of Caius was the only job I ever really coveted and was certainly the one that I most enjoyed doing. Sadly for Jack, not getting the things he longed for gave him more pain than getting them gave him pleasure. He always used to say that when the gongs, (such as his chair, his knighthood and his FBA), did arrive, they seemed rather meaningless. Seven honorary doctorates would be a source of considerable and well-justified satisfaction for most academics but, for Jack, they were merely a reminder that neither Oxford nor Cambridge had given him one.

8. PLUMB THE POSSESSIVE FATHER FIGURE

Impatient with lack of ambition, Jack could be equally impatient with his pupils' devotion to their wives and families. As a bachelor, he tended to judge his colleagues by their single-minded pursuit of their careers. He had always felt free to accept visiting professorships and to take on lucrative lecture tours without the restraints of a family and the requirements of their schooling, their friendships and their examination schedules. I had a quite different set of priorities from his that he found very difficult to understand. He always criticised me for spending too much of my time with my family. He thought that I treated them like protégées and spent too much time plotting and planning their careers when I should have been promoting my own. For someone with such an unerring eye for spotting talent amongst his pupils, he had great difficulty in coming to terms with the talents of their wives and families. He notoriously underrated the wives of all of his friends (with the possible and occasional exceptions of Valerie Winterton and Selina Campailla). I always felt that it took him far too long to appreciate fully the qualities of my wife and daughters. He eventually conceded, when she got a Cambridge chair and a Fellowship of the British Academy, that Melveena really was a very distinguished woman; and when Olivia became Solicitor of the Year before she was thirty and Cornelia came top of her university as her mother had done before her, he conceded that they were all more than capable of achieving their highly successful careers by themselves. If I spent so much time with them it was because nothing gave me greater pleasure. My favourite world tours were those I took *en famille* and I was never happy to be away from my family for long. Jack was baffled by such preferences and such priorities.

He regarded the loneliness and isolation of visiting professorships as the inevitable and acceptable downside to the successful pursuit of his ambitions. Living in Texas he described as like being banished to "a hot Siberia", and he regarded being entertained in Faculty dining rooms on American campuses as "coming close to purgatory". Much as he enjoyed being lionised on his "one night stand lectures", the endless travel involved soon lost its allure, but these disagreeable consequences were all, he argued, worthwhile sacrifices the better to promote his career and to fatten his wallet. His correspondence grew dramatically in these long spells in self-imposed isolation. I received up to three letters a week when he was away from Cambridge – often with no major news to impart. He wrote, he said, simply to induce replies that would assuage his isolation. "Forgive me dribbling on like this", he wrote, "but it is the closest thing to conversation available in my desert exile in Texas". On other occasions he would write to say simply "I am, of course, terribly lonely. Please write." It was a situation that intensified his dependence on his friends. It was a situation that also intensified his possessiveness towards them, and he became even greedier than ever for their time and attention.

He has often been cast as a father figure to many of his pupils, especially to fatherless ones such as myself. Many of them felt that their relationships could more accurately be likened to being the sons of a possessive mother. The stereotype of the Jewish mother (fiercely protective of her male progeny, fiercely involved with their choice of life partners, and fiercely demanding of them in terms of both tribal loyalty and worldly success) was often invoked by his Jewish pupils. "He's worse than my mother when it comes to frightening off what he deems to be unsuitable wives and worse than her in his demands that I achieve material success", said one disconsolate Jewish pupil who had just had his choice of girlfriend publicly denounced and his lack of worldly ambition found seriously wanting. In many cases it was a very appropriate analogy. The emotional charge was certainly equally powerful, the claims on group loyalty were certainly equally strong, the insistence on the "parental" veto was certainly equally vigorously stated and equally rarely conceded. Being "a good pupil to Jack" was very much like "being a good son to his mother" – someone whose achievements could be proudly proclaimed and whose tribal loyalty could be insisted on, even if it required massive doses of outrageous emotional blackmail to insist on it.

Achieving one's independence once one had been adopted into Plumb's "family" circle could be very difficult. Breaking free was analogous to "marrying out".

Like many confirmed bachelors, Jack disliked his friends getting married because their marriages threatened to rob him of their company. For much the same reason he also often took an instant and decided dislike to their newly acquired friends, especially if they became close ones with whom they spent much time. Worst of all in his eyes were those who asked his friends to join them on holiday. Such invitations were a threat to his ability to monopolise their company. He liked his friends to be "on call", as it were – instantly available to respond to his social invitations, preferably as unencumbered as possible with partners or other social commitments.

Many of our friends (intelligent, attractive and in every way delightful company) were quite taken aback, indeed justifiably astonished, by his extremely hostile reaction to the news that we were going on holiday with them. Even if he had previously liked them and asked them to his parties, they suddenly became socially undesirable and were comprehensively dropped.

What they understandably failed to appreciate was that Jack felt that they were depriving him of "his family", interfering with his holiday plans, and diluting the amount of time we had to devote to him. So they were suddenly denounced as being "too talkative", "too dull", "too un-travelled" or whatever other spurious defect Jack could invent. "She talks too fast", "he's too self-involved", "they are both too mean", "God, they're dull", we would (wholly unjustifiably) be told. His intentions were all too obvious. He was like a jealous mother driving away possible suitors to her children to keep them wholly dependent on her. He hoped (I am happy to say in vain) to prise apart newly established friendships and, by doing so, to banish the threat they posed to his plans and his needs.

His efforts to stop his friends getting married were often much more extreme. If I cite my own experiences here, it is to save many of my old friends from knowing what he said about their prospective partners. In my case he was as blunt to my face as he doubtless was behind my back. "You are surely not going to marry that Welsh witch, are you?" was his less than flattering response to the announcement in 1966 of my engagement to Miss Melveena Jones, widely known as "the beautiful Miss Jones of Girton" and "the rising star of the Spanish department". In spite of dramatic and compelling evidence to the contrary, he declared her to have neither looks nor intelligence. This was the woman who was to end her career as Professor Melveena McKendrick, B.A. (London), M.A., Ph.D., Litt.D. (Cantab), FBA, not to mention an Honorary degree from South Wales. She was also for ten years Senior Tutor of Girton College, Cambridge, Chairman of the Faculty of Modern and Medieval Languages, and for five years Pro-Vice Chancellor for Education at Cambridge. In addition she was an internationally acclaimed author, and was also widely regarded as a woman of striking beauty and elegance. Not surprisingly she was approached (and declined to be considered) for the headship of several Cambridge colleges; and turned down the formal offer of one, in spite of being urged by many people (including me) to accept it.

Plumb had been quite without shame in the counter-propaganda campaign, which had preceded our engagement. With breath-taking impertinence, he would say, "I met your Melveena in the street today but I couldn't think who on earth she could be when she spoke to me. She looked so dowdy, middle-aged and plain!" Fortunately such blatant manipulative shamelessness had little hope of succeeding in the face of youth, beauty and intelligence on Melveena's part and undeviating love and devotion on mine. To do him justice he usually quite quickly made the best of a bad job once his friends were married. The time they spent in exile varied but they were almost all finally invited back into the fold. Some were ultimately treated with great generosity. My wife and children certainly were – he commissioned two very successful books from my wife, and generously supported my daughters' finances in their early adult years. I suspect his philosophy was "better a friend encumbered with a wife and family than no friend at all". He was almost excessively generous to some of his surrogate grandchildren even if he some times promised more than he delivered. He promised, for instance, to leave my daughters £150,000 each when he died, but by the time he was ninety they were both working as commercial lawyers for Magic Circle London law firms and enjoying very generous stipends, so he very understandably felt that they had done quite well enough financially without any further help from him.

Fortunately for him, his surrogate grandchildren remained loyal and affectionate to him for most of his mature life. They offered him love and solace for many decades. With the passage of time, however, (as the family obligations of his old friends grew ever more demanding as first their children and then their grandchildren occupied their time and required their devotion), Jack finally began to feel that he might have made the wrong call himself. Then he sometimes admitted that he thought that he might have sentenced himself to a lonely old age. He felt (for all his long service to his college and for all the lustre he had brought to it through his academic achievements and for all the money he had raised for it) that Christ's had never properly appreciated him. He knew that he had made many enemies who were now only too delighted to see him so reduced in health and vigour and so bereft of so many of his old friendships. In some quarters he was sadly proved right – as with the Fellow who said to me with undisguised relish, "He's like a king who has lost his court". Even more grimly, another very distinguished Fellow (and previous admirer of Jack before his sad decline in old age) said, "The best thing that could happen to Jack would be for him to fall down his staircase and break his neck, and if he doesn't, it's your duty to give him a push!"

Fortunately for him, his reputation outside Cambridge was much less subject to such malice, and his influence remained stronger for much longer – especially in the States.

9. PLUMB'S REPUTATION AS PATRON, PROMOTER AND FIXER

Jack was keenly aware that his own reputation as a scholar was higher outside Cambridge than within, and higher outside Britain than at home. His scholarly reputation in the America he so loved was certainly very high – he got many more Honorary degrees there than he did in England, he was invited to give far more named public lectures there, and he found it easier to promote his pupils there than he did back in England. Professorships in distinguished universities seemed to come far more easily for those he backed in America than they did in England. Simon Schama, John Brewer, Roy Porter, Derek Hirst, Clive Holmes, Keith Wrightson, David Cannadine and Linda Colley all first earned the title of Professor of History in the States. Some like Geoffrey Parker did get his first professorship at St Andrew's through the good offices of John Kenyon, but his first established/endowed chair, achieved when backed by Plumb, was in the US. There are those in the historical profession who think that this power and this patronage were ill-used. They certainly excited envy and unhappiness in some quarters. This is hardly surprising. Almost every academic appointment must of necessity be accompanied by a number of legitimate disappointments and some ill-feeling is only to be expected. If, however, one accepts the views of Professor Jeremy Black, the prolific historian at Exeter University, Plumb's methods of promoting his protégés were of a kind and an intensity that inspired real and justified anger – or even "fear and loathing" as another historian put it.

The Plumb archive suggests that much of the angry indignation is overdone. When Bernard Bailyn, for instance, wrote to Plumb asking him to propose possible replacements for Wallace McCaffery's chair at Harvard, it is noticeable that Plumb's suggestions include no one that he had taught himself – indeed, his favoured candidates were Blair Worden and Paul Slack of Oxford. Many of the references in his archive explicitly compare his pupils (to their very clear disadvantage) with their rivals with whom he had no direct connection.

Not everyone recognised that he was capable of such disinterested impartiality. Jeremy Black wrote in 2002, in *The Times Higher Educational Supplement*, "Plumb's skilful use of patronage helped arouse the anger and maybe envy of others. This determination extended across the Atlantic. I recall the head of one Ivy League department telling me about the 'extraordinary pressure' brought to bear to take a Plumb candidate. There was certainly a malignity that was the other side of his active sponsorship of his own reputation and the careers of his protégées. Others were abused, damaged and harmed." It is difficult to judge whether other more deserving candidates were passed over, but most academics would be pretty content to be judged on the basis of Plumb's successful pupils. If there were better candidates for the jobs they got, they must have been a pretty remarkable bunch. It would be good to hear their names so that one could better judge whether any major injustice occurred.

Curiously enough his patronage did not seem to work locally. If the stories of threats and manipulation and denigration of others are true they seem to have been singularly ineffective in Cambridge outside the immediate walls of Christ's. Few of those he taught flourished in the Faculty. Indeed Oxbridge at large was not a happy hunting ground for Plumb's pupils – not at least for those seeking preferment at anything above the most modest level. During his active career, only one pupil taught directly by Jack (Eric Stokes) got a chair in Cambridge and only one (John Burrow) in Oxford, and only one got a Readership in either. Some of Jack's pupils felt not unreasonably that along with Jack's public support they inherited some of his many enemies. Certainly many of his Cambridge rivals took ample revenge on his more vulnerable protégés. I can certainly recall sitting on many Cambridge appointments committees when those trying to block candidates backed by Jack seemed to be motivated by powerful emotions which had nothing to do with the candidates themselves and everything to do with their backer. Some of his more impassioned rivals insisted on recording their votes against his pupils even when they had lost the battle – the record of these votes against in the Minutes of the Appointments Committee in the Cambridge History Faculty now reads like a badge of honour for some outstanding historians. Most, of course, were prudent enough merely to speak against and vote against without leaving any trace of the historical record. Those who voted against Simon Schama, Roy Porter, Geoffrey Parker, David Cannadine and others must surely have been given pause for thought by their later careers. It was not for nothing that Schama has recalled that in Cambridge he was treated as if he had "an infectious disease". Others, too, thought that they suffered from what one of them called "Plumbago" – a debilitating, job-blocking, promotion-stopping disease caught by close association with their controversial mentor.

It has to be admitted that Jack Plumb's support could be a double-edged sword in Cambridge. I certainly profited from it in my early days in Cambridge, but as Jack's army of enemies grew with the passage of time it became less obviously advantageous. I can well recall its effect on my chances of becoming a Syndic of the Fitzwilliam Museum. It was a position that I had modestly coveted and for which I felt, as a ceramic historian and an ardent collector, I was reasonably well suited to. So I was delighted when Philip Grierson, the great numismatist and close colleague of mine in Caius, told me that he had proposed me and that the proposition had been well received. Unfortunately, Jack, who was a syndic himself, enthusiastically took up my cause, at which point my chances nosedived. As the Director of the Fitzwilliam said regretfully to me, "Alas, you were dead in the water once Plumb threw his support behind you". This was a very minor example and a very minor disappointment but it indicates the dangers of being too closely associated with Plumb in Cambridge. Many of his pupils suffered far more significant setbacks in their careers.

Some of those who have worked on Sir Herbert Butterfield's papers in the University Library have even claimed that Jack's pupils were actively discriminated against in more sinister ways. Those of a more paranoid tendency have even alleged that what was sometimes called the Christ's-Caius axis, or the Plumb-McKendrick school of historians, was deliberately under-marked in the History Tripos by examiners in other colleges who were jealous of their success. The most infamous case is said to be that of Simon Schama. Schama was widely tipped to be the star in his year in Part I of the Tripos when to almost everyone's amazement he was given a 2.1 – having, allegedly, been given three alpha marks by three separate examiners and three beta marks by one examiner (Brian Wormald of Peterhouse). How or why these improbably low marks were given we will never know for certain, but in the fuss which followed (largely orchestrated by Jack Plumb) it was decided that in future all scripts must be double marked. In addition no single examiner would be allowed to mark more than a maximum of two scripts from any one candidate. In the following year, under this much fairer system, Schama came top of the university and was awarded a starred First. Schama has proposed a far simpler and less sinister explanation for the dramatic difference between his performances in the two Parts of the Tripos. "I think I just under-performed in Part I" was his modest and un-paranoid view.

It is alleged by some that the Butterfield papers also provide evidence of how Plumb was blocked from getting the Chair of Modern History on the grounds of his atheism, but that is a story best kept for a later date. Not many of the alleged black-listing cabal still survive (they are said to have included Butterfield himself, Dom David Knowles, Desmond Williams and Hugh Trevor-Roper) but the story of their successful plotting and the dash to Jesus through the streets of Cambridge by one of the plotters to tell Charles Wilson, my research supervisor, that he had been elected to the Chair is too good not to be unfolded in all the richness of the surviving correspondence when space and discretion permit. Trevor-Roper was very taken aback when his disobliging comments on Plumb's and Elton's unsuitability for the Chair were leaked.

In a letter to Desmond Williams, he had written: *"Elton would be an unpopular choice. I am told that he has become an arrogant bore (I can believe that too), a stiff opponent of reform, and in general the bane of the Faculty. I don't myself much like what he writes, or the style in which he writes it, but there is no denying his energy and ability"*. As for Plumb, he wrote *"well, I couldn't vote very enthusiastically for him. There is something small about his character, something vulgar about his arrivisme, something trivial about his attitude to history. I do know him pretty well, so it would be embarrassing if I had to say this (and have it reported back by Rowse, who would probably vote for Plumb as a fellow-devotee of the great god Mammon); I do hope I will not!"* Trevor-Roper was understandably horrified when, in the House of Lords, Noel Annan gave him a copy of a transcript of this letter, which had been circulating in Peterhouse and in all likelihood would reach *"Maurice Cowling, who, of course, seeing a chance to make trouble, will pass it on to Elton and Plumb"*. He was right to be concerned – the letter was well and truly circulated and did cause trouble. It convinced Plumb that he had powerful enemies in Oxford as well as in Cambridge.

If Cambridge could be a difficult place for Plumb and his pupils to flourish, there were many other universities where his writ ran strong and his backing could open doors and win promotion for his protégés. No one can doubt that he was a most generous and effective supporter. Fuelled by memories of his own difficult apprenticeship he could be a very committed and enthusiastic referee. He always felt that launching and promoting his pupils' careers was as important as teaching them in the first place, so it is not surprising that it was from his pupils that he most easily earned the full recognition he deserved. They were quick to recognise the influence of his teaching and his generous promotion of their talents. At Christ's alone he promoted the careers of historians of the calibre of Rupert Hall, John Kenyon, Frank Spooner, Barry Supple, Eric Stokes, John Burrow, John Vincent, Jonathan Steinberg, Quentin Skinner, Norman Stone, Geoffrey Parker, Michael Bush, John Thompson, Richard Simmons, Roy Porter, Simon Schama, John Barber, Clive Holmes, Nicholas Wharton, Ted Royle, Dominic Lieven, David Cannadine, Linda Colley, Joachim Whaley, Niall Ferguson, Simon Smith and me. These, and many others, were launched on their successful careers by Plumb's patronage and support at Christ's.

I always felt flattered that a man with such a perceptive eye for academic talent trusted my judgement sufficiently to welcome into Christ's so many of those whom I had taught at Caius. I sent an impressive number of distinguished Caians back to my old college and my old teacher as either research students or colleagues. They included Quentin Skinner, Norman Stone, Clive Holmes, Derek Hirst, David Reynolds, David Feldman and Geoffrey Baldwin. I hope any concern that this was another example of what has been labelled nepotism or cronyism will be mitigated by the fact that forty-two of my Caian pupils achieved Oxbridge research fellowships in colleges other than Christ's.

My role in promoting my pupils in Christ's was mainly the result of the fact that, as Jack increasingly lost contact with the bright young prospects in the History Faculty, he increasingly relied on me to recommend the most promising youngsters. In the days, when I was playing a major role in teaching, lecturing and examining in the Faculty, I could cherry-pick not only for Caius but also for Christ's. As Chairman of the Faculty and Chairman of the Appointments Committee, I had inside knowledge of those most likely to flourish in terms of future appointments. I recall recommending first David Cannadine and later Linda Colley to him and watched with fascination how he persuaded the fellows of Christ's to accept them. Neither St John's nor Girton, where they had respectively held research fellowships, had offered them teaching fellowships. There was no room for them at Caius, but I was sure that if I convinced Jack how good they were, he would cajole or bully Christ's into accepting them. It was not completely straightforward.

Amusingly, David Cannadine allegedly objected to the election of Linda Colley. If so I suspect that he was simply irritated by having to watch Jack continue to run History at Christ's when he (David) thought that he should be allowed to do so himself. But Jack brushed his objections aside, saying, "You will probably end up marrying her". Reader, he did!

Jack's confidence in his judgement (and in mine) and his skill in persuading Christ's to do his bidding, meant that he almost always got his own way in such matters. When I tried unsuccessfully to persuade Caius to elect Niall Ferguson into a research fellowship and failed to persuade my close colleagues to recognise his obvious virtues, I was pretty sure that Jack would be more successful in Christ's. So, since I was not officially handling his application, I conceded defeat and recommended him to Jack. The rest as they say is history – an impressive number of major books and a distinguished career already in the making.

The list of such Christ's stars is a tribute in itself to the Plumb legacy. When I last did a count, he had a remarkable total of 57 pupils holding academic posts. Perhaps even more impressive than the quantity, was the quality. It is surely not without significance that in the run up to one appointment of the Regius Chair at Cambridge, the public prints included as serious runners for the chair such Christ's luminaries as Professor Roy Porter of London, Professor Simon Schama of Harvard, Professor David Cannadine of Columbia, Professor Linda Colley of Yale, Professor John Vincent of Bristol, and Professor Norman Stone and Professor John Burrow both of Oxford, as well, of course, as Professor Quentin Skinner of Cambridge who was most deservedly appointed to that most prestigious post. Obviously there is an element of double counting here: of these eight stars I can claim to have taught six of them myself. Obviously, too, the press does not get everything right. But having listened to the Patronage Secretary run through his more official and admittedly rather different list, I can confirm that no other college in Oxford and Cambridge (not even Caius) came anywhere near Christ's cluster of historians who were held by their peers to be plausibly papabile for the Regius Chair, although I took some comfort from the fact that Quentin Skinner, the ultimate choice, was admitted by Caius, taught by Caius and exported to Christ's by Caius.

Plumb knew all too well the irritation that seriously committed teachers feel when they read in references in support of living academics, or in the obituaries in memory of dead ones, the almost invariable claim that the subjects of the notices are or were great teachers. Most of us know that many such claims are generous to the point of absurdity. In the commercial world many such claims would infringe the Trade Descriptions Act.

Great teachers who influence whole generations of students are very rare indeed. Without question Jack Plumb was one of them.

All the Christ's historians experienced his promotional skills and benefited from his advice and patronage; many of them were the product of his own robust teaching methods in which exaggerated praise and excoriating blame seemed to rain down seemingly at random to keep one encouraged and yet to prevent one from becoming complacent. Plumb, as a supervisor, was not a paragon of all the old-fashioned virtues of charm, restraint and tolerance. He used to cite with approval how the school-master who most influenced him once ended a passionate argument by denouncing him at three in the morning outside the gates of the town gaol with the words – "You've misunderstood your facts, you've misread your psychology, you've got a third-rate mind, and you are probably impotent. Goodnight, Sir!" With the happy certainty that these accusations were unfounded, Plumb interpreted the rebukes as clear evidence that H.E. Howard (the schoolmaster in question) obviously really cared about his education. In Plumb's supervisions, he showed by his ferocious response to the casual or the second-rate, and of course by his extremely generous response to the first-rate, that he too really cared. Nowadays it might be described as "tough love". Some found it too tough. Few people emerged unscathed. Most admitted to being profoundly influenced.

It has to be admitted that not all of that influence was beneficial. Sir John Elliott, a former Regius Professor of History at Oxford, thought, as did David Cannadine, that "Jack's most enduring legacy was his pupils", but he also felt that one should recognise what he called "the downside" to Jack's teaching. In his view, "a really great teacher is one who can encourage the weaker brethren, and I fear that Jack had no use for weaker brethren". He had in mind "those people who did not, in Jack's eyes, make the grade, and particularly Bob Robson. I don't know how many others there were who were similarly dropped, but I think his treatment of Bob was callous and cruel". This is all the more telling a criticism because, although John Elliott recognised very clearly the manipulative and destructive aspects of Jack's character, he also recognised his very real qualities. "I loved and admired him", he wrote, "for his energy, his breadth of vision, and what could, at its best, be a very creative generosity."

Some would dispute Elliott's verdict on Jack's treatment of his less than stellar pupils. Even if he did not rate them amongst his stars he seems (to judge from his archive) to have often continued to support them at the level he felt they deserved. He was certainly very indignant when Bob Robson's manuscript on *The Eighteenth-Century Attorney* was initially rejected and he also commissioned him (alas in vain) to write a book for one of his series. Robson may have fallen in Plumb's estimation (and, in truth, he was never rated very highly by him) but it does not seem that he was entirely dropped or indeed was treated very cruelly. I suspect that the truth was that, given his sensitive and modest nature, Bob Robson listened to Plumb's robust and impatient response to other "weaker brethren" and feared that he would inevitably be included in that class. In my opinion his fears were probably all too justified. Self-confidence was never Bob Robson's strong suit. It is difficult to believe that being taught by Plumb bolstered it.

Geoffrey Parker, although a great admirer of Plumb's inspiring teaching, reinforces Elliott's doubts about some aspects of it. In his own *festschrift* Parker describes Plumb's undergraduate seminars: "every two weeks, Jack Plumb held a meeting at which seven Christ's History undergraduates each had to present a paper. We quaked in our seats while hard-hitting and wide-ranging discussions raged around the highly polished table in Jack's private dining room and gradually, sustained by copious supplies of fruit, claret and port, we improved our ability both to articulate and to defend bold arguments". He added, however, that the only thing he disliked about the seminars was that Jack invited "only the students which he considered 'promising'. This excluded about one-third of our cohort. I always felt uncomfortable with such 'two tier' systems and resolved not to do the same when I became a teacher. It's a resolution I kept." Here was a warm admirer drawing attention to Plumb's highly effective concentration on his most able students and his willingness to ruthlessly relegate those he thought to be the less able to a lower sphere of his attention and concern. He was a brilliant teacher of the very bright, less so for the less gifted.

Less friendly voices than John Elliott's and Geoffrey Parker's have spoken of an even darker downside to Plumb's treatment of his pupils. A savage letter of indictment from that usually most generous of men, Professor W.A. Speck, was published in *The Times Higher Educational Supplement* in response to Professor Jeremy Black's corrective comment on what he felt were excessively generous obituaries of Plumb and their failure to chronicle the malign effects of his power and patronage. Professor Speck wrote "Whether the rule that one should speak no ill of the dead still holds or not, it was certainly breached by Sir Jack Plumb and his cronies in the hatchet job they did on the reputation of the late John Kenyon in their obituaries of that generous, genial and big-hearted historian. Jeremy Black gives Plumb no more than he deserved for that alone".

I confess that I was very surprised at the letters in the *THES*. It is not often that one reads articles commenting on obituaries. It is even less common that one then reads comments on the commentaries. Even if one attributes this strange phenomenon to the powerful reactions that Plumb seemed to arouse amongst his fellow historians – and it is perhaps worth remembering that another letter in the same correspondence column went so far as to refer to "the fear and loathing among historians in respect of the late Sir Jack Plumb" – one is still left with a sense of puzzlement over Bill Speck's letter, partly because I always found him to be such a warm-hearted and generous man.

I could well understand his anger and disappointment on behalf of Kenyon on reading the less than generous obituary by Plumb in the Christ's College magazine, but, in my experience at the time, Plumb's pupils also shared a sense of embarrassment and disappointment with that obituary when it appeared. Their reactions were very far from being part of a hatchet job on Kenyon, indeed they were the very reverse.

John Kenyon and Jack Plumb's relations were, it is true, less warm in later years than in the period when Kenyon was one of his most favoured protégés. Partly this was because Plumb felt let down, even perhaps mildly betrayed, by the mature Kenyon's decisive preference for Elton and the Elton school rather than for Plumb and his coterie, partly it was because Kenyon's failure to get the Chair of Modern History at Cambridge and his later failure to get a vice-Chancellor-ship left him feeling quite unjustifiably suspicious that Plumb had not backed him strongly enough. The combination of the mentor disappointed to have lost the allegiance of his protégé and the protégé disappointed to have (as he thought) lost the backing of his mentor led to some mild paranoia on both sides, but as a pupil of both and an old friend of both and indeed an obituarist of both, I was completely unaware of any concerted or collective hatchet job by Plumb or his cronies, and indeed saw no evidence of one.

As someone who must rank as a crony myself (however unpleasantly pejorative one finds that word) and as someone who wrote more than one obituary of Kenyon myself, I confess I find Professor Speck's comments both unjustified and very unwelcome. It was certainly my intention to be generous about Kenyon's work and affectionate about his character, and I was pleased to receive such warm acknowledgements from many of his friends, family and colleagues that I had done him as much justice as an obituary of 800 words allows.

Fortunately, greatly to the relief of Kenyon's pupils and friends, Geoffrey Parker's provided an excellent corrective follow-up in the Christ's College magazine which firmly put Plumb's very disappointing assessment of Kenyon's work there in perspective, but it is also fair to point out that Parker was also a favourite pupil of Jack's. Here was a case of a protégé (or perhaps, to Professor Speck, a crony) very properly correcting his mentor.

I discussed John Kenyon with Plumb both before and after Kenyon's death and I have had access to Plumb's archival reaction to his old pupil. I remain convinced that he always greatly respected and greatly admired Kenyon's work – both his scholarly work (particularly his life of Sunderland) and his wonderfully generous reviewing for *The Observer*. I am completely unaware of anything that could be regarded as a concerted intention to damage or diminish his reputation. Given their very different characters and personalities and their very different personal tastes, Kenyon and Plumb were never likely to be lasting or intimate soul mates, but of any deep antipathy I saw very little sign. Mutual respect seemed to survive even after they grew apart. Certainly judged by the rancour directed in Plumb's bleak old age at many of his other friends, Kenyon escaped pretty lightly. Kenyon always used to visit me when he came to Cambridge and, when he spoke of Plumb, I always felt that the affection still outweighed the disillusion, and that admiration and guarded respect still outweighed the disappointments.

Rather surprisingly, Plumb could be curiously tolerant of some forms of scholarly disagreements and minor personal disloyalties. He tolerated the hilarious send-ups of both his prose and his opinions in the lectures in Cambridge given by one of his colleagues at Christ's. According to my reports, when this behaviour was first revealed to Plumb at one of The History Society's annual dinners at Christ's, he characteristically exploded into violent anger. Purple in the face with rage, he denounced his junior colleague as "an insolent ingrate" whose career he would destroy.

I was not present at the dinner, but when Jack later reported the event to me, he had calmed down enough to do his best to laugh it off. He certainly winced when he described the heavy-handed satire, but said he could understand both the motives and the methods of the ambitious and irreverent young. He, more than most, knew that young men have their way to make and accepted that ambitious young historians would not be too squeamish about how they made their iconoclastic reputations. Not everyone would have put up with such mockery from such a close colleague who shared his college as well as his faculty, but Jack could sometimes be disarmingly philosophical about the young bulls challenging the old patriarch of the herd. "Such youngsters eventually grow up", he would say, "and when they do they will realise what real achievement is and how difficult it is to amass a substantial body of work. Then they will have a better appreciation of what I have done. They may then be more respectful".

His optimism has certainly proved correct with regard to the close colleague in question, who has not only produced a very balanced assessment of Jack's life's work, but he has also dedicated one of his own books to him along with a very affectionate tribute in the preface. Jack's unshaken belief in his boisterous young colleague's abilities and his continued support for him when he was seeking professorial posts in his more mature years finally earned their proper reward. Some good deeds do go unpunished. Indeed sometimes, as in this case, they are generously rewarded.

Most of Jack's pupils came to acknowledge very generously what he had achieved and what they owed to him.

Others in the profession chose his death to reveal their hostility — as Bill Speck's acerbic anti-Plumb letter richly exemplifies.

Jack wrote very appreciatively and very generously (and in my view very deservedly) about Bill Speck (as his archive proves) but it seems that his generosity was not returned. Perhaps Bill Speck's acid comments were inspired by the false attribution to Plumb of the authorship of such disparaging nicknames as "the infinitesimal Speck" and "the exorbitant Bill". Plumb certainly used these descriptions when he was surveying in comic and light-hearted mood his Cambridge colleagues and his fellow historians elsewhere, but I am pretty sure that these two were not Plumbian coinages. Jack certainly enjoyed the rather schoolboy habit of identifying fellow academics with mildly mischievous labels. One would need footnotes to identify some of the more arcane nicknames but many will remember and recognise all too well "the Dollar Princess" (A.L.Rowse, who boasted so much about his American earnings), "the Egghead with a double yolk" (C.P. Snow after the Two Cultures Debate), "the Delta Queen" (Dr Betty Wood, the historian of the American South who used the delta mark with great abandon when she first examined in the Tripos), "the Chief Clark" (the greatly revered G.N.Clark), "the Office Clark", "the Junior Clark", "the even lesser Clark", "the Examiner Royal" (Christopher Morris), "the Hungarian Rhapsody" (Peter Bauer), "the bouncing Czech", "the endangered Seal", "the Great Sensationalist", "the Anonymous of York", "the Todd everlasting", "the Rabbit with steel teeth", "the very much lesser Fieldmouse", "the poisoned Brook" and "the babbling Brooke", "the broken Cheyney", "the not Sharpe enough", "a little Slack", "the bespoke Taylor", "the off-the-peg Taylor", "the doubting Thomas", "the Norman conquered" and "the blarney Stone", "the Cambridge Pop shop", "Alcock – and no balls", "the Morris Minor and the Morris minus" (they came as a married pair), and two wine-merchants who were known as Gummer major and (rather predictably for the younger and much less respected one) "Gummer minus".

What Jack often forgot to allow for was how rapidly such verbal put-downs were passed on to the victims of them. When Todd, as the Master of Christ's, received his peerage, he would not have been pleased to be told that Plumb was publicly speculating as to whether he would take the title "Lord Christ".

I have to confess that I was mildly flattered to be thought worthy of such gentle mockery when I learned of the use of "McKendrick's Prussia" (invented by my pupil Norman Stone, later Professor of Modern History at Oxford), or "Smash McKendrick's Prussia" (painted in blue paint as a huge forty foot long graffito on the outer wall of Caius by the distinguished historian Peter Hennessy, later Lord Hennessy, when he was an undergraduate at St. John's), or "the Kaiser of Caius" (invented by my Caius colleague, Professor William Frend) or "mon Général" (still affectionately used by my old friend Dante Campailla), but others I know were more sensitive and more easily offended.

One has sadly to admit that malice in fairly mild forms, and infantilism in rather more powerful forms, are not entirely absent from academic life. These nicknames are their consequence, and they in turn foster some of the more absurd forms of paranoia that letters to the editor so often exhibit. Plumb was certainly not entirely free from these absurdities but when it came to pinning his colleagues down with verbal put-downs he always proudly laid claim to those that he had invented himself. His were rather wittier than most and often more unkind. He could also be memorably and unattractively coarse in his reaction to his colleagues. In his defence one should probably concede that a male dominated profession was coarser then than one would easily find acceptable today. Namier's cutting comment on what he regarded as Butterfield's convoluted versions of historical truisms was not atypical of the time: "it is like watching a man swallowing nails", he said, "then shitting screws". Indeed Namier was notorious for using what the Oxford historian John Cooper called "rather adolescent obscenity in exclusive male company".

In today's world of greater political correctness, Plumb's language (and indeed Namier's) can certainly sound startlingly coarse, but forty years ago the vocabulary of abuse could be surprisingly frank and uninhibited. When Margaret Thatcher said that "politicians like nappies should be frequently changed – and for the same reason", Plumb was delighted that his new heroine was reacting so robustly to those of her colleagues who had variously described her as "behaving with the sensitivity of a sex-starved boa constrictor", or as "a great she-elephant" or as "Atttila the hen", or simply as "a cow". In his view, MPs who dismissed her as "the immaculate misconception" or, even worse, "that fucking stupid petit-bourgeois woman", or who shouted in the Commons "Ditch the Bitch" deserved all that they got in return, however coarse it might seem today.

I suppose if you have a name like Jack Plumb it is difficult to resist the temptation to get your retaliation in first. There was something intrinsically comic about it. It sounded like a character in a nursery rhyme. One cannot imagine that he would have resisted the opportunity to invent cruel and childishly clever clerihews involving the words "thumb", "bum", "rum" and "plum" or "hack", "back", "lack", "sack" and "jack", if any of his rivals had been burdened with his name. He knew very well than an unkind phrase mocking the Oxford Regius professor of history, Archbishop Stubbs and his ally Freeman could survive for over a century. The two great medieval historians are still remembered in the lines:

Ladling butter from alternate tubs
Stubbs butters Freeman, and Freeman butters Stubbs.

He knew, all too well, that his surname alone made him vulnerable to such memorable mockery. He got very upset if unintentional typos led to him being addressed as "Professor Plump", and one Cambridge antique dealer claims to have lost his patronage forever as a result of this simple and innocent error. Both Snow and Plumb complained of the double indignity of being born both poor and with names that were irresistible invitations to mockery. Snow would often complain about the number of words beginning with the letters "Sn" which had unattractive associations – snide, sneer, sneaky, snarl, snob, snub, snivel, snoop, snore and such like. But when it came to unfortunate rhymes, Jack Plumb had surely drawn the shorter straw.

No one can deny, however, that he liked to make fun of people himself. He dearly loved to mock, and his mockery could be cruelly accurate about those he disliked or those he found wanting. Even his close friends and pupils were not immune from his dismissive comments – of one long-standing friend who was an outstanding cook, he used to say "I suppose the pleasures offered by her cooking just about compensate for the pain inflicted by her conversation"; of another who was extremely generous with her favours, he once wrote "her lack of morals just about makes up for her lack of sense"; of another, he wrote crudely "her talents are as small as her tits".

One has to concede that there were those amongst his pupils who were found wanting by Jack's exacting standards and who were mercilessly mocked, but I still like to think that the majority vote of those he taught would be a favourable one.

Many have reminded me that he not only encouraged them to aim high but also offered solace and sympathy when they failed immediately to succeed. Professor Barry Supple, his pupil who became Master of St Catherine's College, Cambridge, after narrowly failing to be elected to the Mastership at Christ's, pointed out in his autobiography that Plumb's standard reaction to his failure to get the promotion he sought or the job he had applied for was to remind him that "when one door closes, another one always opens". In recognition of this positive encouragement from Plumb, he called his autobiography *Doors Open* when he published it in 2008.

Indeed many of his pupils would readily admit (as would I) that he was the greatest single positive influence on their early lives and careers. Many have told me what an inspiration he was in their days in Cambridge and many count it as one of the great pleasures of their lives to have basked in his company. Not that it was always a comfortable experience. Jack Plumb did not earn the title of being the rudest man in Cambridge without inflicting some hurtful verbal wounds. Many of the insults and rebukes have become part of the Plumb legend; many of them are treasured almost as much by the victims as by the onlookers. As one who had suffered more than most said, "What will we have to talk and complain about when Jack has gone?" I suspect I shall miss the sense of outrage almost as much as the positive side of Jack's friendship. In spite of having known him for over fifty years I have never quite come to terms with what C.P. Snow called "the complex and contradictory nature of Jack Plumb."

10. PLUMB IN FICTION

Novelists, who used Jack as a model, have found it no easier than his friends to capture all aspects of his complex personality. Since his circle of friends included some very insightful novelists who had ample opportunity to observe him in action, it is not surprising that many did not want to waste such excellent novelogenic copy. C.P. Snow was a life-long if ultimately somewhat ambivalent friend, Angus Wilson was an equally ambivalent friend, William Cooper (Harry Hoff) was a friend who became an enemy, and R. Philmore (Bert Howard) was a mentor who knew at first hand Plumb's vices as well as his virtues. All four of these novelists based characters on Jack, while Pamela Hansford Johnson (Snow's wife and a most accomplished novelist) was a friend who had a very clear-sighted view of Jack but never to my knowledge made direct use of him in her novels. Perhaps she thought that there were enough fictional versions of him already in print, and I have never heard that his lover, the novelist Michael Ramsbotham, made use of Jack in his novels.

One is certainly, however, not short of choice.

Does one choose the character who Angus Wilson so memorably pinned down as John Hobday in *The Wrong Set* (1949), or does one choose one of the various versions of Jack Plumb who are said to flit through Snow's later novels such as Lord Ryle in *In Their Wisdom* (1974)), or does one plump for the two splendid portraits of him which dominate William Cooper's two best novels *Scenes from Provincial Life* (1950) and *The Struggles of Albert Woods* (1952), or does one go back to the first fictional portrait of him in R.Philmore's *The Good Books* (1936)? My vote would go to the Cooper fictional portraits. They give the best physical description of the young Plumb and the best insight into his personality, which could be so engaging and so maddening at the same time.

Sometimes it would be difficult for the uninitiated to recognise him in some of his fictional forms and impossible for those who knew him well not to recognise him immediately. The first that I came across was in Angus Wilson's brilliant and devastatingly insightful short story, entitled "Realpolitik" published in *The Wrong Set* (1949). This was the first high profile fictional version of Jack. In it he is the sparkling young director of a museum ruthlessly weeding out what he cruelly decides is the dead wood amongst the senior and distinguished members of staff and marking down his secretary for equally ruthless removal when she shows sign of less than total devotion to him. When she says: "*Golly you do tell some lies, don't you? Or have the Board ratified your staff changes?*" The John (Plumb) Hobday reply is "*How many times must I tell you, Veronica, that truth is relative*". But her fate was sealed when, after years of loyal service, she feels the need to warn him about his relentless ruthlessness with the words: *"You're getting too fond of bullying, it interferes with your charm, and charm is essential to your success"*. His reaction is thoughtful but decisive. *"What Veronica said was very true, thought John, and he made a note to be more detached in his attitude. All the same these criticisms were bad for his self-esteem. For all her loyalty Veronica knew him too well, got too near home. Charm was important to success, but self-esteem was more so. His imagination began to envisage further staff changes, perhaps a graduate secretary would really be more suitable now."*

Angus Wilson had seen Jack Plumb's highly effective manipulation of his career advancement at Bletchley, where his success far exceeded his own, and could not resist depicting his skilled and ruthless self-promotion – first as a short story in *The Listener* and then in his first book, which received rapturous reviews and rapid reprinting. First published in March 1949, it was reprinted in April '49, reprinted for a third time in June '49, and reprinted many times thereafter.

It must have been very difficult for Jack Plumb to stomach the brilliant depiction of him as a skilful bully ruthlessly trampling on the scholarly ideals of the expert, if old-fashioned, staff that he had inherited with his appointment as Museum and Gallery Director, but that is what Angus Wilson offers:

"John Hobday sat on the edge of his desk and swung his left leg with characteristic boyishness….and then spoke with careful informality. It was not going to be an easy meeting, he decided… None of the three who formed his audience made any response. Veronica, who remembered him taking over new departments at the Ministry during the war, thought he hasn't got the right tone, he doesn't realise that he is coming up against deeper loyalties with these people, loyalties to scholarship and ideas….". "As you know", John went on, and Victoria could tell by the loud, trumpeting, rhetorical note of his voice that he was once more the confident salesman lost in the dream world of grandiose schemes he was putting before them, "I've got some very big ideas for the Gallery. I'm not an expert in any way as you people are, but I think that's possibly why (they) chose me for the job. They felt the Gallery had already got its full weight of scholars and experts….That's why they got me in."

"The faces in front of him were quite unresponsive…. The damned fools, thought John, they have the chance of turning this tin pot, cranky provincial gallery into a national institution and they won't play ball. Well if they can't see which way their own chances lie, they're not getting in the way of mine. They'll have to come to heel or go."

He then, in a tone which was "purposely patronising and offensive", pointedly probes their individual weaknesses, and expertly provokes them into threatening to resign when he explains that they are likely to have to work under rather than with the new staff he intends to appoint. It is a *tour de force* of expert cruelty and passive aggressive bullying.

When I got to know Angus Wilson well, after reviewing him very favourably for *The Bookman*, I asked him if he had not had doubts about the effect his devastating fictional version of Plumb would have. After all he knew him pretty well and many friends would find it difficult to forgive such a cruelly insightful portrait. He replied that he could not resist the opportunity. He argued that only those who knew Plumb very well would recognise his portrayal. As he not unreasonably said, what he depicted was only one facet of Jack's multi-faceted career and only one side of his many-sided character. Most people, he felt, would not recognise his source. In this he proved to be correct. For most people this would remain simply another part of the hidden life of Jack Plumb.

It was not, of course, hidden from Jack himself and his relationship with Angus was not as warm as it once had been. Fortunately Plumb's genuine admiration of Wilson's major novels, and Wilson's genuine admiration for Plumb's major histories, led to a rapprochement marked by Angus Wilson's eulogy of Jack's work as an historian when he was awarded an Honorary degree by the University of East Anglia. In that eulogy Angus painted a portrait of someone who was "at once a very sensitive and a very tough-minded man" and someone who was "outstanding among contemporary historians in fighting the diminished scope of his chosen profession". It was as generous about Plumb's strengths (both as a man and as an historian) as his short story had been so insightful about his shortcomings. Not entirely surprisingly it was the vivid portrait of his personal shortcomings that remained more vividly in Plumb's mind.

Understandably, Jack never fully forgave Angus for the portrait of him as John Hobday, and hostility between then often bubbled up. Jack was jealous of Angus's success as a novelist and Angus was even more jealous of the wealth that Jack had achieved through his writing. I recall Angus leaving a lunch given by Melveena and me in a tantrum, when Jack boasted of the huge earnings he had received from *Royal Heritage*.

The appealing description, given by Margaret Drabble in her biography of Angus, of Plumb's reaction to Angus's oration at the Honorary degree ceremony, was quickly squashed by Jack's response. Drabble wrote: "Angus presented an Honorary degree to Jack Plumb, speaking warmly of Bert Howard, and Plumb seemed moved to tears." Plumb replied, in a letter bristling with indignant corrections: "my eyes did not fill with tears when I got an honorary degree at East Anglia. I was nearly hysterical with suppressed laughter as Angus looked and spoke like Margaret Rutherford in drag."

Perhaps here was Plumb's belated opportunity to take his belated revenge on two authors, now both dead, for their devastatingly insightful fictional portraits of him. That he could do so when writing to rebuke and correct another distinguished novelist probably added to his satisfaction, not that Drabble seemed to be conscious of the use that Wilson and Howard had made of Plumb in their work, which in turn had inspired his ambivalent attitude to them.

The revenge motive is further suggested by the fact that in the same letter he dismissed Harry Hoff as a source of reliable evidence about him because he was always "paranoid about me"; said of Snow, "your account of Snow and the presence of Bert Howard at Bletchley is pure fiction"; and followed up with a letter saying that "the major reason for his (Angus) poor sales was that most people found his books distasteful or unreadable." In a single brief correspondence with Margaret Drabble in 1995, he had managed to be dismissively disobliging to all four of the novelists (Hoff, Howard, Snow and Wilson) who had written about him.

In earlier years he had sustained an apparently amiable relationship with Angus and Tony and frequently entertained them in Cambridge (where I first met them in 1953) and at Westhorpe in the 1960s. As a result Melveena and I also often met them and were not infrequently invited to lunch. We were always delighted to accept. They were brilliantly entertaining hosts and their tiny garden set in the middle of a wood in Suffolk was a horticultural jewel – understandably rated by many famous judges as one of the finest private gardens in Britain in spite of its minuscule size. My daughters, when they were still little girls, were entranced by Angus Wilson's expert garden tour of his flowers, ranging from a spectacularly flowering dogwood to the tiniest double-flowering columbine.

Our most significant visit was when Tony followed up his invitation by saying that he had to warn us that the lunch was to be televised and that this was because Angus was going to publicly announce the nature of their relationship. We said we would be honoured to be there and were surprised that he thought that we might not. He said that he had been surprised and disappointed by those who had accepted but then withdrawn when they learnt of the nature of the lunch. In those unenlightened days, when even being associated publicly with the openly gay set was regarded by many as unwise and best avoided, some were too protective of their reputations to risk attending the lunch.

At the lunch when Angus asked us whether we thought Jack was ever likely "to come out of the closet himself", we replied that in all honesty, if he did, we did not know what he would come out of it as. At the time, unlike Angus, we were all too well aware that he was currently involved in an intense affair with the wife of one of his old friends. What we did not say was that Jack thought that Angus's decision to go public on the nature of his relationship with Tony was irresponsible and self-indulgent and risked Tony losing his successful and very valuable career as a social worker – which it did.

If Plumb had understandably not warmed to the Wilson fictional incarnation of him in 1949, he was very soon to be faced with another fictional version of him, which was unmistakeable to many more people and which annoyed him even more.

In 1950 Plumb's personality was explored in fiction once again. This time it was explored at greater length but equally brilliantly in William Cooper's *Scenes from Provincial Life (1950)*. In this wonderfully high-spirited novel, our hero Tom (Plumb) pursues hilarious amorous adventures rather improbably disguised as a predominantly gay but also bisexual, red-haired, Jewish chartered accountant. In the opening pages Cooper (who in real life was Harry Hoff, once a personal friend of Plumb's who became an ardent enemy) pins down his fictional subject as vividly and as accurately as a butterfly collector pins down his specimens: "*Sometimes what a man thinks he is can be just as interesting as what he really is. In Tom's case it was just as interesting and decidedly more wonderful; it had an endearing romantic grandeur. Tom saw himself as a great understander of human nature, a great writer, a great connoisseur of the good things of life, and a great lover*" of both sexes.

It was an incisively accurate introduction to the Tom/Jack character and Cooper went on to say "*Tom possessed a formidable capacity for psychological hustling. In an easy agreeable way he hustled other people into doing what they did not want to do. He was always trying to hustle me, especially for instance over our country cottage*". Cooper then explores the two friends' different attitude towards their sharing of the country cottage. One relied on his "*unusually strong legal right*"; Tom (Plumb) "*made in a different mould did not see it that way. In a style more heroic, more passionate, more expansive, more wonderful than mine, he systematically tried to hustle me out of my turn*". Anyone who has shared a property with Jack Plumb (as I have) would at once recognise and accept the accuracy of this fictional depiction of him.

Tom's friend, in a delightfully ironic way, concedes that "*there was some basis for Tom's picture of himself. He was courageous and he had a great fund of emotion: he had a shrewd down-to-earth insight into human nature and tireless curiosity about people. He was the ideal listener to one's life-story – the only trouble was that in order to encourage the next person to tell his life-story Tom was liable to repeat under the seal of secrecy one's own*". Once again the fictional portrait (both the positive and the negative aspects) remind one irresistibly of Jack Plumb.

The novel proved to be a great and well-deserved success. The *Daily Telegraph*, the *Evening Stan*dard, the *Daily Express* and the *Manchester Guardian* all sang it praises, and in the *Sunday Times* Snow gave his novelist friend an enticingly encouraging review: "*Scenes from Provincial Life has given me more pleasure than any book I have read this year. It is told with immense high spirits, with poetry, subtlety and humour and with remarkable technical command...The story is often* *hilariously funny, always true, sometimes joyous and sad. But the only sadness with which the book leaves one is simply that youth must end...This novel is not suitable reading for anyone easily shocked, for anyone shocked, say, by the Satyricon or by Colette. All others are advised to get hold of it...I believe that the strength of his work resides ultimately in his knowledge of human beings and his power to depict them."* Jack Plumb, the main human being who was being so brilliantly depicted, was understandably less appreciative than Snow.

Other distinguished critics were, however, equally impressed. V.S. Pritchett called it *"the rarest thing in English fiction – a falling-out (of) love story"*. Stevie Smith called it *"a most touching and brilliant piece of work, every one is so young and full of life and affection"*. Angus Wilson saw it as a story told *"in the spirit of Fielding and Smollett, with a dash of Petronius Arbiter"*.

John Connell in the *Evening News* was equally flattering: *"Mr. William Cooper's first novel is a highly diverting piece of work. Its title is demurely and mischievously reminiscent of George Eliot. The mischief is unrepentantly predominant throughout the book, and I fancy that George Eliot would have been thoroughly scandalized by it ... I recommend the book firmly to everyone who wants to be shocked. Every now and again the middle-aged encounter the loves of their youth – did one really believe that that pudding-face hid brains and noble character ... Such an experience, with its wry twanging of the heart strings, it is to read Mr. Cooper's novel."*

Not surprisingly the book sold well. When I bought it in 1950, the year it was published, it was already in its third impression, and the more of Jack Plumb's friends who read it, the more of them there were to tell him how accurately and brilliantly Cooper had depicted him. He was not well pleased. He was all too well versed in the falling-out of love or falling-out of lust process to want to be depicted so brilliantly experiencing it. He, too, often looked back at some of the many people he had bedded and asked himself what he could possibly once have seen in them, and he did not enjoy being seen as a character being so accurately mocked for his self-flattering and self-deceiving ability to reinvent himself into someone much grander and more romantic than he really was. So he robustly denied being the real-life prototype for Tom.

He was even less pleased when Cooper published his second novel, *The Struggles of Albert Woods*, in 1952. In this third fictional incarnation, he is a brilliant research scientist, humbly born, richly gifted and highly ambitious (both academically and socially). In this version he is uxorious, creative and, although often on the brink of disaster, ultimately satisfyingly successful. In some Cambridge colleges this novel was for many years a set book for research students in their first term, and deservedly so, for it teaches one a great deal about those seeking advancement and promotion in academic life. This time the physical description of Albert Woods is unmistakably that of the young

Jack Plumb. He is described much as he was in youth and in many ways much as he remained (although admittedly without the hair) all his life: "*By the time he was twenty-one our subject had reached his full stature physically, that is to say five feet six inches. He was a sturdy young man inclined to be plump. He had a fair amount of muscle sleeked over by a layer of thin fat that gave his body a faintly pneumatic look. He had a hefty chest and buttocks and a high waist. His body was strongly-made, tough and resilient, but there was nothing of the carthorse about it. He had a certain fineness of grace. The flick of his eyelids was rapid, the movement of his hands was delicate. His head was round like a ball and he had long dark silky hair. His face was broader than it was long. His big grey eyes protruded so far that he swore that his eyeballs got sunburnt in summertime – he was short sighted and wore spectacles. His nose was short and rather stubby, his mouth wide with red slightly pouting lips. It was a good, clever, homely, sensitive, pleasing, English lower middle-class face – not specially beautiful.* "

Many people would be pleased, even rather flattered, to be depicted so centrally in three distinguished works of fiction published within the space of only two or three years, but Jack most certainly was not. William Noblett (the future librarian who is now the most expert guide to the Plumb archives in the University Library in Cambridge) loves telling the story of coming across *The Struggles of Albert Woods* by chance when staying at Westhorpe and (having delightedly read it) saying to Jack's not inconsiderable fury: "Albert Woods is pure Plumb". The more people who told him the same thing the crosser he became.

Although he maintained an on-off relationship with Angus Wilson, his friendship with Harry Hoff was fractured for good – not helped by the fact that Hoff discovered that Jack had rather casually seduced one of his lovers – apparently in Jack's version of events just for the fun of it, but in some peoples' eyes just for the revenge of it. Hoff never forgave him. When my wife and I met Hoff at a party given by the Snows many years later, it was almost all that he wanted to talk about – and in the most unforgiving terms. Hoff did admit, however, that Plumb had provided him with the inspiration for what he described as his two most vivid fictional portraits and his two most successful novels, not that that made him like him any better.

Although there was a lukewarm attempt at reconciliation in later life Jack never really forgave Hoff. He had many reasons to feel aggrieved, not least the jealousy of a novelist manqué. Just imagine how he must have felt when he read the ecstatic reviews which welcomed *The Struggles of Albert Woods*. A rave review such as John Betjeman's in the *Daily Telegraph* was like a dagger to the heart for the young man who had once longed to leave academia to write novels himself, but whose own two novels had been rejected for publication.

Betjeman wrote: "*I do not often enjoy a novel as much as The Struggles of Albert Woods by William Cooper. Certainly the books I have read since, competent and entertaining though they are, seem an anti-climax. "Restrain yourself, my dear Betjeman," my business acumen tells me, "don't lose your head and start using words like masterpiece and genius. Think of the book in the perspective of ten years hence." "Yet", my intuition replies, "this is a book comparable in its affectionate humour with the famous Diary of a Nobody. It deserves to be read ten years hence" .... It is so easy to write a humorous novel like this sneeringly. There are laughs if you do, but they are not the deep laughs which Albert Woods gives us. They lack the touch of pathos which the best comedy has: the difference between a Chaplin film and a Wilde play. Mr. Cooper's first book, Scenes from Provincial Life, has stuck in my memory as a remarkable picture of English character. Albert Woods will remain in it longer still. It is a firm defence of English individualism and a first class comedy. I have no doubts about it."*

Jack might well have taken solace from the ample evidence that he was such a beguiling and intriguing character who had starred in such brilliant works of fiction, but he did not. He always denied that he was the real life prototype for Albert Woods in spite of overwhelming evidence to the contrary. He tried to convince his friends that Woods was actually based on Philip George, once a scientific fellow of Christ's, but very few were even partially convinced.

Some have argued that he also appeared in fictional form in the later works of C.P. Snow.

I find this somewhat problematic. In 1973, I wrote "none of these fictional portraits is by his old friend, C.P.Snow. Despite frequent assertions to the contrary and feverish searches through *The Masters* and *The Light and the Dark*, Plumb does not appear in the *Strangers and Brothers* sequence. Indeed at Jack's fiftieth birthday in 1961 Snow explained why he had never written extensively about him. He was often asked why he had not exploited one of the most novelogenic of his friends, and the answer, he said, was very simple. Jack was too difficult, too complex, too contradictory. No one would believe him if he were faithfully written down. I think this is perhaps true and explains why the existing portraits are somewhat one-dimensional. They have explored only bits of the man, and, therefore, though they are often revealing, even brilliant, they are not wholly satisfying – not, that is, to historians seeking an accurate version of J.H. Plumb; to the ordinary reader they are marvellously satisfying."

When I delivered my valedictory tribute to Jack in December 1973, Snow had assured me once again that he had never attempted more than a fleeting use of Plumb as a character in his novels. He said that he thought that it would be too difficult to do full justice to what he called "his complex and conflicted personality". Since that date, some have suggested that he changed his mind. Certainly Snow's novel *In Their Wisdom*, which appeared in 1974 (the same year that my tribute appeared and when he was assuring me that he had never made major use of Plumb in his novels), contained a character called Lord Ryle who had some striking similarities to Plumb. He was *"a historian by trade, inquisitive by vocation"* who *"had travelled up through layers of society"*, and his considerable wealth *"was all self-made. Comfortable professional jobs over a life-time, but that didn't explain it all or nearly all. Histories which had sold well, especially in America, and used as text books. Consultancies with publishers, investments which had started early for a poor young man. It had accumulated and been well handled"*. In addition, he *"had written books about the Industrial Revolution"* and he *"hankered after"* other people's women. In addition, Ryle had been a *"Chairman of Royal Commissions, one of the first Life Peers"; "he sat on the board of a merchant bank, and a couple of others";* and had a face *"like a picture of W.M.Thackeray or a retired pugilist"*. Of these defining features of Lord Ryle more than half were shared with Jack Plumb. More significantly this novel by Snow contains no insightful or detailed concerns with typical Plumbian behaviour, but there were enough superficial similarities for friends such as Professor Leslie Green and Sir David Cannadine to see at least part of him in the depiction of Lord Ryle. Indeed Cannadine sees the name Lord Ryle alone as a rare Snovian joke and a wry pointer to the man who riled so many in his lifetime.

Superficial similarities to Plumb can also be found in Snow's portrait of Reginald Swaffield who is described as *"a formidable self-made"* man who enjoys exercising a *"kind of personal imperialism"* over people within his orbit, and is *"hoping for a peerage"*. Lord Swaffield, as he becomes, certainly displays a Plumb-like eagerness to take over and direct other people's lives but he is very far from a fully fleshed-out version of Plumb.

Like so many of Snow's fictional depictions of the Fellows of Christ's in *The Strangers and Brothers* series of novels, Lord Ryle and Lord Swaffield may well have been a hybrid version of more than one living character. In *The Masters* it is almost impossible to miss part or even complete portraits of many of the most prominent college contemporaries of Snow and Plumb. Snow was not one of the most creative or imaginative or inventive novelists when he came to depicting his main characters. One can easily recognise, for instance, the use he made of Canon Charles Raven as the character Paul Jago. His brother, Philip Snow, called Jago "a superbly drawn portrait" of Raven, and Snow himself said that "Jago is a good picture of Raven, though considerably transmuted". Other fictional portraits (such as Roy Calvert and Arthur Brown and Eustace Pilbrow) are obviously based on the real-life Fellows (Charles Allberry and Sidney Grose and J.B. Trend respectively). Many others amongst Snow's fictional characters were clearly hybrid versions of other Fellows because Snow frequently combined aspects of different real-life figures in creating his fictional characters. By his own admission, Alec Nightingale in *The Masters* is based partly on the mathematician Stourton Steen, and partly on the classicist and College librarian Arthur Peck. Revealingly Peck took his real-life revenge by refusing to have any of Snow's books in Christ's library.

For all these part or whole examples of fiction borrowing from real life, Snow never claimed to me that Ryle was either all or partly based on Plumb, but one cannot deny that there were some striking surface similarities.

Plumb certainly never spoke to me of recognising himself in either *In Their Wisdom* or *The Malcontents*, the two Snow novels in which some have claimed he appeared (as Lord Ryle and as Lord Swaffield), nor did very many of his friends.

He and they may well have thought that any passing similarities were insufficient to compare with the detailed and forensically accurate dissections of his character and personality that Angus Wilson and William Cooper had so devastatingly produced, and therefore were not worth fussing about.

He also made little complaint (at least to me) about his portrayal in R. Philmore's *The Good Books* published in 1936. Philmore was the pseudonym of Bert Howard and although his novels were respectfully and respectably reviewed they remained pretty obscure when compared with the writings of Angus Wilson, William Cooper and C. P. Snow, and Plumb may well have hoped that their relative obscurity would save him from any undesirable public exposure.

He may also have felt that few would recognise this fictional version of him. After all it would seem highly improbable that a schoolmaster would portray his prize pupil as an academic fraud and a murderer. It would also seem improbable that a close adult friendship would explode into such a savage indictment by one of the other. In fact, they always enjoyed a somewhat fractious relationship. Both were men much given to anger. Both could explode into towering rage. Both could be unforgiving, and with Jack Plumb there was often a lot for Howard to forgive. Few would know that Plumb seduced and then dumped Howard's sister – a fact that perhaps inevitably complicated their relationship. Few would know that the love of Plumb's life (who was also a friend of Howard's) committed suicide when faced with Plumb's explosive rage on discovering that they were both sleeping with that same sister. Few would know that Howard and Plumb fell out so badly at Bletchley. Few would know that, when later Jack seduced the wife of a very close friend of Howard's, a furious Howard warned him off from endangering a marriage and risking causing a mental breakdown for the cuckolded husband.

Enough of these ruptures in their long-term friendship happened early enough to explain why Howard's portrait of Plumb in the 1930s was not so very surprising. Early in life Howard had been an inspiration for the youthful Plumb, later in life Plumb had generously helped to fund an ageing Howard when he was in disgrace and in exile in Holland, but no one can deny that it was often a troubled relationship. So perhaps Howard's portrait of Plumb in the 1930s was in some ways very understandable, although in later life their friendship was partially repaired.

I was first alerted to this portrait of him (the first time Plumb was immortalized in fiction) when Bill Noblett lent me his copy of *The Good Books*, which had once belonged to Marjorie Howard, the sister of Howard and the one-time mistress of Plumb. Inside the book she had written "Marjorie C. Howard" in ink, and then helpfully inscribed in pencil a list of the main characters and their real life identities. The list identifies Snow as a character called Swan, Harry Hoff as Harry Colin, Jack Plumb as Jack Pope, and Bert Howard as Garner.

Snow might well have been flattered to be portrayed as the all-knowing, all-seeing, super-intelligent solver of the central mystery; Harry Hoff might well have been pleased to be portrayed as a sympathetic character and to have the book dedicated to "My Candid Friend H. S. Hoff"; but Jack Plumb would have to have been astonishingly magnanimous to have welcomed being portrayed as the deviously cunning if highly intelligent Jack Pope, both an academic fraud and a cold-blooded murderer.

He is first introduced to the reader as "a brilliant young scientist" but his detailed depiction is that of a morally dubious character (a verdict softened only by his willingness to put himself at greater risk of detection as result of an elaborate attempt to protect his close friend, Harry Colin). It is this act of kindness and affection that saves him from the gallows, but it does not save him from a pretty comprehensive character assassination in the final chapter.

Amongst other character flaws, he is accused of "loose living"; of living "a life of aggressive freedom"; of pursuing a life "independent of any moral restraint"; and of being "a scientific rogue" who produced "false results", not to mention being a murderer and planning to be a double murderer. Indeed his motive for his first murder was to prevent his academic fraud being exposed by the man he murdered. He then plans further multiple murders when he fears exposure for the first.

Swan (Snow) is convinced that a jury would find Jack (Plumb) Pope guilty: *"They would be prejudiced against you from the start ... they would make up their minds to hang you. You are one of those unfortunate people who suggest in their own person all that the average man understands by loose living. Your general mode of life, your suggestion of independence from any moral restraint, your manner – all would go against you."* Even his close friend, Harry Colin, refers to Jack Pope's spasmodic attempts to be *"a gigolo"*. Nevertheless the magisterial Swan does not intend *"to have you sentenced to death because you have lived a life of aggressive freedom"*.

He does, however, insist that the Jack Pope/Jack Plumb character gives up his academic career. It is because *"producing false results is the great scientific crime"* that Swan/Snow concludes that *"you must get out of science. I demand that, at least. Try writing."* The irony of this verdict for Jack Plumb, who, in the 1930s, was desperate to get out of academia to pursue a writing career as a novelist, cannot have been lost on him, but he can scarcely have welcomed this dissection and depiction of his character.

Whether read individually or judged as a group of fictional portraits, the authors who used him so revealingly in their work did not offer a judgement of his character that Plumb would be delighted to see widely recognised. Both individually and collectively they offered a view of him that not surprisingly he largely preferred to keep well hidden.

11. PLUMB'S PAINTED PORTRAITS

If Jack understandably always felt that his novelist friends had done him less than justice, or at the very least been less than kind to him in their fictional judgements, then he was equally critical about the image produced by those who tried to capture him on canvas.

He was particularly scathing about the portrait that Christ's commissioned to mark his Mastership. The college had consulted me about Jack's taste in portrait painters – as a Trustee of the National Portrait Gallery he not surprisingly had decided views on the subject. I had suggested Brian Organ, a Leicester artist of whom Jack then approved highly, and when personally consulted Jack in turn confirmed to the college authorities that he would be delighted to be painted by Organ. The proposal went to the College Council, which was appalled to learn that such a portrait would cost £4,000. One helpful member of the Council said that he knew an artist friend who would do one for £400. This cheaper option was gratefully embraced and the poor artist, Jenny Polack, was faced with a furious Plumb, deeply insulted at being "done on the cheap" as he called it, and much put out to be faced by a young woman painter of whom he had never heard. The resulting picture shows a rather purple faced Plumb glaring furiously out of the canvas – "the only thing good about it is the polish on my shoes" was his unforgiving verdict and he arranged for it to be hung in an obscure part of the college where it would very rarely be seen. Some insight into the personal antipathies involved can be judged from the conversation I overheard in the SCR between Fellows of Christ's: one said that it made him "look like an enraged toad". "Yes, you're so right", said the other, "isn't it excellent – absolutely true to life!"

Jack sulked so determinedly that Christ's decided to try again and were rewarded with a very pleasing painting of Jack's room with a very tiny Plumb lurking inconspicuously in the middle of it. This time the artist, Lawrence Gowing, was a name that Jack could quite contentedly acknowledge, and he took solace from the fact that the painting was a remarkably agreeable picture, but he was less than happy that the space occupied by his actual image was the smallest in the college's collection of former Masters.

I had some sympathy with the college. He was not an easy man to please and when I arranged for the wonderfully gifted artist, John Ward, to produce a portrait of him to mark his eightieth birthday I prudently asked John to produce two different versions, saying I would keep one for myself and the other would be given to Jack. It was a strategy born of long experience of the difficulty of pleasing him. Having travelled all over Europe with him, I knew from many past experiences that the first room that he was offered, even by the grandest hotel, was never good enough. He always insisted on seeing another. He always took the second offering – much to my family's delight because we always inherited the first one, which was almost invariably the bigger and better of the two. I guessed that the same would be true of the portraits, so when, in a private room in Raymond Blanc's renowned restaurant at *Le Manoir aux Quat' Saisons*, his friends met to celebrate his birthday I had the two portraits placed on easels and carefully draped. When the first was revealed (which incidentally I much preferred, as did most of those who saw them) Jack immediately declared that it made him look "like Toad of Toad Hall", so we rapidly unveiled the second – this was declared to be "satisfactory" and was the one specifically directed in his will to be left to the National Portrait Gallery.

The "Toad of Toad Hall" version now hangs in my home next to a portrait of me by Michael Noakes, and next to Michael Ayrton's portrait of Joseph Needham, which I bought when the College Council of Caius equally foolishly rejected it. John Ward's rejected portrait is now hugely admired by many of my more discerning visitors.

It is true that, for most of his life, Jack's face and physical appearance changed remarkably little. If, as the cynics say, there are three stages of life – youth, middle age and "you haven't changed a bit" – then he occupied the period of "you haven't changed a bit Jack" for about fifty years. The image he chose to present to the world did, however, undergo some very revealing changes. Here the formal portraits are of only limited help. They do, of course, give some impression of how he dressed in later life. Both the John Ward portraits come complete with Jack's unmistakable headgear – an overlarge velvet hat that became his trademark in old age.

One has to rely on photographs and oral history for how he dressed throughout the rest of his life. According to that evidence he went through four phases: the radical, Bohemian student of his Leicester youth with long hair, canary-yellow sweaters and purple corduroy trousers; the earnest young Cambridge academic sporting appropriately shabby tweed jackets and even fleetingly a pipe; the dapper dandy of late middle age, by now the possessor of a formidable number of expensive bespoke suits from his Saville Row tailors, usually worn with a bow tie; and finally what David Cannadine has called the caricatured Club-land swell, with suits of ever more pronounced pin-stripe, shirts of ever bolder colour and stripe, expensive silk ties which loudly announced their designer status, even more expensive and to my taste garish designer cuff-links, dapper little bespoke shoes and very large bespoke hats. He almost invariably wore a rather too tight waistcoat. He really did at times take on a Toad of Toad Hall appearance.

He would have been thrilled to learn that the Victoria & Albert Museum have chosen a selection of his clothes to join their Costume Exhibit. One can only hope that they do not restrict themselves to showing his clothes from his later years – by then his dress sense had become exaggerated to the point of near absurdity.

In his eighties he became ever more a caricature of the eccentric elderly don. Frantically sensitive to draughts, he now wore a hat almost all of the time. His favourite was the huge wide-brimmed velvet fedora. This he wore to cross the court in, to shop in and even to dine with his friends in, but he had an impressive array of alternatives, mostly bought from Locks of St James's. He even wore a hat when dining in Hall, rather pedantically donning his velvet doctoral bonnet as the only proper accompaniment to academic dress. He got so used to wearing this bonnet in the evening that he even turned up in Caius to celebrate his ninetieth birthday wearing it at an absurdly rakish angle and declined to take it off even when eating indoors on a warm August night.

In many ways, Jack and his distinctive clothes were easier to caricature than to paint. In the fifties, I recall some brilliant cartoons of him by Craig Barlow, a gay pupil of his who was then reading history at Emmanuel College in the 1950s. They were based on a series of circles. Round body, round head, round face, round spectacles, these together with a bow tie and a dapper suit were the raw materials. In the middle of the largest sphere, beneath the imposing dome of his high forehead, his neat features clustered together as if for warmth. The result was unmistakable. When he had his cataracts removed in later life he discovered for the first time that he no longer needed glasses, but he was so disconcerted by the change in his appearance without them, that he had a pair made with plain lens so that his characteristic image would be restored.

To be fair to those who tried to catch his likeness, it has to be admitted that his highly mobile features and his rapidly changing moods made the task of the formal portrait painter much more difficult.

He always complained that he would have made a lousy poker-player, and a less than accomplished ambassador, because he could not hide his powerful emotions. His facial expressions betrayed all too clearly what he felt. It was one of the reasons that he made friends and acquired enemies so easily.

12. PLUMB AND THE SECRET WORLD AT BLETCHLEY PARK

When people speculated as to why an obscure young Cambridge don, working during the war at Bletchley Park (or Station X as, for security reasons, it was then called), should have the good fortune to be billeted with the Rothschilds and envied the evenings he spent perfecting his palate on the Lafites, the Moutons and the Yquems from Tony and Yvonne Rothschild's ample cellar, they probably simply cursed his outrageous good luck.

They should have cursed, or rather admired, his outrageous boldness. His mother used often to complain that "the trouble with our Jack is that he's always been too mad-'eaded", and it was his mad-headedness or his bold and instinctive anger on their behalf which earned him the Rothschilds' gratitude and hospitality. When an English peeress married to an influential Minister of State gave vent to a spiteful and anti-Semitic remark about Yvonne de Rothschild, the young Plumb was so outraged that he ordered her out of the party (not his!) and out of the house (not his!) and then hurled her fur coat after her into the snow. It won him a bitter and long-lasting influential enemy but also an enduring friendship, because, as he later wrote, "Yvonne was so grateful that when I lost my lodgings because the absurd husband of my landlady thought, wrongly, that my attention to his wife was not honourable, Yvonne asked me to stay with her and her husband. However, in tight wartime conditions with mandatory billeting, it was only prudent to do so if I became the Rothschilds' billetee, which meant paying them 35 shillings a week and having the payment entered into my billeting book. We (Tony, Yvonne and Jack) lived in the groom's house in the stables – small but beautifully furnished with a glorious Stubbs and a glowing Cuyp, which never ceased to lift my spirits no matter how desperate the news was in those gray years of 1940-43". Little wonder that Asa Briggs, in his *Secret Days: Code-Breaking in Bletchley Park*, described Plumb's lodgings with the Rothschilds at Ascott House, Wing, as "the best of all the Bletchley Park billets".

Not surprisingly, Plumb always admitted that he had a good war. He did not much enjoy flying round the world on Bletchley business in unheated transport planes without the benefit of pressurized cabins, but he greatly enjoyed the exotic places he visited – he particularly enjoyed his visit to

Colombo in Ceylon. He did not greatly enjoy the long periods of boredom interspersed with periods of intense excitement, which, he said, was the reality of wartime code-breaking in Hut 4 Naval Section. He did not enjoy the agonizing decisions about whether or not to use the information made available by the Enigma machine and by his own work on *Reservehandverfahren* (the code used by the German navy) when Enigma broke down. Men's lives hung on such decisions but so did keeping the Germans ignorant of what the Bletchley code-breakers had achieved. No-one, however, could be indifferent to the excitement that Alan Turing's work evoked at the highest levels of government. And he had the comfort of knowing that he was proving to be a success in this strange world of academic code-breakers.

Jack's mind was not of the kind to prosper on the technical side of their work alone (he did not shine at chess or cryptic crosswords or mathematical problems or even foreign languages) but he was a born entrepreneur, a born communicator, a born promoter of what the code-breakers had achieved and he flourished in the sphere of analysis and presentation of the evidence that the code-breakers had deciphered. In doing so he quite quickly built up a successful personal power base for himself. Almost inevitably he became head of his own Section. Another Cambridge historian, Harry (later Sir Harry) Hinsley, flourished to an even greater extent, but many of Jack's friends were complete failures: Angus (later Sir Angus) Wilson was a flop, as were H. E. Howard, who spent all his time chasing the secretaries, and Bentley Bridgewater, who spent too much of his time chasing Angus.

After the war, extravagant claims were made about the varying significance of what individuals had achieved. Some bordered on the absurd. In Margaret Drabble's biography of Angus Wilson, she poses the question "How important was his work? Some say it was routine; 'somewhere way down the line': others claim that it was high powered. One enthusiast believes that Angus Johnstone-Wilson and Bentley Bridgewater between them won the war." She also quotes Snow's almost equally extravagant insistence that Bert Howard "was one of our great men of genius, one of our real men of genius. When still quite a young man … he was still infinitely more useful to us in the war than any General."

Plumb's response to these claims was devastating. First he pointed out those words of Snow's were very appropriately said of Alan Turing not Bert Howard. In the same letter he was once again completely dismissive about the value of the work of Angus and Bentley Bridgewater and Bert Howard at Bletchley. In spite of admitting the trouble he had taken to get Howard into Bletchley because of his quite exceptional memory, he presented all three of them as worse than useless: "We had trouble dealing with Angus and Bentley before Howard arrived – they were always late, at times failed to turn up, had no interest in their work. They often chased each other across the lawns, behaving indeed like children with tantrums. For those of us doing 70 hours a week, it was not tolerable. For me and others Angus's breakdown was a godsend. The *on dit* was that it was due to Bentley introducing him to practices which terrified him. That I did not believe. They were both temperamentally unfitted for office work. The boredom, which was constant at Bletchley with its seemingly meaningless jobs, was too much for him. Howard proved to be a dud. He chased the Wrens remorselessly, then fell overwhelmingly in love with a secretary and spent most of his time trying to persuade her to marry him – in office and out of office hours."

This frank exchange of views about Bletchley between Plumb and Drabble did not happen until 1995. By then the cloak of secrecy, which had for so long shrouded the code-breakers' work in mystery, had been lifted, and more and more of what had been achieved there was being revealed and applauded.

It is often said how remarkable it was that Cambridge, the home of the famous post-war spy scandal that swirled around Kim Philby, Anthony Blunt, Guy Burgess, Douglas McClean and John Caimcross, should also have been the dominant student home to what Churchill called "the geese that laid the golden eggs but never cackled". He was, of course, referring to the code breakers at Bletchley, and there certainly were those, like Asa Briggs, who kept almost totally silent right up to the present day about what was achieved there. His book *Secret Days: Code-Breaking in Bletchley Park* (published in 2014, nearly seventy years after he left Bletchley) was dedicated to his wife Susan with the words "To whom *all* is now revealed".

Others were more talkative. In the decades after the war as the need for secrecy faded, bits of the story gradually filtered out.

As the years went by, my school-teacher Bert Howard, and Harry Hinsley, Peter Laslett, Christopher Morris and Jack Plumb, who all taught me in Cambridge, were all willing to discreetly hint at and even take modest credit for the huge importance of what had been done at Station X. Since he was the one that I knew best, Jack was probably the most forthcoming of them all about the sensational secrets and about the drab huts in which they spent heroically long and often mind-blowingly boring hours pursuing those secrets, but even he was uncharacteristically careful about what he revealed.

To be fair to them all, they mainly talked about which of their academic contemporaries had shone most brightly at Bletchley and which of them they expected to shine in public life thereafter. Harry Hinsley and Asa Briggs were the two who were predicted to play a major part in British political life – Bert Howard even predicted that Hinsley would be a future Tory prime minister and Briggs a Labour Cabinet minister. Instead they remained in academia and went on to triumph there – Asa Briggs as Vice-Chancellor of the University of Sussex and President of Worcester College, Oxford; and Harry Hinsley as Vice-Chancellor of Cambridge University and Master of St John's College, Cambridge. It was generally conceded that Plumb had also been a success at Bletchley. Others were less highly thought of. Only Plumb predicted much for Peter Laslett. He told his pupils, such as Geoffrey Parker, that at Bletchley "Laslett was repeatedly on the point of being fired for some shortcoming or other – but would then propose some idea of dazzling brilliance and simplicity that had occurred to no one else. 'And that's what he's done now with his population project', Jack exclaimed: 'Laslett has come up with something completely new and it's brilliant'. As Geoffey Parker concluded: "All of us "Plumbstones", as Parker called Jack's pupils, "sat up and took notice because Jack so rarely bestowed unqualified praise on any one but also because English social history was his own field of expertise and so his praise carried even more weight". It is greatly to Plumb's credit that he immediately recognised and paid tribute to what were to develop into the singular achievements of what became known as the Cambridge Population Group. It was also greatly to his credit that he generously equated that achievement with the flashes of brilliance at Bletchley of his maverick Cambridge colleague. He always argued that Laslett (who was remarkably never given a chair at Cambridge) never received due credit for the originality of mind that played such a major role in such projects as the Open University and the University of the Third Age.

When he was actually working at Bletchley, Plumb was far more interested in things very distant from his future colleagues at Cambridge. He was much taken up with and also remarkably frank about the physical attractions of the vast cohorts of young women who proved to be so adept at acquiring the necessary foreign languages, so stoical in putting in the demandingly long hours of concentrated work, and so willing to seek solace with and provide comfort for the male code-breakers. In Margaret Drabble's words, these young women "included debutantes, bright young graduates and 'call-up' girls – a potentially explosive social mix.... There were love affairs and emotional dramas. Marriages were made and broken.... Some of these unions lasted some did not".

As Gorley Putt, later the Senior Tutor at Christ's, put it: "In the hot- house secret confinement of Bletchley Park, personal relations were as grotesquely falsified as in an Iris Murdoch novel. Sexual infatuations and personality clashes alike became obsessional. One after another, in one way or another, we would all go off our rockers.... We shot up and down from elation to despair and back again".

In this febrile and highly pressurized atmosphere, tough personalities like Plumb prospered whilst frailer men like Angus Wilson were sent off to discreet rest-centres. Others, as Gorley Putt explained, "nerves, tautened to breaking-point by round-the-clock speedy exactitude, would fumble in off-hours, for emotional nourishment".

Even Alan Turing, who was very conscious of his own homosexual tastes, got engaged to a fellow mathematician, Joan Clarke (later Murray) played by Keira Knightley in *The Imitation Game*, but it proved to be very short-lived relationship. As one of his contemporaries said, it was just as well that Turing did not advertise or practice his true sexual preferences too widely at Bletchley, because "if he had he might well have been sacked and Britain might well have lost the war".

Jack Plumb, who must have been very conscious of his own rich bisexual life to date, also got engaged, but Plumb's Bletchley engagement did not survive the end of the war and his return to Cambridge. I can, however, recall his fondly nostalgic reminiscences about Nina, his blonde fiancée. He used to say that only the declaration of peace and his departure from Bletchley saved him from a conventional married life.

He frequently spoke of the girls he had known at Bletchley, although it was often to make gentle fun of them. I can well recall his satirical memories of the majestic Hilary Brett-Smith, who, he said, was so stately that she seemed to glide between the huts as if she was on miniature roller-skates. She married the brilliant and glamorous Harry Hinsley, who not only thrived at Bletchley but hugely enjoyed the life style there. In Richard Langhorne's *Memoir* of Hinsley we are told: "Congregated at Bletchley was a group of young, highly accomplished men and women, living a completely secret life in conditions somewhat resembling a physically uncomfortable University Senior Common Room. 'It was a lovely life', Hinsley later recalled, 'Bletchley was like a University. We lived the anarchic life of students. There was a tremendous social life, parties, amateur dramatics, lots of young ladies and lots of young men'. Young as he was, Hinsley became the leading expert on the decryption and analysis of German wireless traffic. Hinsley's interpretative skills became highly significant after May 1941....Young as he was, his insights came to be respected – they called him the Cardinal".

It is worth remembering that Hinsley (born in 1918) was only in his early twenties in his early days at Bletchley and Plumb (born in1911) was only in his late twenties. Many of them and the hordes of young women who joined them were remarkably young for the responsibilities they were burdened with.

When Plumb joined the code breakers at Bletchley, the organisation was less than 300 strong; when he left it numbered 10,000. They were overwhelmingly female – by 1945, there were 8,000 women working there. Even at the end of the war they look alarmingly young and beguilingly attractive. A photograph of Asa Briggs with his colleagues from Hut Six taken by Bletchley Park lake in 1945 shows an engaging group of thirty-two (nine men and twenty-three women) in a mix of uniforms and civilian clothes "paying no more attention to rank than our working lives did". Asa described their relationships with characteristic discretion: "Some did not understand women. Some fostered personal relationships with women that lasted. A few flirted. I preferred flirting". So did Plumb.

The numerical dominance of women at Bletchley is rather sweetly illustrated by the undated, home-made Christmas card, entitled "Happy Festivities and Plum Pudding!" which was carefully preserved in Plumb's archives. It was illustrated with a cartoon of a line of eight little figures, rather bizarrely all dressed in football kit, headed by an unmistakeable Jack Plumb as a small boy. The women – greater in number by six to two – were mainly from the Japanese intelligence section. On the back was a typed list of eight surnames and also a handwritten list of nine which identified the women by their first names. Both lists are headed with the name Plumb with no additional forename. On this occasion he seems very cheerful in his leadership role – his cartoon is the only one distinguished by a huge grin. It was probably the only time in his life when he was surrounded by young, largely unmarried women, and, according to his excessively graphic reminiscences, he greatly enjoyed their company. That was the aspect of Bletchley that, together with the Rothschild's claret, made his wartime experiences bearable. In his charming privately printed *Vintage Memories*, he paid fulsome thanks to the Rothschilds for making his war-years so bearable; in private conservations he paid ample tribute to the many young women who made his love life rather more straightforward, if less emotionally intense, than it had been in the nineteen-thirties.

More seriously he had the satisfaction of knowing that he had played a significant part (although highly secret) part in what many sound judges regarded as the greatest single achievement of Britain during the wartime years 1939 to 1945. Estimates of how much it shortened the war by, and how many lives were in consequence saved, vary from 2 to 4 years and from 8 to 21 million lives, but even if one accepts the most conservative estimates, one cannot deny the huge significance of the code breakers' work.

According to Plumb, the real heroes at Bletchley were men such as Alan Turing, Gordon Welchman, and Bill Tutte but there were many, many unsung lesser heroes who could be legitimately proud of their lesser contributions. Jack Plumb was unquestionably one of them, but a combination of the Official Secrets Act and the appalling treatment of Alan Turing after the war meant that a proper appreciation of the code breakers at Bletchley was shrouded in the deepest secrecy for many decades. So, for much of Plumb's life, it remained a further hidden aspect of his multifaceted career.

Now that Turing has received a posthumous royal pardon in 2013 and an official apology from Gordon Brown in 2009, and has been the subject of a popular (if not wholly accurate) film of his life played by Benedict Cumberbatch in *The Imitation Game* (2014) and another earlier version played by Derek Jacobi, in *Breaking the Code* (1996), both of which were based on Andrew Hodges' biography *Alan Turing: the Enigma*, (1983) and now that we live in a world of same sex marriages, and now that very many of our most popular film, television and sporting celebrities are openly gay, and now that even successful political careers can be enjoyed outside of the closet, it is worth remembering that, in the decades after the war, Turing's life and achievements were shrouded in scandal and illegality as well as in officially imposed secrecy.

In a world in which a major war hero, then working at Manchester University, could be arrested for a consensual sexual relationship with a nineteen year old young man and then subjected, after being found guilty, to "chemical castration" in lieu of a prison sentence, and hounded into depression that led to his suicide by cyanide poisoning at the age of 41, it was clearly not the most appropriate time to highlight and celebrate his extraordinary achievements even if the Official Secrets Act had permitted it. Some more sensational versions of his death even suggest that he was poisoned by government authorities because as a homosexual man, who knew so much about national security measures, he was dangerously open to blackmail. One does not have to believe such fanciful elaboration to accept that someone who deserved the status of a national hero was appallingly badly treated.

In a time of such officially imposed secrecy and at a time when the iconic hero of Bletchley was so publicly tainted, it is not surprising that those like Plumb involved at Station X kept that part of their lives discreetly well hidden.

13. PLUMB: HIS TASTES, HIS COLLECTIONS AND HIS ENTHUSIASMS

Jack liked to describe in great detail how he had the extraordinary comforts of staying with the Rothschilds to return to when his long hours at Bletchley were over. The tastes he developed then and the interests which grew out of his visits to Houghton as the guest of Lady Cholmondeley when he was working on the Walpole archives were to last all his life.

Houghton had fired him with a passion for porcelain. As he admitted, he "had always loved objects but rather like a child or a magpie – a piece of furniture, a print, a piece of china would catch my eye and realizing at once where it might go in my house, I would buy it. Except for wine, I rarely felt compelled or driven to collect consistently". Having grown familiar with the Cholmondeley collection, his collecting took a quite new direction. "In all their houses there were great old masters, superlative furniture, bronzes and sculpture, but what really trapped me was the collection of cups and saucers, plates, tankards, and vases of Vincennes and Sèvres porcelain". Introduced by the Cholmondeleys to the great Bond Street dealer, Hans Weinberg, Plumb began his collection with a modest Sèvres green cup and saucer for £75. The next week he was back to buy a beautiful Vincennes *gros bleu* large cup and saucer for £200 – double the advance he had received for *The First Four Georges*. He was well and truly hooked. The eighteenth-century porcelain craze, which he later wrote about so brilliantly, had reached forward two hundred years and captured another addict. When he fell out with Weinberg, he continued to buy from Winifred Williams and his collection grew and grew.

It has become fashionable with many today to decry these remarkable triumphs of ceramic art as the products of an unjust *ancien regime* society. They are denounced on social as well as aesthetic grounds as vulgar, ostentatious and excessively showy. The prevailing taste, particularly in academic circles, is for pseudo folk-art, studio ware in the style of peasant pottery. But pine furniture and peasant pottery were very definitely not to Jack Plumb's taste. He loved the rich lustrous dark blues, the Rose Pompadour pinks, the brilliant apple green, the turquoise, the fabulous yellows of early Vincennes and Sèvres. He adored the stream-ice fragility of the glowing white china and he knew what a technical marvel it was that the eighteenth century could produce such wonders.

Later he justified his addiction in financial terms, writing "I decided that porcelain was infinitely more beautiful to look at than share certificates. Somewhere about 1960, I decided to put most of my money into French china, English silver and Dutch paintings but that china was to be the dominant theme". So it was to remain until his great sales of the 1990s, but there was an even more central thread to his collecting life – the one that he claimed was also the best financial investment he ever made: his cellar full of claret.

This was inspired by the years he spent as "the only paying lodger the Rothschilds ever had" and surely the most lavishly victualled lodger in the land. As a result of Anthony de Rothschild's extreme generosity, Jack was given a remarkable education in drinking fine claret. "Year after year we drank the first growth clarets of 1920, '24, '26, '28 and '29 – very rarely we drank 1921 (the Mouton Rothschild was outstandingly good). Naturally we drank mainly Lafite, indeed I suppose as much as two or three times a week when I was staying there; on other nights it would be Mouton, Latour, Haut-Brion and Margaux in that order. In summer time there might be a bottle of the two superlative Yquems, the 1921 or the 1899. Through Tony Rothschild's generosity the highest standards were indelibly impressed on my memory: for years afterwards as their aroma came from the glass, I could recognize the wines I had drunk at Ascott. I was determined that, as soon as the war was over and I had a little more money to spare, I would build up a cellar that would be as rich in wines as Tony's but more varied".

Jack was willing to include second and even lesser growths and took delight in such favourites as the Ducru '29, the Gruard-Larose '20. the Rausan-Segla '29, the Domaine de Chevalier '24, the Brane Cantenac '24 and many others. Once Jack had taken a shine to something, he was determined to pursue it with all the force of his ardent nature and his formidable stamina.

For the five years that I lived in the attic rooms on O staircase in Christ's, I was the happy beneficiary of much of this wine. I was far too insignificant to be invited to Jack's dinner parties, which were held in his dining room immediately beneath my rooms, but almost invariably when they ended, I would be summoned down for a post mortem on the party and to help him finish off the left over wine. These "dregs" as he called them were my initial education into fine wine. Whilst Jack grumbled about the deficiencies of his guests as connoisseurs of fine claret, I was only too happy to listen and learn and, of course, to taste. I rapidly came to realise that either he was an excessively generous host or he was right to complain about the folly of his guests in leaving decanters half full of Lafite and Latour and Yquem. Fortunately, I had a good and a receptive palate and (in those days) an even better memory so that I could soon discuss the wine at an informed and intelligent level – which to Jack was half the fun. For academics assessing and arguing about the quality of students and colleagues and their work occupies much of our lives. Doing the same for wine seemed an almost natural extension of the game – deciding to award a wine an alpha plus mark was as rare as awarding one to an examination script. Those who diluted the honour by giving them too readily were despised for their lack of proper standards, those who never awarded the accolade at all were pitied for their meanness of spirit. In one sense wine tasting was yet another form of competitive sport – with the added attraction for Jack that it was a sedentary game.

One of the things I rapidly learned about Jack, Bert Howard and Charles Snow was how much they loved any form of competitive game; especially, in later life, games which they could play sitting down and exercising only their minds and their memories. Exercising their judgement and rehearsing their knowledge was their idea of play. As they sat watching cricket at Fenner's, Plumb and Snow would while away the time constructing "World XIs" consisting of great men whose names began with the first two letters of their own names and those of their friends. Plumb, who could open the batting of his team with Plato and Plutarch, open the bowling with Pliny the Elder and Pliny the Younger, and play Max Planck and Plautus as two all-rounders, was much more favoured than poor Snow who had to struggle with his miserably under-strength "Sn" team, so he obtained a dispensation to captain a "Go" team in which God and Goethe invariably opened the batting and invariably did pretty well. So well that Snow could refuse to pick Goering and Goebbels on grounds of good taste – indeed they were given a life ban.

Invited to join Snow and Plumb at Fenner's when I was an undergraduate, I managed to impress them by arguing that McKendrick included an assumed "a" and therefore opened my batting line-up with Marx and Mahomet, with Macaulay at number three and Mao at number four. My spin bowler was Machiavelli, my three fast bowlers were Clerk Maxwell, Marlborough and Mark Antony and I could choose the rest of my team from an impressive squad of Malthus, Macadam, Mahler, Manet, Mazzini, Mallarme, Magritte, Mantegna, Marconi, Thomas Mann and many others, and still keep Harold Macmillan and General MacArthur as my non-playing captains to take strategic decisions. They declared me to be a most accomplished cheat but also knowledgeable enough to be allowed to play the game. With Plumb and his friends a good memory was a vital passport with which to gain entry into their private world. They exercised their memories with the same repetitive dedicated regimes that athletes follow in exercising their muscles. An ability to argue adroitly was a further attraction to them. The whole point of the Cricket XI game was to initiate an argument to decide which of the chosen teams would win. Rather like a real cricket game, it could take a very, very long time, because one had to justify why the wiles of, say, Machiavelli's "spin bowling" would be sufficient to unsettle, say, the solid "batting technique" of Plato. To justify such a claim, one had to know enough about their respective philosophical positions to sustain one's argument. It was a game in which the person with the most encyclopaedic knowledge and the most cunning deployment of argument (whether sophisticated or merely sophistry, whether using accomplished verbal skills or merely a dominating and aggressive personality) would win. Not surprisingly Jack was very good at it. As indeed was Snow. They both liked someone to join them in verbal sparring just as good squash players like to play someone capable of giving them a testing workout. It hardly needs saying that they also liked to win. It hardly needs saying that, when they played me, they almost invariably did.

When Bert Howard wrote about Snow (as the character Swan) in his novels, he often made him an obsessive player of the Cricket Team game. "Swan not only talked cricket, he talked about other things in terms of cricket. That morning at breakfast he had insisted on compiling a team of Immoral Statesmen against my team of Moral Statesmen, and I was annoyed to realise that he had been certain at the beginning that he would win."

There were many other such teams: English Publishers, for instance, with Victor Gollancz opening the batting. There were even teams of murder suspects, and when asked, "Who is Professor Beaton?" the murder victim in *The Good Books*, Swan replies "I should put him in number one in my team of English Anthropologists. He'd probably open the batting with young Pope. I should probably play him at number five or six in my team of English Scientists with Inflated Reputations."

As I learned to my cost, in real life, as in fiction, Jack, Howard and Snow could effortlessly produce more and more obscure team lists to keep less well informed players in their place.

To be fair to Snow, in spite of his appearance (described by the kindly Asa Briggs as "the ugliest man he had ever met") he was, in his youth, a remarkably talented sportsman – he represented both his county, his college and his university at tennis and table-tennis, and his school and his college also at cricket. Unlike Plumb who lacked the hand-eye co-ordination or the peripheral vision to play any ball sport at a respectable level, Snow (in spite of a most un-athletic appearance) played with obsessive concentration and considerable skill and dexterity. Plumb used to tell the story of how he was once upbraided by an umbrella-wielding old lady who saw him playing tennis with Snow. In spite of the fact that Snow was only 26 at the time and was giving him a comprehensive thrashing, he looked so old and untidy and shambling (in Jack's words "so physically disreputable"), that Jack was denounced for making "the poor old man run around like that". His protestations that it was he who needed the sympathy and the protection cut no ice with the indignant spectator, so Jack wisely confined himself in future to competing in sailing or driving – activities in which he could compete sitting down and in which a superior boat or a faster car or a quicker brain could make up for his sporting deficiencies.

Jack was not slow to realise that, given the genetic hand that he had been dealt, he was born to write and read and talk and theorise rather than to waste his time on sporting activity. He was happy to discuss sport and he actively liked watching it, but he realistically recognised that theory and erudition were always likely to be a better bet for him than trying to play. So he wisely pontificated on the qualities that made for sporting success and left it to others to sweat away at trying to achieve it. As he used to say "the race is not always to the swift and the strong, and success does not always come to the clever and mentally agile, but that is the way to bet". From similar convictions he always advised one "never to play poker with someone richer than oneself". Assuming that they were not irremediably stupid, he argued, the rich man could always bluff for longer and afford to risk more and so would inevitably win in the long run.

Plumb was also greatly drawn to systems of explanation. He was a great advocate of the Sheldonian system of body types as a key to personality. All his friends were immediately assessed according to the Sheldonian typology. They were declared to be ectomorphs, mesomorphs or endomorphs or some intriguing mixture of the three main body types. Since the system allowed for precise numerical assessments of the constituent elements, there was endless opportunity for arguments and heated disagreement. The most desirable thing to be was an equal mixture of all three types but it was conceded that only God, and, in his own assessment, Snow, could claim to have achieved this ideal. Some – such as tall, long-limbed, thin, introspective mathematicians were dismissed as pure ectomorphs; others – rounded, sensuous, soft-skinned, self-indulgent types were regarded as pure endomorphs; whilst the muscular, athletic, big-boned, insensitive types were classed as pure mesomorphs. I was rather unsatisfactorily classed as an endo-ecto mixture, that is, self-indulgent and almost wholly lacking in muscle. Jack classed himself more attractively as an endo-meso mixture. This, in his judgement, allowed him both the "masculine" virtues of muscle and stamina, together with the more "feminine" virtues of sensitivity and a heightened response to feeling. As far as I can recall, Snow's portfolio of characteristics was comprised of all the virtues known to man – as befitted, in is own assessment, such a God-like creature.

Almost needless to say, Jack was also a passionate believer in Freud. It suited his own preoccupation with sex and offered him endless opportunities to speculate on the sexual experiences of others and how this had influenced their behavioural make-up. He had been converted to a belief in Freud early in life and was very reluctant to give it up in these post-Freudian days. Once smitten with an enthusiasm – as with wine and porcelain – it took a great deal to dissuade him from its virtues. In print he dismissed the follies of "crude Freudianism" but in life he continued to draw conclusions from its teaching.

He could take to countries and cities as ardently as he took to porcelain and wine and ideas. To America, he took with a vengeance. Seeing an advertisement for "topless snooker" as he drove into Los Angeles filled him with delight – the sheer incongruity of it seemed to him to be irresistible. He took to New York with even greater enthusiasm. In his "Love Letter to New York", he asked "Where else can you buy second-hand food, or consult a cat psychiatrist, or buy false eyelashes for your dog?" When his love affair with New York was briefly threatened after he was mugged on Brooklyn Bridge, he very soon rallied. The incident tells one much about Jack Plumb.

When a large black man grunted a curt demand for his wallet, Jack, as Simon Schama has written, was not about to let poor enunciation pass unchallenged and uncorrected. As if addressing a tongue-tied undergraduate, he barked "Speak up, I can't understand you". "Well understand this!", said his mugger pressing a large bayonet at his throat. For once, Jack was speechless and sensibly handed over his wallet and returned, understandably shaken, to his brownstone house in Schermerhorn Street. My pregnant wife and I, who were staying with him at the time, expressed suitable alarm and sympathy, and said that we should all give up our customary daily stroll across the bridge. "Don't be ridiculous", said Jack who was rapidly recovering his spirits, "nobody is going to bother to mug you. You are young and tall and poor. You are not worth the risk of mugging. I am old and small and rich. I was really worth mugging". This conclusion seemed to cheer him immensely as did the knowledge that the mugger had accepted the wallet in which he kept only a modest amount of money whilst the one stuffed with dollars remained safely in Jack's possession. By now the drama of the event was starting to take on an altogether more attractive glow. Jack was not going to miss looking from Brooklyn Heights at the skyline of lower Manhattan, which he regarded as one of man's supreme architectural achievements, because it might cost him a few dollars. So he went upstairs and wrote up the story. He soon returned in triumph to say he had turned a pretty profit on the whole episode. From somewhat dejected victim of New York crime to triumphant essayist of the irresistible vitality and urban fizz of Manhattan had taken him a mere couple of hours

14. PLUMB'S WEALTH – ITS SOURCES AND ITS SIZE

Jack's insouciant attitude to his successful wealth creation served only further to irritate his more hide-bound colleagues.

In his mature years, he made a formidable amount of money from his pen and only punitively high rates of tax prevented him from becoming a very wealthy man, at least by the modest standards of academia. He increasingly became an historical entrepreneur rather than simply a narrowly committed academic scholar.

Fat editorial fees from the American journals *American Heritage* and *Horizon*, even fatter royalties from his TV series *The Renaissance* and, most of all, from *Royal Heritage*, and substantial earnings as a prolific newspaper journalist led him further and further away from the narrower preoccupations and more frugal life-styles of most of his academic colleagues. This was all the more the case when he used his high-profile journalistic platform to lambast what he regarded as their more constipated efforts.

Academics are used to waspish and nit-picking reviews in the decent obscurity of scholarly journals, but mockery in the public prints was more difficult to bear. It is easy to imagine how the authors felt who were on the receiving end of such very public criticism of their efforts, but Plumb was on a journalistic roll. He found American journalism an exciting new world to exploit. American editors responded warmly to his punchy prose and his unfettered opinions. They encouraged his aggressive freewheeling approach. Even better they paid well. The *New York Review of Books,* the *New York Times* and the *Saturday Review* all paid much more than their English equivalents and *American Heritage* and *Horizon* paid even better. Jack was a born journalist and rightly prospered in this appreciative and rewarding world of letters.

His Cambridge colleagues were less appreciative and it did not help that Jack kept them fully informed about his earnings. I remember him proudly showing off the letter he received from the BBC, which began, "Dear Dr Plumb, We are not sure if you are used to receiving royalties of this order, but you should warn your accountants to expect an income in excess of £1 million in royalties this coming year from the sales of *Royal Heritage.*" Later letters (recounting the royalties from the nine different translations of *Royal Heritage),* which were produced to accompany the television programmes all round Europe, only compounded the sense of outrage and envy which many seemed to feel. These fat royalties were being earned by him nearly half a century ago, when £1 million a year was enough to create an even more powerful sense of envy than such a sum would today, and how Jack relished creating it. One needs to remember that in those days there were still many unworldly dons who richly deserved their "remote and ineffectual" labels.

Those were the days when the BBC used to say that if they wrote to a Cambridge professor to say that his talk had been accepted for the Third Programme for a fee of £25, there was a high likelihood that he would reply with a letter of effusive thanks ending with the words "I enclose my cheque for £25". Little wonder, therefore, in that era before the ubiquitous tele-don of today, that many of Jack's colleagues were baffled and dismayed by his entrepreneurial moneymaking skills. Many obviously thought such skills were slightly distasteful – "not really gentlemanly" as one of them put it to me. I vividly recall the sense of outrage from other dons who were supervising me as an undergraduate in 1955 when Jack wrote (I thought entirely reasonably) that "Men write history for many reasons; to try to understand the forces which impel mankind along its strange course; to justify a religion, a nation, or a class; to make money; to fulfil ambition; to assuage obsession; and a few, the true creators, to ease the ache within." In this catalogue of motives it was quite clear where Jack's sympathies lay, but even including the phrase "to make money" was thought to be a betrayal of the academic historian's higher calling. "We are here to pursue truth – we are not in trade", was the indignant response of one of my supervisors.

Some thought that Jack was just lucky and said that anyone who wrote about royalty was bound to be excessively well rewarded. But without his enterprise the programmes that became *Royal Heritage* would have been an obscure antiquarian event of only very modest interest. The initial approach to him was to do a late night BBC2 programme on "Some Selected Objects from the Royal Collections". His response to this was to propose a BBC1 series with each programme dedicated to an individual monarch and their distinctive acquisitions. Typically he was as interested in the personalities and motives of the monarchs as he was in what they had bequeathed to the royal collections. His approach proved to be hugely successful and the programmes attracted massive audiences. Their popularity owed less to luck and far more to his imaginative adaptation of a rather routine, not to say boring, project. Once again, he had proved that he was a natural communicator, a born popularizer and an instinctive entrepreneur of quite exceptional quality. He was a Schama or a Starkey or a Ferguson or a Mary Beard or a James Fox more than twenty-five years before they followed in his wake.

Jack, of course, loved the fact that he had earned his newfound wealth from his pen. There had often been much mildly malicious speculation about the source of his wealth. Did it come from Dr Plumb's pipes (then a well-known brand)? it was snobbishly asked. No. Did it come from Plumb's bedding? No. Did it come from an underwear factory? No.

I have often been told, by many different people, of Hugh Trevor-Roper's sneering dismissal of Jack's wealth as coming from a knicker factory. "He likes to pretend that he earned his money by his pen", said Lord Dacre, "but it actually comes from his 49% holding in his brother's knicker factory in Leicester." Wrong on every count. Jack's brother did not have a knicker factory, and even if he had had one, Jack would have put no money into it. The brothers did not get on. They rarely saw or spoke to each other. Jack's scrupulously kept accounts and his meticulously preserved bank statements confirm that there were no financial transactions between them. As Jack said when he heard of Dacre's comments. "He has always done malice and snobbery better than I have. He has worked the preferment system better than I have too. What he can't forgive is that for all his talents he has never produced a significant book or any significant pupils. As for his scholarship, his comments on my income are about as accurate as his judgement on the Hitler diaries".

Not surprisingly he loved nailing these disdainful put-downs by telling those who sneered that such handsome sums were readily available to anyone who could write accessible prose. His innocent encouragement to his colleagues ("I don't know why you don't all do it") effortlessly provoked the desired effect. Pure envious rage. It did not help either that he so obviously enjoyed his newly found wealth. He loved spending it and loved giving it away.

The fact that he consistently gave so much away, and so consistently spent so lavishly on entertaining his friends, explains why he left only £1.3 million.

This was more than A.J.P. Taylor's modest legacy of £309,082, or Geoffrey Elston's £739, 494, or Joseph Needham's £899,478 and far more than Angus Wilson's very modest "less than £125,000", but it was less than Trevor-Roper's £1,638,119, less than Eric Hobsbawn's £1,835,341, and far short of Philip Grierson's £5,189,096. One needs to read these figures with great caution, for whilst Plumb was notorious as a lavish spender, Grierson was notoriously careful with his money. One also needs to allow for the fact that many of his contemporaries inherited substantial family money and family houses, whereas Plumb always used to boast that he had inherited nothing. When one also allows for the fact that Plumb's philanthropic giving before his death greatly reduced what he had to leave, one realises how misleading such legacy figures can be.

15. PLUMB AS A PROLIFIC EDITOR

There were other sources of wealth, which did contribute very significantly to Jack's growing income levels. They had nothing to do with knickers, but they did owe something to Plumbian enterprise. I am not sure whether all those young scholars of promise whose early publications came as a result of Plumb's editorial recommendations knew that he took a cut of the royalties on the books which sprang from them. He found lots of young authors for both English and American publishers. The more winners he chose for them the better off he became. His judgement was excellent and the more successful the books which stemmed from it became, the more his earnings rose. I know of no other academic who negotiated a contract as fiercely and as ruthlessly as Plumb. He demanded and got generous annual payments as both consultant and editor, but he always insisted on a royalty not only on each book he wrote or edited himself but also on each book he recommended or acted as general editor for. He watched the returns like a hawk and his archive offers more than ample evidence of how ferociously he reacted to those publishing houses that he felt were not adequately promoting his books and those of his protégés. If they were slow in handing over the royalties, his letters would be incandescent with rage. His archive is packed with evidence of how effective such rebukes could be. His bank accounts reveal a tidy income-flow over many years from the efforts of those he promoted.

It is worth remembering that he had what has been called "a dazzling portfolio of (editorial) appointments, which gave him formidable powers of patronage". He was simultaneously historical adviser to *Penguin* books, European editor for *Horizon*, editor of the *Fontana History of Europe*, and general editor of the *Hutchinson History of Human Society*. He proved to be a shrewd and impressively impartial editor in those he chose to commission books from. Few would have predicted that he would choose his arch-rival Geoffrey Elton to write what turned out to be arguably the best volume in the *Fontana History of Europe* series. Those who knew him only in his mature right-wing days would have been surprised to see that he backed such left-wing historians as Eric Hobsbawm, E.P. Thompson, Christopher Hill and E.H. Carr for paper-backing at Penguin. Others he asked to write for him included such major figures as Walter Ullmann, John Hale, Hugh Trevor-Roper, John Elliott, Olwen Hufton, C.R. Boxer, J.H. Parry, Raymond Dawson and Donald Dudley. More and more British historians came to recognise that Plumb was a powerful source of publishing patronage. John Elliott recalls Trevor-Roper saying to him "I guess we are just two prawns in Jack Plumb's aspic".

Inevitably, Jack also had Trevelyan's *English Social History* reprinted in four lavishly illustrated volumes.

Forgivably, he commissioned books from youngsters from amongst his own pack of friends and protégés – including Norman Stone, Geoffrey Parker and Melveena McKendrick. Geoffrey Parker generously acknowledged that "Jack persuaded Penguin to commission *The Dutch Revolt*, and Little Brown to commission *Philip II* for his "Library of World Biography" series. I would surely not have landed either title myself, and I certainly would never have thought of including a chapter on "Philip II in legend and history", which Jack had made a series feature." The success of this commission can be judged from its translation into six languages and from the fact that the Spanish version – *Felipe II* – alone sold over 500,000 copies and led to King Juan Carlos conferring a knighthood on Parker. As Parker wrote in his own *festschrift*: Plumb admitted him to Christ's on the basis of only two A levels (he failed the third) and "having secured me travelling scholarships and a four year research fellowship, Plumb steered three books my way, not only *Dutch Revolt* and *Philip II*, but also *Europe in Crisis*, a volume in the "*Fontana History of Europe*" series that he edited". When Plumb knew that he had found a star historian, he stuck with him.

On the basis of these commissions, few could argue over the merits of his choices. On the basis of the reception given to their books and the sales they achieved, few could argue that he did not deserve the income they brought him. I know from first-hand family experience that *A Concise History of Spain*, which he commissioned from my wife, sold 50,000 copies in hard back and ultimately sold in even greater numbers when it appeared in seventeen editions in paper back. Given that she accepted a modest one-off payment for the book, it was left to Jack to profit alone from the royalties from all the many later editions. Given the standing of many of his other authors and given that many of the books appeared in paperback, one would have been able confidently to predict even more substantial sales for many of the books he commissioned. His bank accounts show that such predictions were not often disappointed.

The huge number of letters preserved in his archives, which tell the story of these editorial appointments, suggest that perhaps he deserved the financial rewards they brought. Over four thousand letters as editor of *American Heritage* (4171 letters), nearly two thousand as editor of the *Fontana History of Europe* (1971 letters), over two thousand as historical advisor to *Penguin Books* (2024 letters), approaching two thousand letters as editor of the *History of Human Society* (1717 letters) – these and many others demonstrate the energy and commitments that he brought to all these appointments. Naturally his personal wealth grew proportionately.

It is easy to see from his correspondence why his editorial skills were so much in demand and so widely appreciated. His crisp judgements (both positive and negative) were promptly delivered; his wide range of contacts in both England and America were rivalled by very few professional historians; the originality of his ideas for individual books and whole series never seemed to dry up; and he had the energy and the stamina to keep the most demanding publisher contentedly satisfied.

William Noblett's very valuable article in *The Penguin Collector* (December 2016) on Jack's role as Advisory Editor for History for Penguin, demonstrates very clearly why he held this position for thirty-one years between August 1961 and December 1991.

Jack's verdicts on the quality of proposed publications were rarely ambiguous. Opinions such as "it is quite frightful"; or, of another, "flabby, certainly not a book for us"; or, of another, "it may be short...but the prose makes the reading of it as wearisome as toiling through quicksand" left little room for doubt as to whether they were worth publishing.

When he approved, there was equally little room for doubt. Of Ronald Blythe's *Akenfield,* he wrote it is "one of the most poignant and moving books which I have read in years"; of Barbara W. Tuchman's *The Proud Tower* his verdict was simply "a brilliant tour de force"; of J.J. Scarisbrick's *Henry VIII* his opinion was "it is absolutely magnificent"; and of E.P. Thompson's *The Making of the English Working Class* he correctly predicted that it "will fly off the shelves (and) would go like wildfire".

He could also be helpfully pragmatic: of one proposed publication, he wrote "this is an admirable book and would add prestige to any list, but I doubt whether it would sell sufficiently at the price we would have to charge for so large a book"; of another he wrote "as an historian, I admire the book: it is excellent. But as a publisher I would have cold feet. It is not a paperback"; of another, written by a close friend and very distinguished historian (Dick Hofstadter), he wrote regretfully and impartially "it is a sad book, it is unfinished and in consequence unbalanced ... I am sorry to be so unenthusiastic for a man who I greatly admired and who was my closest professional friend in America, but piety and profit are often at variance. I think we should lose money."

Valuable as such discerning and decisive judgements were to Penguin, his more important role was to commission new authors and new projects. In his first year with Penguin, he had contacted fifteen potential authors, and after five years, he had approached sixty-eight historians, and, of those sixty-eight, forty-one had agreed to write a Pelican. Not surprisingly in his search for potential future stars, he commissioned books from his favourite former pupils, such as Simon Schama, Roy Porter and Geoffrey Parker. He pursued with great determination other young scholars whom he particularly admired, such as J.H. Elliot, even though on this occasion he had to settle simply for reprinting in paperback Elliot's *Imperial Spain,* accurately described by Jack as "a superb book, beautifully written". Given the future stature achieved by Sir Simon Schama, Sir John Elliot, Geoffrey Parker (knighted in Spain) and what surely would have been Sir Roy Porter but for his premature death at the age of 55, it would be difficult to question Jack's good judgement in commissioning work from his friends.

In addition to the single works he commissioned, Jack was also fertile in proposing new series. His proposal of a series on the history of British institutions was welcomed by Tony Godwin as "a master stroke" and within twelve months, Jack had signed up for books on eleven institutions – the Village, the Church, the Universities, the Justice of the Peace, the Navy, the Royal Academy, the Royal Society, the Press, the Gentry, the Army and the Treasury. Not entirely surprisingly, given the usual casualty rate in commissioned academic works, not all of these were to appear.

Other proposed series – a series of brief national histories, a six volume history of European Thought, a two volume economic history of England, a two volume documentary history of England, and a seven-volume social history of Britain – were also welcomed by Penguin. From these proposals some notable successes appeared: Eric Hobsbawm's *Industry and Empire* (still selling after over half a century), Walter Ullmann's *A History of Political Thought in the Middle Ages* (which sold 52,000 in the first six years), and E.N. Williams' *Documentary History* (which sold 9,2560 in the first five months of publication) all did well both critically and commercially.

I am greatly indebted to Bill Noblett's invaluable work on Jack's editorial work for Penguin for this detailed information, which demonstrates the prodigious energy and skill he brought to the task; yet this was only one of what has been described as an "enviable and formidable array of editorial appointments". It was indeed "a dazzling portfolio of editorial positions". It would have constituted a lifetime's work for most men.

A comprehensive study of the whole array of these editorial positions would leave few people in any doubt of Jack's skills as a perceptive judge of talent and a creative potential publisher. Such a wide-ranging study would also leave very little room for surprise that Jack was able to live a very prosperous life in his mature years. Coming on top of his basic academic appointments and the handsome royalties from his own publications, his frequent American lecture tours and his well-paid journalism in the States, the rewards from his prodigious editorial work help to explain how in years of absurdly high tax rates he was able to live so well.

16. PLUMB'S AMERICAN JOURNALISM – AMERICAN HERITAGE AND HORIZON

It was not only as an editorial adviser to book publishers that Plumb excelled, and thereby profited accordingly. It is well known that he was a prolific journalist in his own right especially in the States where, for instance, he had a regular column in the *Saturday Review*, but it is less well recognised that he was equally active in promoting the journalistic endeavours of his pupils, his friends and his colleagues to American journals.

He had always enjoyed reviewing for the *New York Times Book Review* and the *New York Review of Books*, but it was his monthly column for the *Saturday Review* that proved to be the mainstay of his newspaper journalism in America. In 1967, he began to do a monthly column called "Perspectives" about books of his own choosing. Far away from the disapproving eyes of more narrowly focused Cambridge academics, he wrote: "books on every conceivable subject landed on my desk – Japanese gardens, sexuality in boys, the Negro family, the Incas, the historiography of Indonesia, Nelson's letters to Emma Hamilton, tomb sculpture, the influence of Europe on Asia in several volumes, quantities of eighteenth-century history, heaps of biographies; indeed history of every kind. I never knew what new exotic fruit would land on my desk". Articles on this vast range of subjects poured from his pen, and his crisp accessible prose won him a very wide readership in the States.

That fluent journalism on a vast range of subjects (far beyond any claims to specialist expertise) tells us a great deal about Plumb's attitude to history writing, but his work in commissioning articles for publication in America tells us a great deal more – both about Plumb the historian and Plumb the man.

As an editorial adviser of *Horizon* and *American Heritage*, he was his characteristically active and energetic self. He was also characteristically generous to his friends and pupils. He was also characteristically trenchant in his judgements of his colleagues – both positive and negative.

The details of his successive roles as European editor, advisory editor, and member of the board make it very clear why he was so valued by *Horizon*.

Of the 4256 items relating to *American Heritage* and *Horizon* preserved in his archive in the University Library, 95 per cent of them were written by Plumb; in the first two years of *Horizon's* existence he (in his own words) "drummed up a number of very good authors for them – Veronica Wedgwood, Hugh Trevor-Roper, Moses Finley, Oliver Millar, Christopher Hibbert, Nancy Mitford and others"; he also recommended as potential authors for *Horizon*, four young and unknown Cambridge scholars (John Burrow, Jonathan Steinberg, Michael Biddiss and myself – all lavishly praised by Plumb for our literary skills); many more senior and better known scholars were ruthlessly dissected to reveal their shortcomings; and, in sharp contrast, many other leading historians were strongly recommended and quickly signed up by Plumb. As a result, he was not surprisingly hugely valued by his American employers – "We weep in gratitude" was their response to one article.

Their gratitude was very understandable.

He introduced them to young scholars that they otherwise would never have known about but whom they went on to use for years afterwards – I was commissioned to write three articles, and John Burrow was commissioned to write seven articles, for *Horizon*. He warned them off those grand names who were unlikely to produce. When asked if Julian Huxley would produce a piece on Charles Darwin, Plumb replied "I think Julian Huxley would do quite a good article if he set about it, but he is old and famous and therein lies the difficulty…if you are prepared to go to a brilliant, scarcely known young man then I would suggest John Burrow."

Whatever the subject *Horizon* wanted an article on, Plumb always had a suitable author to approach on their behalf. In the early days of his relationship with *Horizon* when they wanted an article on Thucydides, Plumb commissioned the brilliant Cambridge historian, Moses Finley. When they wanted articles on "How armies have been raised" and "How nations take defeat", he commissioned Correlli Barnett. Fortunately, after starting on such a high note, he had the huge reserves of almost endless academic contacts, constantly replenished by new stars emerging in Cambridge, to keep *Horizon* well supplied with new authors. Fortunately, too, he never ran out of ideas for new subjects for them to write about. Small wonder that his American employers were so delighted with him.

He warned them of the dangers of approaching certain prima donnas such as A.L. Rowse who "will burst with fury if a comma is changed and in return for suggestions you will get vituperation. I like Rowse, admire much of his work, but I would hate to do business with him". He warned them off established scholars whose work he did not rate – "No. Seton Watson far too dull". He warned them off scholars with doubtful scholarly reputations – writing of one proposed author "Sir Peter Medawar, England's leading biologist, tore him to shreds the other week in the NYRB. I do hope we shall never see D……. in the pages of *Horizon*. Historical journalists, I like to see there, but historical charlatans, NO". He warned them of the difficulty of persuading

Antonia Fraser to write for them, saying "she is rich and immensely social so I have my doubts. Bur I will do my best" and his best proved successful. He warned them of the difficulty of dealing with his friend, Glyn Daniel, writing "Daniel is the most velvety of men, but beneath the urbanity and courtesy and charm there are claws as strong and sharp as a hawks". So Plumb's advice was "whether you like or not what he writes pay him in full because he loves money as much as food and he could be a dangerous and influential enemy if we cross him". He warned them of the problems of dealing with A.J.P. Taylor who made it clear that he expected payment in full for whatever he wrote whether it was published or not, saying a "guarantee payment of one half" for a rejected piece brings an automatic refusal.

He worked very hard to smooth the way to successful completion of commissions by warning British historians of how hyper-active and pernickety and sometimes how slow to act American editors could be. He wrote to his old adversary G.R. Elton when commissioning an article from him, which, in fact, was never published: "You will doubtless be aware that American editors are weird. They took a piece from Moses (Finley) and published it three years later! And, of course, they always have to justify their monstrously high salaries by asking for, at least, one paragraph to be changed or one added".

He worked even harder to ensure success by the enormous trouble he took over each commission. In William Noblett's as yet unpublished work on *J.H.Plumb and the Early Years of American Heritage's "Horizon Magazine"*, he writes: "With most of his authors Plumb liked to discuss in person the form, structure and content of their articles. If the authors were Cambridge based, he would entertain then for lunch, a drink or dinner, the telephone was heavily used and on some occasions he would visit the authors in their houses or offices".

When he commissioned a piece on the House of Lords, he arranged through Lord Cholmondeley for the author to be given access to the State Opening and be given a guided tour by Cholmondeley himself, and followed this up with a lunch with Lady Cholmondeley to deal with any detailed queries the author might have.

When the editors raised queries about Plumb's own article on "De Mortuis", which referred to the Arundel Tomb made famous in Philip Larkin's poem in *Whitsun Weddings*, Plumb wrote to Larkin himself to solve the problem.

When the *Horizon* picture researcher, searching for an illustration for Plumb's own article on "Political Pornography", wished to find a cartoon which depicted "the unbreeched royal backside of George II descending towards the expectant face of Sir Robert Walpole", Plumb was quick to reply "the cartoon of the royal backside is in Paris. It is to be found at the Quai d'Orsay, Archives Affaires Etrangeres, Memoires et Documents Angleterre, vol.xxxix, folio 127."

He very rarely failed to help, although in his dealings with the Keepers of the Royal Collections he had to admit defeat, writing to *Horizon:* "although I would dearly have liked to tell (them) to go to hell I have restrained myself (and) consistently met rudeness with courtesy", but I "have rarely received a more offensive epistle from any public official". With admirable restraint, he replied to the author of the "offensive epistle" to "thank you for your kind and helpful letter", and for once gave up the unequal struggle.

Such help was invaluable to, and always much appreciated by, the editors at *Horizon.* Their relationship with Plumb had begun in 1957 when he was at the height of his creative and publishing powers. *American Heritage* had commissioned an introductory chapter from him for a book on the American Revolution for what he regarded as "a princely sum" and both had been delighted with the outcome. Joseph Thorndike, one of the original founders of the company had written to congratulate Plumb on the chapter, called "The world beyond America at the time of the revolution", and after commissioning another article by him on the English Country House, wrote to say that "it would be very valuable to us to be able to draw upon you for editorial advice and contact with British and European authors". Plumb was only too happy to agree and thus started a hugely successful relationship.

It did him no harm, of course, that his work with them started with a spectacular success. The first book to be published by *Horizon* – *The Italian Renaissance* – which was overseen by and half written by Plumb enjoyed extravagant sales. Plumb had signed up an impressive roster of star names –Bronowski, Mattingly, Trevor-Roper, Mack Smith and Iris Origo – and, by insisting on a sliding scale of payment, snaffled Kenneth Clark, the starriest art historian of them all, by offering him $1 a word for his 3,500 word article.

His insistence on choosing the best paid off in spades. The book sold 225,000 books in hard back. It was translated into every Western European language, including Finnish. The paperback edition did equally well. It still enjoyed steady sales some twenty-five years after its first appearance.

As Plumb wrote of its huge success: "It confirmed my position with American Heritage for the next twenty-five years and made my name known in America. But more importantly it released me from the confines of eighteenth-century British History. This new freedom allowed me to range widely over European and American History. I became fascinated by the interplay of cultures not only in ideas but in things".

Not surprisingly, these were the years in which he first fell in love with New York and most things American. In 1960 he had been a Visiting Professor at Columbia and he had hoped to negotiate a shared existence between Cambridge and Columbia.

Columbia, supported by the Ford Foundation, was very keen but Cambridge was characteristically slow. In Plumb's words they found the idea "alarmingly original" and the problems almost "insuperable". "Urged and prodded by Columbia, they moved, but very slowly. By the time they came to a reluctant agreement, over two years had elapsed and naturally the Ford Foundation had gone cold. It would have suited me to perfection". I do not think that he ever forgave Cambridge for their tardiness, but it made him cherish his connections with *American Heritage* even more. He loved their energy, their enterprise, their enthusiasm and their generous-hearted response to problems. He loved the opportunities they gave him for frequent trips to New York.

He had visited New York as an Intelligence Officer from Bletchley in 1945. Then he had sailed on the Queen Mary, very aware from decoded German agents where German U-boats still lurked. He knew that "a lone wolf" U-boat was lurking off the approaches to New York – but he was equally conscious that the Queen Mary could comfortably outpace it. Excited as he was by this first experience of American life, it was his visit in 1960 (once again on the Queen Mary) that confirmed his lasting devotion to New York.

I had introduced him to Richard Hofstadter in 1958 and they became close friends and admirers, so when Columbia needed a visiting professor in January 1960, Hofstadter invited Plumb. He was met on arrival not by his academic contacts but by his journalistic ones from *American Heritage*.

His eloquent tribute, written in 1989, to the significance of that first night in January 1960 spells out just how much it meant to him. "It had been very kind of the Jensens to meet me off the boat. And that night I did not realise how closely the lives of those I was meeting for the first time – James Parton, Joseph Thorndike, Richard Ketchum – would become a part of my life as an historian. Nor did I realise that from then until now I would visit America several times a year, sometimes for long periods, or that over the next few decades I would lecture in most American States; that I would get to know innumerable universities and colleges; make some of the deepest friendships of my life in New York; or that America could make me a prosperous man. But that first night was like a moment of crystallisation in a human relationship. I was first entranced and then committed. America was my 'Newfoundland'. I wanted to see it, live in it, learn everything I could about it, and try to understand its history without which I would be lost in its complicated present."

This deep involvement with America and American historians had grown ever deeper over the thirty years before he wrote that tribute, but this part of is life was to remain hidden from most of his colleagues in Cambridge. His almost endless lecture tours were a chapter of his life that were largely hidden from all his old friends. Few of them knew much about his literary work in New York, but Plumb had become a really very close friend of Joseph Thorndike and Oliver Jensen and James Parton, the Company's President, and, even eight years after he had resigned from his role, he wrote to Parton to say "I still recall my years with *Horizon* as one of the high spots of my career", and stated in volume two of his *Collected Essays* that *Horizon* "was one of the finest magazines ever produced in America, both for physical beauty and literary content".

Plumb had greatly profited from the relationship. He was handsomely rewarded financially and he was able to handsomely reward those he commissioned. His junior pupils like me received payments of $500 an article and his more senior colleagues received $1,000 an article, which were indeed princely payments back in the 1950s and 1960s.

I am hugely indebted to Bill Noblett for much of the information in this chapter. Few people know the details of Plumb's American literary career. They were yet another aspect of his largely hidden life. They also go a long way to explaining why he was able to live so indulgently and spend so extravagantly in his middle years.

They also help to explain why Plumb loved New York so much and why he preferred the company of American historians rather than his colleagues at home in Cambridge. In 1989, he wrote: "For the last thirty years I have been deeply involved with American history, American historians, and American universities. Although most of my time has been spent in New York, I have lectured in almost all of the states of America, missing only Alaska, North Dakota and Idaho. It was one of the most rewarding aspects of my middle age, for it gave me what I needed most: hope – hope about the future, hope about history as an aspect of our culture, and hope about myself. The American scholar is still far more generous than his European counterpart, freer from malice or personal paranoia, and the vast majority of American scholars believe that anyone who has devoted his life to the writing of history is engaged in a serious purpose, trying to make the best of his talents to illuminate the problems which he has set for himself. This does not mean that American scholars do not criticize. They do. Apart from a few, these criticisms are usually constructive and always made with good manners. Certainly, temperamentally I was happier in academic society in America".

He concluded this tribute with the words: "America became a refuge as well as a stimulant and I am deeply grateful for the generosity with which I was treated. I hope for many years to come my heart will lift as the mid-town skyline comes into view from Triborough Bridge. "New York", I say to myself with joy, "here again".

Plumb in Litt.D. gown

REGISTRATION DISTRICT		LEICESTER		
1911 BIRTH in the Sub-district of **Leicester South**		in the **County Borough of Leicester**		

Columns: 1 2 3 4 5 6 7 8 9 10

No.	When and where born	Name, if any	Sex	Name and surname of father	Name, surname and maiden surname of mother	Occupation of father	Signature, description and residence of informant	When registered	Signature of registrar	Name entered after registration
359	Twentieth August 1911 65 Walton Street U.D.	John Harold	Boy	James Plumb	Sarah ann Plumb formerly Timson	Shoe Clicker	James Plumb Father 65 Walton Street Leicester	September 1911	Herbert George Cooper Registrar	

Plumb's birth certificate

Plumb's birthplace and first home
– 65, Walton St., Leicester

The youthful Dr. J.H. Plumb aged
25 in 1936

Plumb aged 39 – his favourite self-image

Plumb with Craig Barlow, Angus Wilson and the author in 1956

Plumb aged 90

Plumb aged 60 – chosen for his Festschrift

Plumb with the author in 1954

A Christmas card cartoon of Plumb and colleagues at Bletchley Park in the early 1940s

Happy Festivities — and Plum Pudding!

Plumb with the
author in 1964

Plumb: a portrait by Lawrence
Gowing, commissioned by
Christ's in 1980

Plumb: a portrait by Jenny Polack, commissioned by Christ's in 1978

Plumb: a portrait
by John Ward,
commissioned by the
author in 1991

Plumb's country home from 1958-1992 – The Old Rectory, Westhorpe

The author in 2000

Plumb in the garden at the Old Rectory, Westhorpe

Bert Howard – scoolmaster mentor
of Plumb and the author.

Plumb drinking a 1911 Perrier-Jouët at a
Bordeaux Club dinner at Hugh Johnson's
home at Saling Hall, Saling.

The author in 2005 painted by Michael Noakes

Plumb's favourite photograph of his surrogate family – the McKendricks.

Hugh Johnson, John Jenkins, Michael Broadbent, Jack Plumb, Neil McKendrick and Daphne Broadbent – before a Bordeaux Club dinner hosted by Hugh Johnson at Saling Hall.

Plumb – celebrating Christmas dinner with the McKendricks in the
dining room of the Master's Lodge in Caius.

Plumb walking across Brooklyn Bridge in New York in 1972

Plumb on holiday in France.

Plumb's holiday home for many years – Le Moulin de la Ressence, Plan de la Tour.

The author in 1949 when he first met Plumb

The author in 1953 when he went
up to Cambridge

C.P. Snow - Plumb's oldest friend and mentor

The author in 1964

17. PLUMB'S APOLAUSTIC LIFE STYLE: EXPENSIVE CARS AND THEIR DESTRUCTION

It was in these years that Jack earned his reputation as an impulsive and at times an extravagant buyer – amongst other things he bought large cars, which he drove excessively fast. Jack always liked doing things at speed. He ate rapidly, he talked rapidly, he worked rapidly and he travelled rapidly. He enjoyed taking decisions rapidly. It was once said of him that, while others are still admiring the landscape, Jack has bought it. Inevitably he loved to fly on Concorde and in his newly prosperous years he started to indulge his taste for larger and more luxurious cars. Cars such as the modest Morris Oxford of which he was so proud in the early 1950s were now dismissively disdained. Eventually he was to decide that the largest kind of Jaguars and Daimlers suited him best, but, before settling down for a succession of these, he tried a Lanchester, an Armstrong Siddeley Sapphire, some top of the range Rovers and even, the ultimate cliché for the naturally ostentatious, a huge Rolls Royce. The Rolls proved altogether too stately for Jack. It did not last long. Jack liked to drive his cars, if not exactly to destruction (although there were some notable crashes involving more than one complete write-off), then at least to well beyond their natural limits.

My wife and I still vividly recall a nightmare drive over half a century ago from Cambridge to Venice and back in 1967. Every *autoroute* and every *autostrada* was transformed into a racetrack on which Jack was unwilling ever to finish second best to any other car. A half-century ago Jack could not yet afford more than a brand-new three-litre Rover. Keeping ahead of the Porsches and Alfa Romeos and even the Maseratis (which it manfully did, to our driver's great delight) took its toll on the poor over-strained Rover. By the time we were returning through Switzerland, the car was showing obvious signs of distress and the white-coated mechanics of the Rover dealership in Geneva pronounced the brakes and the engine to be the victim of disgraceful car abuse. Six immaculately dressed Swiss engineers (they looked more like surgeons than car mechanics) turned on us like an accusing lynch-mob and demanded to know which of our party had ill-treated this car so badly. Suitably

133

impressed by their ferocious concern, Bill Noblett, Melveena and I bravely left Jack to face the music, saying quite correctly that he was the only one who had been allowed to drive. Even he was slightly taken aback to be accused so publicly and so ferociously of wanton engine and brake abuse. Instead of being nursed through its first few thousand miles of its running-in period, the car-doctors said, it showed all the marks of having just been subjected to the rigours of a remorseless speed test on the Le Mans racing circuit. It certainly felt like a white-knuckle ride at the time: my wife and I cowered in the back seats in terror and gave thanks every evening that we had, against all the odds, survived yet another day.

Even negotiating a comfort stop was extremely difficult. Melveena would politely ask whether we could possibly stop at the next service station, but Jack would invariably flash by, saying irritably "No, we'll stop at the next one". This phrase was repeated so often that when we passed a terrible accident and Melveena asked Jack if he would stop so that we could see if we could do anything to help, I could not resist saying "No, he'll stop at the next one!" After that, he drove faster than ever and never seemed to stop except for fuel. We had to learn to calibrate and synchronise our bladders' needs with his fuel tank's requirements.

The poor Rover was not the only car to suffer burnout at the hands of Jack, the demon-driver. I recall a Morris Oxford (being driven at excessive speed under the influence of excessive drink), which rolled over spilling out all his passengers as it rolled – in contrition, a crest-fallen and hugely hung-over Jack insisted that his passengers should all sue him for negligence. I recall being with him in a head-on crash in the Armstrong Siddeley, and a further head-on crash the day after it was repaired, and a further head-on collision with a motorbike, all three the result of rather adventurous over-taking on narrow roads. Even in his eighties he managed to get a rather staid Daimler to rollover and finish upside down on the opposite side of the motorway when he was driving along one dry, sunny Monday morning. He was driving alone and a burst tyre was the charitable explanation but, knowing Jack's characteristic driving style, there are some of us who suspect that excessive speed played its part.

He regarded speed limits as a source of mild advice rather than legally enforceable constraints, more like an opening bid in a friendly negotiation than a rigid road rule to be obeyed without question – certainly not something to be taken too seriously by free spirits and dashing drivers such as himself. I recall one occasion when he was caught breaking the 60 miles per hour speed limit twice within the space of thirty minutes – once in Suffolk and once in Cambridgeshire. Even more remarkably, after hiring an expensive lawyer and playing the absent-minded professor in court, he escaped scot-free.

More typically I recall a stately Lanchester, which failed to survive a hair-raising trip through the Alps in the 1950s. By the time we reached Calais on the return journey, the car would only go in reverse. With admirable ingenuity, Jack refused to give up and backed it onto the car-ferry, leaving his passengers to worry about how it could be got off when we reached England. During the crossing, Jack managed to bribe someone to examine the engine and the gearbox and produce a partial repair. Miraculously the car was declared to be just about road-worthy as long as it only went forwards and was driven very slowly. This seemed a huge improvement on being able only to go backwards very slowly, but it led to a wearyingly slow trek back home. Exhausted as his passengers were, there was little hope of sleep. Understandable anxiety about the state of the engine, understandable worries about what speed Jack would decide was slow, and the ever-present fear that he might drive into a situation which would require the car to be manoeuvred in reverse kept most of us watchfully awake.

If Jack was an over-enthusiastic driver, he was an even more over-enthusiastic and excessively involved passenger. As a passenger, he believed firmly in audience participation, giving out urgent instructions to anyone foolish enough to be driving him whether it was a friend or a professional chauffeur. Taxi drivers, even in Paris, New York and London, were bullied into following his routes not theirs. Chauffeurs were even more at his mercy. Being driven by a professional is for most of us a mercifully passive role – one lies back and lets the driver take the strain. Not Jack.

From the moment he got into a hired car, he would begin the interrogation about the chosen route and insist on changes. The whole journey would be accompanied by a running commentary on alternative routes that would avoid possible hold-ups and delays. To be fair, he had a remarkable topographical memory and he was more often than not in the right. He claimed that when he could not sleep, he used to set himself journeys to negotiate in his mind. He would visualise each route rather like an early linear road map consisting simply of a list of the names of the villages and towns one needed to go through to reach one's destination.

It was the kind of memory test that Bert Howard used to encourage in his pupils. Howard himself could list every constituency in the country and name the members of parliament and their majorities for each one. Jack's party piece was to ask his friends to name two distant towns and then challenge him to reel off every village between them for whatever part of the country one chose. He very rarely failed. The downside was that he not unreasonably came to assume that he always knew the way. Modern motorways seem to be designed to fool a sense of direction and one does better to rely on the signs rather than on one's geographical instincts. Jack remained true to his instincts and his encyclopaedic knowledge, and even when he was wrong, there were few who could resist his ferocious insistence that they should follow his instructions. I well remember his pupil Dr Simon Smith, (now Senior Tutor of Brasenose College, Oxford) being forced to take Jack's advice over a turning in the Algarve, which resulted in a very silent forty-mile drive back the way they had just come on a motorway.

18. PLUMB THE BIG SPENDER: HOUSES, HOLIDAYS AND OTHER INDULGENCES

These were the years when Jack also learned to shop at speed. I learned never to ask Jack for advice about whether I should buy some much coveted picture or much admired piece of furniture, because almost invariably he would rush out and buy it himself, saying that I could not possibly afford it anyway. When I had learned to buy first and tell him afterwards, he found other ways to put me in my place. When I bought a Sidney Nolan, he promptly bought two; when I bought three fine antique parrot prints, he promptly bought four; when I bought three Graham Sutherland lithographs, he immediately bought five. In our purchases of silver and ceramics, it was simply no contest. He could afford comfortably to pay in multiples of thousands. I was lucky if I could buy in multiples of hundreds.

All this was in stark contrast to his income in the 1950s. A typical letter in late 1953 read "This afternoon I shall try to write 400 words for a *Sunday Times* review and pick up 4 guineas – which, My God, I shall need. No news of Chatham sales & I am totally blank for ideas for the BBC or *History Today* & yet I want money badly for I'm on a basic payment of £35 per month now. So I hope you'll buy me some drink & a little food on occasion. Don't forget to go & get the apples from my mother's garden & bring them up to Cambridge with you." This was a letter written to an undergraduate from a don who in the same letter gloried in his established status. In it, he wrote "I'm boring everyone with lengthier & lengthier descriptions of Yugoslavia. I watch the junior fellows blench when I enter the combination room but I don't spare them a word – oh, the joys of being old & established."

Clearly the financial rewards of being old and established were not yet great. Even in his late forties, when he bought The Old Rectory at Westhorpe in Suffolk in 1958, he felt the need to ask me to share it with him – not only out of friendship, but also because he thought he might be over-reaching himself in acquiring a four-bedroom, three-bathroom, three-acre property. It cost only £3,600, probably because all the prospective local buyers were put off by its reputation for being seriously ghost-ridden (far beyond any amiable picturesque haunting), but in 1958 that sum gave Jack sleepless nights about whether alone he could afford the cost of up-keep as well as the mortgage repayments. I was the one who actually chose The Old Rectory. I chose it on the grounds that he could not afford an alpha-plus country house so he ought to buy an alpha-plus country cottage. That it certainly was. It came complete with a fine eighteenth-century coach-house, a substantial carp-filled moat or dewpond and many fine specimen trees. It was extravagantly pretty – it had the best thatched roof in Suffolk (as confirmed in a national competition), it had wonderful Regency *cottage orné* windows set in a handsome sixteenth-century shell and it had a fine Regency staircase and six lovely beamed sixteenth-century rooms at the front. It was neatly split in two with two kitchens, separate staircases and separate entrances so that it could function as two separate houses, but it soon became clear that it would be a far handsomer house and a much more enjoyable one as a single entity. So one of the kitchens was banished (and became Jack's study) and the divisions disappeared. Jack, with extraordinary generosity (as he was very much the senior partner in the enterprise), took the less attractive (but admittedly much warmer) nineteenth-century back of the house for his bedroom and gave me a much larger (but admittedly much more frequently haunted) one in the much more beautiful sixteenth-century front.

In 1958, many of his friends thought that Jack had "bitten off more than he could chew" in acquiring his modest country estate, but as his income grew it soon became clear that he could live there in comfort and some style. A large Sidney Nolan and a Picasso in the entrance hall with two fine Picasso dishes welcomed the visitor and a fine seventeenth-century portrait of Clarendon dominated the beamed drawing room. Interesting silver and ceramics started to flow in and Jack entertained with increasing ease and frequency. There was a rather over-the-top period when one was served off solid silver plates, but he soon grew out of that phase and reverted to less ostentatious English and French porcelain. These were the years when he was best looked after domestically. Mrs Adams, his admirable cook, produced ample meals throughout the day. A full English breakfast, a three course lunch, a huge tea with memorable home-made chocolate cakes, followed by a four course dinner and the contents of a very acceptable cellar ensured that his guests were well looked after. Mrs Filby, his housekeeper, took early morning tea to his indulged visitors and first "Old Finch" and then Kenneth Kinsey, his two gardeners, kept the household well supplied with fresh young vegetables from a huge kitchen garden. It was so peaceful that guests said that they "could hear the silence" and, apart from a tiresome female ghost who troubled young unaccompanied male guests, it was a blissfully comfortable house to stay in. It was easy to find secluded corners in the grounds and many good books were conceived and even written there. Several friends (including Bill and Lesley

Noblett) claim fondly that their children were also conceived there.

The house was probably always more to my taste than to his. Although he lived in it for over thirty years and watched it grow in comfort and comeliness (the gardens which were always my concern blossomed into a three acre show piece which was on occasion opened to the public, and the one and half acre wood which I planted in 1960 is now a striking addition to the landscape), it was never really grand enough for Jack. He grumbled for years that my lack of ambition and indeed lack of vision had landed him with a mere country cottage when he deserved and should have had a fine country house. It is true that in his prosperous years he could have afforded something far grander, but it is probably the place in which he enjoyed his happiest years – certainly they were his most creative and most productive.

My children regarded it as their second home and for years we spent nearly every weekend and every vacation in it as a family, often with Jack presiding over us like a fond and benign grandfather. It is very touching to read in his diaries how much he delighted in my children ("the delightful Olivia and the enchanting Cornelia") when they were at "Westhorpe" as the house was always called.

At one stage, he offered to give the place outright to our family, but Melveena, who was well versed in the ambiguity of what a gift from Jack might mean, urged me to gracefully decline the offer, arguing that Jack would inevitably still think that he had first call on the use of it even if we were now responsible for the whole upkeep. Anyone, she said, who had read William Cooper's fictional account of what sharing a cottage with Jack would be like in *Scenes from Provincial Life*, would be very ill-advised to think that it would be straightforward or unproblematic. Greatly to Jack's surprise, I took her advice. When he offered to give the cottage opposite the Old Rectory to Gordon and Valerie Winterton, they too gracefully declined. They, too, knew Jack very well. They, too, knew that gift exchange with Jack Plumb could be a complicated business. They, too, had read *Scenes from Provincial Life*.

He finally gave up the Old Rectory after it was comprehensively burgled on 23 October 1992 – the burglars smashed in the heavy oak front door with a ram-raider and emptied all the contents of the ground floor into a large lorry. Not surprisingly, ageing and increasingly unwell as he was, Jack could not face refurnishing the whole place, and our lives had largely out-grown it. Rather despairingly, he sold it at the very bottom of the property market slump of the early 1990s for a mere £200,000 – it had been valued at over £330,000 only a few years before and when it last came on the market it had climbed well above that figure. Now the whole property would be well worth a substantial seven figure sum, but it has been split into two – with the handsome eighteenth-century coach house converted into a separate new house with its own separate drive and the sixteenth century Rectory substantially extended to the West.

By the time of the burglary and subsequent sale, Plumb had for some time increasingly taken to entertaining his friends abroad. From the early 1970s to the early 1990s, Jack's burgeoning prosperity led him into being almost excessively generous to his friends in terms of the lavish house parties he organised every summer. Spending September in France had long been a habit but now it could be done in much greater style.

In the early to mid-1950s, his rented villas had often been rather run-down and even rat-infested bastides without running water or any other comforts – they were to be reached half way up mountains without roads or even paths. I recall carrying all his Walpole papers through almost impenetrable cork forests with brambles tearing at my skin and sweat almost blinding me as I stumbled up hill in my search for La Vieille Bastide. My other humble role was to collect all the water needed for the house from a distant and impressively deep well (I had to wear thick leather gloves to prevent the rope ripping my hands), but my problems paled into insignificance compared with those of Dante Campailla. Dante had joined the party late and all the bedrooms were taken and so he was offered the dark unused ground floor room in whose dusty recesses an old divan could just be discerned. All life was lived out on the vine-covered terrace, and, because the grapes were said to attract wild boar, it was explained to Dante that he would be safer if we locked him in from the outside. Dante, who hated most animals even most tame ones, was only too happy to be safely locked in, and the rest of the party rather drunkenly disappeared up the stone staircase, which was on the outside of the ancient bastide, and locked themselves in upstairs. The next morning a white-faced and trembling Dante was released from his nightmare prison. The divan on which he had gratefully lowered himself the night before, turned out to be as lively as a strangely warm water-bed, even livelier in fact because the divan was one huge rats' nest and Dante's terror can be well understood as his bed writhed and heaved and squeaked in protest when he lay down on it. Like a punctured waterbed, it sank ever lower as the larger rats deserted the sinking mattress – but, since the younger rats sat tight squeaking their disapproval and there was the constant fear that the larger ones might return, Dante understandably left his bed and cowered in a corner for the rest of his sleepless night. He could not be persuaded to return to his mattress and everyone tended to drink even more wine to suppress the thoughts about which other rooms the rats might decide to decamp to next.

Wine played a big part in these early all-male, all-adult parties. Perhaps Pernod before dinner, but throughout dinner and after dinner, cheap red wine flowed without stop or stint. I, as the youngest member of the party, usually had the task of keeping it flowing. Any suggestion that the supply was drying up and I would be sent to fetch more, sometimes with unfortunate results. I have often been reminded of the night when, having been dismissed to get more wine, I did not return. Apparently there was much grumbling about the idle bastard sloping off upstairs to bed and someone else had to get more wine. Not until the next morning was I found lying face down in a bed of scarlet geraniums, seriously hung-over, and head to head with a gigantic European toad the size of an inflated poussin.

In later years, after the arrival of wives and children, the living was much less rough and ready, the drinking was much more controlled and the villas were much more opulent.

It was, in fact, an altogether different situation which met Jack's friends in the last twenty-five years of his holidays in Provence and the Algarve, when they joined him in his superbly furnished holiday homes consisting of up to twelve en-suite bedrooms, with huge pool-houses and near Olympic-sized swimming pools. For between the mid-1970s to the mid-1990s, he could afford to preside in much grander fashion over a much larger "family".

Vast gatherings met up in the South of France to be entertained royally in a wonderful Provencal olive-mill near Ste Maxime and a huge and handsome villa near Grasse and later still in the airy, spacious Quinta Rebecca on the Algarve.

Jack may have mocked the perils of family life but there can be no doubt that he greatly enjoyed this peculiar form of family gathering which he had devised for himself. It was like a rolling house party of up to eighteen in which his most favoured friends stayed all the time and the currently less favoured ones flitted through to be shown what they were missing. Jack would occasionally spice up the action by inviting over Leonard and Elizabeth Wolfson and their younger daughter, or Antonia Fraser and Harold Pinter. I well remember Antonia Fraser's elegant breaststroke, as she cruised in stately fashion up and down the pool, whilst wearing a huge straw hat. I well remember too Lord Wolfson's open-mouthed incredulity at the elegant pool-house setting – "Good God", he said, "you academics live better than I do!"

Sometimes Jack would leave us and set off alone to join some grandee on his yacht in Cannes or Port Grimaud but the staple diet was his chosen family of academics and their offspring. For something like twenty years, my daughters were invited to join him entirely at his expense. In later years they were even urged to invite their boyfriends (and their female friends too if they so wished – again all at his expense) to make up the marvellous mix of generations that Jack so enjoyed. While the elegant young bodies frolicked in the magnificent pools and the middle-aged ones took refuge in the shade to talk and read and write, Jack exercised total control – ordering and indeed paying for all the food and wine, choosing the menus, bullying his servants and bossing about his friends, refusing permission to distinguished old friends to leave the grounds until he said they could, vetoing visits from anyone currently out of favour, interrogating the young on their relationships, re-organising all our careers and predicting disaster and disappointment if we did not take his advice. If he was exasperated beyond bearing, he would retire in disgust to his library. It was rather like living with a cross between the bullying of Mr Barratt of the *Barratts of Wimpole Street* and the exasperation of Mr Bennett of *Pride and Prejudice* in a setting designed for Scott Fitzgerald's *The Great Gatsby*.

Invitations to join Jack on his holiday jaunts were extremely difficult to resist. As one frequent member of his summer house parties put it, it was like receiving an offer you could not refuse from the Mafia.

The invitations came very early before one could reasonably claim already to have fixed holiday plans. They came dressed in the most flattering guise (that you were the very first and most important guest to be approached). They were astonishingly generous (it would cost one nothing, parents could bring their children, children could bring their partners – all at Jack's expense). The attractions were always very considerable (all one's old friends were being invited, the villa would be lovely, the food and wine would be lavish, the service impeccable, the pool irresistible). And if flattery and the appeal of hedonism did not work, then the approach would switch effortlessly to emotional blackmail (surely one was not going to let him down after so many years of friendship). For the last twenty years of his life, friends who had firm family plans of their own would be cajoled into cancellation of their plans and acceptance of his by the pitiful plea that this would certainly be the last year that he would be well enough to travel. Needless to say, more often than not his old friends dutifully fell into line. It really was very difficult to say no, and, in truth, the parties were hugely enjoyable as long as one submitted to the will of the Master-planner and dictatorial host.

Over a period of several decades my family missed only one year when we had to spend the summer in Cambridge overseeing the repair to the roof of our home. In spite of this being a matter of pressing necessity, we were told later that in our absence we were constantly denounced as incompetent ingrates with no sense of loyalty who should be able to plan ahead to ensure that essential repairs to our house did not clash with his holiday requirements. This denunciation came in spite of the fact that we were the most loyally committed of all of his friends when it came to answering the call to join him on holiday. Not that this was any hardship.

When Jack was entertaining the food and drink were usually (except for a few notable exceptions when with exaggerated emphasis he was making a pointed show of economy) hugely generous. For many years, he rather grandly took the College chef and the College butler with him on holiday to look after his guests. Food was in many ways just as important as wine was in his life. He was a founder member of the Academy of Gastronomes as well as a Member of the Wine Standards Board, he was an excellent cook in his younger days, and he pored over the *Michelin Guide* like a cricket lover poring over *Wisden*. He loved to "collect" visits to Michelin three-star restaurants and there were very few of France's great restaurants at which he had not eaten.

Jack also knew how to get the best out of them. I once lunched with him at *Le Pyramide* at Vienne in its three-star glory days when many well-informed judges placed it as the best restaurant in France. The lunch consisted of eleven courses of exquisite food. It was probably the best meal I have ever eaten – certainly it was the best back in the 1950s. A delighted Jack declared it to be the best meal that even he had ever had, and then, in characteristic didactic fashion, explained to me how he had set up the ecstatic welcome, the sycophantic service, the respectful sommelier and the super-attentive chefs. He had arranged for an impressive number of letters to be posted to him to await his arrival at *Le Pyramide*. They were all addressed to Dr Plumb, The President of the English Wine and Food Society, The President of the Cambridge Wine Society, The Founding Member of the Bordeaux Club and whatever other mixture of truth and gastronomic fantasy Jack thought would impress the great French restaurant. So it was perhaps hardly surprising that we were met by the great Monsieur and Madame Point themselves.

19. PLUMB AND HIS NEW FRIENDS: A CASE OF SOCIAL MOBILITY

Jack's new prosperity also led him into an ever-increasing preoccupation with a more fashionable and more cosmopolitan life-style.

These were the years when, along with his summer holidays in France and Portugal, he took winter holidays in the Caribbean and spring holidays in New York.

These were the years when he got to know Ben Sonnenberg, Drue Heinz and Brooke Astor in New York and revived his old friendship with Pat and Liz Moynihan in Washington. These were the days when he loved to drop ever more impressive names – "When I was in the White House with Pat, he introduced me to the President" or "Jackie Kennedy really is as beautiful as everyone says, but she is embarrassingly unintelligent".

These were the years when he was taken up by Colin Tennant and Princess Margaret in Mustique and St Lucia. These were the years when it seemed more important to him to become a social diarist than a historian. Bizarrely to those who knew the young highly professional academic Plumb, the diarist 'Chips' Channon became his much admired role model rather than the great historians he used most to revere. He was now more interested in writing up the great social and public events he attended than writing a scholarly article. Vivid depictions of the exotic excesses of Colin Tennant's sixtieth-birthday cruise through the Caribbean, or the party which preceded Prince Charles's wedding to Lady Diana Spencer, show that he did not cease to write when his major historical writings started to dry up in the mid-seventies and early eighties. He simply wrote privately about different subjects. Charming privately printed little pieces, such as *In Search of China* (1986) and *Vintage Memories* (1988), showed that he had lost none of his literary skills. He had simply found new subjects on which to hone them. His diaries showed that he had lost little of his compulsion to write and not all of the stamina that enabled him to do so. His portraits of those who inhabited these new social worlds show that he had lost none of his ability to pin down in memorable prose the personal quiddities and social excesses which he once wrote about so memorably when he was describing eighteenth-century society and politics.

So he slipped easily into a world peopled by Johnnie and Raine Spencer and by Colin and Anne Tennant: he took great pleasure in attending the same parties as Mick and Bianca Jagger; he reported with almost adolescent enthusiasm the sayings of Jerry Hall; he spent whole days sitting on the beach with Princess Margaret. He used his position as Master of Christ's to entertain both major and minor royalty, both current and past political leaders – and inevitably he had to entertain all their hangers-on.

Many Cambridge academics were bemused by his interest in Marcia Falkender and Princess Michael of Kent, Harold and Mary Wilson, Princess Margaret and Roddy Llewellyn. They were understandably surprised when Princess Michael of Kent (addressing a dinner table packed with distinguished academics of the calibre of Asa Briggs, Jack Plumb, Quentin Skinner and many others) referred expansively but without a hint of irony to "We historians". They would have been even more baffled if they had known of his hour-long (sometimes literally hours long) phone calls from Raine Spencer, and the twelve-page long letters he received from Princess Margaret; but Jack found this new social world endlessly fascinating. He really was intensely interested in their private lives and public woes.

Fixing them with the full force of his attention he would listen for hour after hour to their emotional outpourings and then faithfully record them in his diaries – all for now sadly embargoed. He could be a most effective listener, and a most dedicated recorder of what he had heard.

Good old-fashioned snobbery doubtless played its part in dictating Jack's taste for such unlikely aristocratic company but he did seem to be genuinely interested in their lives. He fully recognised how manipulative and acquisitive Raine Spencer (especially in her "Acid-Raine" years) was and how appallingly ruthless Ruth Fermoy could be, but he was fascinated to watch them and their like using their titles and position to jockey for further advancement up the social ladder. He watched with horrified concern how Lady Fermoy used her friendship with the Queen Mother to dangle her granddaughters in front of Prince Charles, and he presciently predicted disaster when the Prince of Wales finally succumbed to the ever-increasing pressure to find a virgin wife by accepting Lady Diana Spencer. Even her doting and delighted father, Johnnie Spencer, was worried about her many shortcomings as a future Princess of Wales and potential future Queen of England. "Jack", he said, "could you try to educate her? She's bound to put her foot in it if she does not get some help. She really is wholly uneducated, spectacularly ignorant even by our country house standards!"

Jack was only too happy to respond to his aristocratic friends' trusting dependence on his knowledge of the constitution or his scholarly addiction to our royal heritage and, of course, his knowledge of it. He knew the pitfalls and disasters that littered the history of the English monarchy and he was quite prepared to play the role of the wise old mentor generously making available his profound scholarship to guide the next generation towards survival and popularity. Unfortunately, the Royals themselves (Princess Margaret apart) were less impressed by his credentials as an advisor than the Spencers were. For all his boasted friendship with the royal family, he mainly had to make do with the lesser royals and the more ancient members of the aristocracy. He certainly gave them his full and sustained attention. He often seemed to know more about their family histories, their houses and their possessions than they did. He would ask one to lunch to meet three aged dowager duchesses and wax lyrically about the jewels they paraded in old age and the colourful love lives of their youth. "She was the toast of London sixty years ago", he would proudly pronounce of an elderly female guest, and be very disappointed if his young guests did not share his excitement. For a man with such a remarkable eye for talent amongst his pupils, I thought that he showed an equally remarkable blindness to the deficiencies (in interest, intelligence or talent) in his strange collection of the faded flowers of the English aristocracy – many of whom seemed to do little more than boast about how old were their families and how large were their houses and how valuable their jewels were.

He would invite me to dine with a duchess, to converse with a countess, to stay with a marchioness and to take drinks with a princess and then be bewildered by my failure to match his obvious delight in their company. I simply could not respond as ecstatically as he expected to the attractions he found all too evident.

I could, of course, readily see that his first and longest standing aristocratic friend, Sybil Cholmondeley, was a woman of great distinction. She had taste, intelligence and beauty. I found her company and her hospitality quite delightful from the 1950s to the 1980s when she last invited my family to Houghton – characteristically, she wanted to show my young daughters what a great house, then still unopened to the public, was like. I remained disappointingly unresponsive, however, to the attractions of many of his other aristocratic friends.

As for Princess Margaret, to whom he always remained loyal (and she, I believe, to him) I found her a very sad and unsettling creature. Unlike Prince Philip and Prince Charles, both of whom I entertained several times in the Master's Lodge in Caius, and both of whom I found delightful company – highly intelligent, hugely entertaining and completely relaxed – Princess Margaret seemed effortlessly to put everyone on edge. Unable to come to terms with a passionate desire to assert her royal status and an equally powerful need to indulge her desire to be a free spirit, she could switch in an instant from being vivacious and charming and lively, to being aloof and distant and icily regal. It was a disturbing combination. Many have commented on how the palpable tension between these two needs led to tragedy for her and extreme social discomfort for everyone else. It simply filled Jack with sympathy for her. He shamelessly indulged her every peccadillo.

The most ferocious defender of his claret I have ever known would smile indulgently whilst she smoked throughout the splendid dinner parties he put on in her honour. She ruthlessly rejected his Lafites, Latours and Yquems and demanded Famous Grouse instead, and ostentatiously repaired her highly perfumed make-up between courses, but all was forgiven. Her wonderfully loyal friends such as the enchanting Janie Stevens and the charming Anne Glenconner helped enormously to make entertaining her much more than acceptable but I could never share Jack's uncritical delight in her company or his endless fascination with her psyche. He loved entertaining her in Cambridge (or bullying his friends such as Patrick Bateson in the Provost's Lodge at King's and myself in the Master's Lodge at Caius into doing it for him). He loved even more being entertained by her. He loved what she called her "jollies" – elaborately informal visits to the Tower of London or to Hampton Court or to Janie Stevens's lovely house in the country, but most of all he loved listening to her accounts of her eventful love life. He thought that travelling with her lover as Mr. and Mrs. John Brown was wonderfully witty and the fact that Roddie Llewellyn was "kind" to his royal mistress immediately invested him with profound interest for Jack. He thought that they were both "extremely vulnerable" and Jack always found vulnerability very difficult to resist. Royal vulnerability was, of course, completely irresistible.

Most of what Princess Margaret confided to him (and which he recorded in his diaries) is safely protected in the University Library, but to close friends he would hint at physical abuse, and when met with disbelief, he would drop enticing titbits, such as stories of lighted matches being flicked at her by her husband that threatened to set light to her glamorous dresses, and of her finding lists of "the forty five reasons he hated her" being left on her dressing table by her serially unfaithful bisexual husband. Such stories (and the leaked information that both Charles and Diana had tried in vain to back out of their ill-starred and ill-advised marriage) were like irresistible catnip to Jack. They excited his sympathy as much as they inflamed his curiosity.

Indeed one of the reasons for his wide circle of friends (ranging from royalty and the English aristocracy to the humblest freshman at Christ's) was his empathetic response to their problems. His sympathies were easily and quickly aroused by the psychologically fragile – they appealed equally to his need to instruct and to help, and his need to interfere and to control. His surviving letters and his diaries show his extraordinary capacity to establish an intimate knowledge of those he befriended and helped. His curiosity about other people's lives was boundless and his ability to get them to confide in him was just as remarkable, as his archive vividly demonstrates. Part of this ability came from the beguiling (not to say hypnotic) effects of his undisguised fascination with the details of his friends' life-stories and their relationships; and a further part came from his willingness to ask the "un-askable" questions about their private lives (effortlessly flouting the usual taboos about money, sex, politics and religion). A yet further part of this success came, too, from his own undoubted ability to entertain and to amuse and to charm and to intrigue. It is abundantly clear from his diaries that he managed to extract the most remarkably intimate details from even the grandest in his circle of friends and acquaintances. It is not for nothing that his revelations about Princess Margaret, Princess Diana and Prince Charles are under restricted access until the death of the youngest grandchildren of the Queen.

Loyal as he was to his close royal friends, there were outlying parts of our royal family that seem more dysfunctional than ever when seen through the sharp eyes and the vivid words of Jack Plumb, the royal diarist. In some ways he was the ideal confidante – inquisitive, sympathetic and shocked by nothing, he was capable of describing their miseries in the memorable prose of one who was exceptionally familiar with such royal problems. He could also judge them in the light of historical perspective. The man who had written with such verve and insight about the sex-life of George IV was, after all, already well versed in the most florid versions of the psycho-pathology of everyday royal life.

His judgments now seem pretty solid. He predicted trouble for the Diana-Charles match from the very beginning and when Princess Margaret was still welcoming the new Duchess of York as "a breath of fresh air" for the Royal Family, Jack was quite sure that she would prove to be a disaster. Many other perceptive insights will be revealed when the more private parts of his archive are made available.

It is easy to see why Jack was so welcome in this normally exclusive circle. He gave intellectual respectability to their meetings, he knew more about their history than they did, he gave generous parties, he was both entertaining and erudite, and he loved to gossip. They certainly thought that he was odd and they came to know that he could be difficult, but his generosity more than compensated for his oddity and his erudition more than compensated for his difficult temperament. And, unlike when he was with his old friends, he was much more often on his best behaviour with his grand friends. One must not forget that he could be remarkably charming when he wanted to be. He was willing to be court entertainer, even court jester, if necessary. He was so endlessly attentive and so fulsomely admiring that more than one of them thought that he must be in love with them.

He could also be very useful. When appropriate presents were needed,

Jack was very good at finding them and if necessary paying for them. When Johnnie Spencer, for instance, declared that he would like all his friends to join together to give him a single significant piece of silver for his sixtieth birthday, Jack volunteered to track down a suitable piece and to write round to all of Johnnie's friends to collect the necessary funds – when he failed to extract the sum needed, he claimed that he had generously made up the shortfall himself.

His archive demonstrates all too clearly how willingly he worked his passage into acceptance into this new social world, which would have seemed so alien to him in his radical, republican and rebellious left-wing youth. His archive contains the formal printed record of all those who contributed to Lord Spencer's birthday gift. Jack had had 150 copies printed in Cambridge in November 1984, and the list was presented to Johnnie Spencer along with the handsome gift of a silver salver by Robert Abercrombie. Jack was delighted that the list of givers started with five Royal Highnesses and contained a healthy sprinkling of Dukes and Duchesses, not to mention a predictable mass of lesser titles.

The Plumb archive also contains Jack's much more revealing record of how much each of the givers actually gave, and incidentally how very modest some of the gifts were. There were a surprising number of £10 offerings in the £4,071.42, which he had raised by the 8th of June 1984.

Both lists are very long and showed how many donors Jack had been required to approach for gifts. Each gift required Jack's detailed involvement – from the initial approach seeking a donation to the acknowledgement and letter of thanks for each gift. The whole process must have been a hugely time-consuming interruption into a busy man's life, but to Jack it seemed a worthwhile investment in cementing his role in the Spencer circle. Johnnie Spencer may have ungratefully thought that "this fellow Plumb is an odd little chap", but Raine Spencer became a firm friend and fascinating confidante for Jack to cultivate, and to use as the key to open up many more useful social contacts.

Whatever the reasons for his acceptance into this strange new social milieu, he certainly was accepted. I remember vividly the eightieth birthday party (one of about eight parties that celebrated this particular milestone), which was given for him by Princess Margaret in Kensington Palace. Princess Margaret provided the setting, the Queen provided the venison, the Rothschilds provided the Lafite '76, and the Glenconners provided the flowers, flown in specially from the Caribbean. It was a splendid party – generous, warm-hearted and sparkling. The guest list was suitably impressive – I recall my daughter Olivia, who was still an undergraduate putting on plays in Oxford, being thrilled to meet Harold Pinter – and Jack was in his element. The Princess gave a charming speech and Jack gave a most accomplished courtier's reply (on reflection it was the last good speech I heard him give). By the time of the speeches he made at my sixtieth birthday at Waddesdon in 1995 and his half-century as a Fellow of Christ's in 1996, he had lost command of his old eloquence, and at later occasions he was but the palest shadow of his former self. After dinner, the guests grew from our original thirty diners (three tables of ten) to something which seemed to be approaching an appropriate eighty but (according to Jack's record of the party) seems to have been rather less. Later in the evening, I heard Princess Margaret doing a brilliant impersonation of Jack. I had never heard him mimicked so well (other than, hilariously, by Angus Wilson and Tony Garrett in a brilliant duet). When I congratulated her, her reply was "Oh, her Majesty does him much better than I do!" As Jack so often said of his life, "It was a long way from Somerville Road, Leicester".

Not surprisingly Jack absolutely loved this royal party. As he wrote in his diary: "And so to the great birthday party at Kensington Palace – one of the great days of my life because not a note jarred, everything was as near perfection as I could expect (the only small flaw was the defection of David Cholmondeley at the last moment) – but his present of a plate of Sir Robert Walpole's Chinese Armorial Export Service c.17725/30 made a kind of amend." The level of generosity of this gift can be judged from the fact that it made £1900 as lot 158 in the Cheffins' sale after Plumb's death in 2001. In some ways, this splendid party marked the pinnacle of Jack's relationship with the royal family. His close friendship with Princess Margaret continued for many years but his eightieth birthday party was probably the most spectacular and the most public display of it.

I find it horribly unpalatable to believe that Jack justified his courtship of Princess Margaret (as Sir Roy Strong has claimed in print) with the words "The best way to the Head Girl is through her sister". I certainly hope he didn't, but I suspect he may well have said it. It would be idle to pretend that he was not capable of such cynical throw-away lines. It would be equally idle to pretend that he did not take great delight in being summoned to Clarence House to lunch with the Queen Mother and even greater delight to be invited to Sandringham to dine and to stay with the Queen.

Delighted as he was to be the guest of the Queen, I think that he always felt more comfortable in the company of the Queen Mother – he was deeply impressed that in their shared old age she drank far more than he did. As he put it when describing her warmth and vitality, "She always seems to be two or three gin and tonics ahead of the rest of us, because she is two or three gin and tonics ahead of the rest of us". He would then add knowingly – to show that he was really in the know – "actually it was usually gin and Dubonnet". More seriously, I think it was simply a case of one life enhancer appealing irresistibly to another life enhancer. Also, as an historian of the English monarchy, he knew how difficult it was for someone in her position (the last Empress of India no less) to combine an unerring sense of dignity with a seemingly unfailing sense of familiarity and friendliness. This was the rare combination which Queen Elizabeth the Queen Mother seemed have mastered quite instinctively and to have effortlessly maintained throughout her long life. He also always relished her style of entertaining, which he much preferred to the more abstemious example set by the Queen. He could respond very easily to the Queen Mother's unembarrassed enjoyment of the good things in life. He also greatly relished her taste – much preferring her taste in clothes, paintings, gardens and ceramics to her daughter's. Few could be excited by the stolid interiors of much of Buckingham Palace or the uninspired Palace gardens, but it was easy for Jack to respond to the Queen Mother's superb collection of early Chelsea botanical plates or indeed her collection of Wemyss. Having seen her collection he rapidly acquired a matching collection of his own – characteristically concentrating on Wemyss pieces decorated predictably with green and purple plums – with which to decorate the entrance hall of the Master's Lodge in Christ's. When he left the lodge, he soon sold the whole collection to his old friends, Dante and Jan Campailla.

He was always quick to copy the things he admired in the lives of his grander friends. Just as he had taken his taste in claret from the Rothschilds and his taste in French porcelain from the Cholmondeleys, he now took his taste in Wemyss from the Queen Mother, and his taste for Caribbean holidays from Princess Margaret and the Glenconners.

It must be said that he took his regular winter holidays in the Caribbean in the 1980s, not simply to be with his new smart friends and to cement his relationship with them, but also to introduce his old friends to a new world, which he thought they would otherwise never see. He invited a succession of them to join him at La Jalousie in St Lucia where he sat on the elegant balcony surrounded by tropical gardens like an old colonial planter entirely at ease in this exotic setting. He appeared quite undisturbed by men with huge machetes wandering through the house and grounds, saying dismissively "they're just my security guards" if one asked who they were. Alas he seemed equally undisturbed by the fact that his cook seemed to live in what looked little better than a large kennel.

He was determined to share the delight he took in this new-found world and arranged for many of his friends to visit all the places he had most enjoyed. Mustique was a must and the Grenadines were an equal imperative. When Melveena told the Fellows of Girton about the wonderfully generous visit to Petit St Vincent, the minute private island in the Grenadines, which he had laid on for us to celebrate my fiftieth birthday, they said incredulously,

"If your friend needs any more friends to spoil, please tell him we are all available!" He was capable of extraordinary acts of generosity to those he was genuinely fond of and many of his old friends were more than generously spoilt on more than one occasion.

The indulgencies which he lavished on them included trips for them and their families to the States and to the Caribbean, financial support to their children on their "gap years", in addition, of course, to his annual invitations for them to join him on the Mediterranean coast. It is little wonder that he was often described by his friends as "the most generous of men".

20. PLUMB'S REPUTATION AS A SCHOLAR AND WALPOLE III

I know that there are some professional historians who see Jack as someone corrupted by money and seduced into a meretricious world of jet-setting socialites. They see him, too, as being diverted from finishing Walpole and quitting the field of professional scholarship because he was unable to reply to the scathing personal and scholarly attacks on him by scholars such as J.C.D. Clark.

Clark, egged on by Geoffrey Elton, did at one stage seem to be trying to demolish Plumb's life's work and to undermine his scholarly reputation. In an article in *The Observer*, Clark wrote that "only the workings of academic patronage were keeping Plumb's scholarly reputation alive". According to David Cannadine, in response to this, a letter was organised in which he had a hand. It was Cannadine informed me, "signed by Owen Chadwick, Quentin Skinner and Barry Supple, and Plumb got costs and an apology. But Clark took terrible revenge, reviewing the first two volumes of Plumb's essays in the EHR, and merely quoting his own cross and bitter words against him".

I knew nothing of this at the time and in my experience Jack ultimately seemed remarkably unmoved by the attack.

Obviously he cannot have liked it. Who would? His initial reaction was as always one of fury. He certainly discussed taking serious legal action himself, but after the usual flurry of furious letter writing, which was his standard response to most things (from a disputed laundry bill upwards), he soon calmed down. He always said that Clark's attack was motivated by Plumb's refusal to supervise Clark's Ph.D. because he "did not take on 2.2s from Downing". And, having dismissively explained it, he very rarely mentioned it to me again.

When urged by some colleagues to write a considered personal reply defending his academic reputation against other hostile reviews and more general critical assessments of his work, he rather loftily said he really could not be bothered. There was more to life than academic squabbles. He had always despised those who made their reputations by constantly re-writing the same material as part of a polemical debate. He had himself dished out plenty of gratuitous insults in the course of the formal peer assessment, which is such an essential part of the academic life. The man who had dismissed as "unreadable rubbish" the work of the hugely influential and greatly admired Sir Lewis Namier was not well placed to decry robust academic criticism of established historical elders. The man who mocked Namier's "myopic methodology", who dismissed John Brooke as "a rat-like, poor, depressed, Ultra-Tory Namierite hack", and who lambasted F.R. Leavis for his "senseless diatribe" against Snow, which he described as full of "folly", "arrogance" and "sheer blind ignorance" was equally ill-placed to complain of personal animus from junior critics. When reminded of the unforgiving tone of much of his own criticism of his peers, he would wryly concede that in such matters what goes around comes around.

One did not have to look far in his writings to find a host of uncharitable judgements: he described Arnold Toynbee as "lurching from campus to campus lecturing for succulent fees"; he described Maurice Cowling as "an endearing comic figure, but intellectually disastrous"; he patronisingly characterised some of Owen Chadwick's books as being "surprisingly good"; he characterised Geoffrey Elton as being a man of "implacability of vision and total rigidity". And, when asked to choose the greatest blunder of the twentieth century, he suggested Oswald Spengler's portentous *The Decline of the West* for its malign influence on the intelligentsia. Pessimists such as Spengler and Toynbee, he argued, "warped history with their verbosities". He could hardly complain when he was on the receiving end of similarly waspish comments.

Having dished it out on his way up, he was, he claimed, quite prepared to take what came back to him in his pomp or indeed on his way down. Fury was his normal initial reaction to hostile reviews, but he usually calmed down pretty quickly. On mature reflection, he said, he saw no point in wasting his energies on what he regarded as trumped-up controversies. To take seriously those who snarled and snapped and surreptitiously bit would, he said, be like an elephant getting upset by what he rather bizarrely called "a bite from barking-mad mosquitoes", or a lion getting upset by "an attack by over-ambitious rats". To stamp on such gnats or to seek revenge on such rats would, he said, be to give them more importance than they deserved. For a rich scholar to sue those he called "academic non-entities" (and win as he might well have done in the case of some of the more personal attacks) would merely offer a probably not unwelcome martyrdom to the "non-entities" in question. Such gadflies, he argued, lived on the oxygen of attention. They would disappear into limbo, he felt, without his bothering about them. So far he seems largely to have been right, but he knew that he would probably have good reason to fear the attention of posthumous revisionists. His death removed the threat of libel suits against his attackers and his absence will doubtless embolden the hidden assassins to emerge from the shadows to take their revenge.

He seemed equally unconcerned with those who chided him for "not finishing Walpole". "What they do not realise", he used to say, "is that I have finished Walpole. I have finished all that needed doing. I have said all that I wanted to say. A third volume would add almost nothing new, so why should I waste several years of my life writing what is already known just for the sake of symmetry". "Anyway", he used to add, "it gives my enemies something to criticise me for. Such things allow you to distinguish between your real friends (who ask you about what you have successfully done or what you are currently doing) and your false friends (who needle and niggle away at what you haven't done and what you are not going to do)".

As with so many things, Jack was not entirely consistent on the question of Walpole. There were certainly times when he talked of finishing it to me, and it would seem from Jeremy Black's testimony that he actually claimed to have finished it in the late 1970s. Professor Black has written that "I was too young to have anything to do with Plumb, but in 1978 I was summoned to see him in order to be told there was no point persisting with my graduate work of Walpole's foreign policy, as he was going to publish the third volume of his life the following year and any other work would be redundant. He must have known that he was lying about volume three. There is a difference between attempting to finish a book and knowing through the absence of a finished text that it is not forthcoming."

I think he genuinely felt that there was nothing much new to say and I am certain that he had no appetite for going over the familiar later years of Walpole's career when he had more exciting things to do. I suspect also that the wickedly effective jibe of his Oxford critics, that the first two volumes had added almost nothing to what Archdeacon Coxe had already written, hurt him more than he would ever admit. The last thing he would have wanted to do would be to give real credence to their witty verdict that his most substantial and arguably his most important piece of professional scholarship could be summed up as " Post Coxe, praeter nihil est". He was well aware that many a career had been blighted by such effective bits of academic malice. Oxbridge common rooms are littered with examples of scholars who were stopped in their multi-volume tracks by a bitchy review from an anonymous non-entity. If it contained a well-turned, easily quoted put-down the effects could be devastating. One could not absolutely rule out the suspicion that the real reason for the non-appearance of Walpole III is to be found in that cruelly effective "Post Coxe, praeter nihil est" crack.

He sometimes felt the need to explain to his admirers why he wasn't working on it. He told Bill Noblett, who was then working as his research assistant, that he did not want to write about the last years of Walpole's life until he himself had experienced the rigours of old age and could then write about it with authority. He told Geoffrey Parker that "he had completed all the research but would wait until his declining years to write it". There is little evidence in his archive of any completed research – a box file entitled "workings on Walpole" contains little to suggest any advanced research. Unlike his work on *The British Seaborne Empire*, which he abandoned when he fell out pretty violently with Knopf and which has left three completed chapters in his archive, *Walpole III* has left no substantial evidence of being started, let alone finished.

Whatever the motives involved in this story were, back in the 1970s, he seemed with the passing years to have few regrets about not completing the planned three-volume life. Significantly Simon Schama, one of his closest confidantes, has recorded that "he never, in my 40-year friendship, betrayed the least sign of even wanting to talk about its completion". Since many obituaries described the two completed volumes as "his greatest work" ranking it "with the greatest examples of political biography", "brilliantly conveying the essence of a politician", perhaps he was right to stop when he did.

21. PLUMB'S HEALTH AND HIS DECLINING PRODUCTIVITY

Jack could reasonably say that he had published quite enough to satisfy most critics and there were good reasons why he was less prolific in old age.

Those who have charted and attempted to explain his decline in productivity often fail to make due allowance for his declining health. Rather than quitting the field in the face of disappointment and hostile attacks, it could be argued that he retreated to a large extent in response to new attractions and in the face of a formidable and crushing catalogue of health worries. He was diagnosed in his early seventies as suffering from myeloma, a particularly unattractive form of blood cancer, with the accompanying promise of a short life and a painful death. It was a diagnosis that understandably led him to review his life's priorities. After he had survived an unexpected ten more years, a new consultant pronounced the original diagnosis to be incorrect. At the very end of his life, I believe that yet a third consultant confirmed the original diagnosis, but by then it was really too late to matter.

He did not fare well at the hands of his doctors. He always insisted on paying for expensive medical advice and even more expensive medical treatment but he rarely seemed to profit from either. His prostate operation was bungled so badly that he was incontinent for the last twenty years of his life. It can have done little to improve his temper – as he put it to me "Peeing yourself when you are being shown the crown jewels by the Queen is not the ideal recipe for social ease and relaxed enjoyment of life". Even worse were the medical consequences of such incontinence. The bulky padding he had to wear to get him through his social life led to frequent bladder infections and all too frequent hospitalisation. His urinary infections seemed to upset him more than some of his more serious medical problems. Urinary tract infections are notorious for causing mental confusion in the elderly, and Jack often seemed close to delirium when they occurred.

Fortunately these attacks of delirium were very short-lived, but there were many other medical problems for him to cope with as he aged. A serious heart condition and chest problems added to his woes. The number of pills he had to take mounted to comic proportions – my daughters, when they were very young, used to like to count them out and line them up for him in differently coloured rows on the breakfast table. But for all the medication, his trips to Addenbrooke's Hospital and then to the Evelyn Nursing Home in Cambridge grew more and more frequent. He was hospitalised in the States and in Portugal as well as in England, and his health became an increasing cause for concern for all his friends.

I was summoned to Christ's in the early hours of the morning to get him a doctor or get him to Addenbrooke's on more occasions than I can count. A combination of cancer (even it was a falsely diagnosed cancer), decades of incontinence, two operations for prostate problems, recurrent attacks of pneumonia, a series of minor strokes, a longstanding problem with angina, minor operations on his eyes for cataracts and over-active tear ducts, appendicitis in his late seventies followed by debilitating infection after the operation, a major fall which led to a fractured spine – these were but part of his medical problems in his seventies and eighties. To add to his medical woes, he had to undergo repeated and agonizing operations on his teeth and gums. Little wonder that he was less productive – and indeed less genial – than in his prime.

Nevertheless, it would be difficult to disagree with those who argue that, given his output in the fifties and sixties and early seventies, the last quarter of a century can be seen as a decline from those enviable levels of quite astonishing productivity. It can also be argued that, given his gifts, he will have left less of a mark than he could have done on English historiography. I recall Jonathan Steinberg, a Fellow of Christ's and later a professor in America, saying back in his Cambridge days, that Jack Plumb was the most naturally gifted historian he had ever met. Blessed with an astonishing memory, an acute analytical mind, an unusual gift for shrewd psychological insights, a remarkable ability to produce prose that was as memorable as it was accessible and a quite unusual ability to hold his audiences' attention, he was also blessed with formidable stamina and an ability to work at speed. Given all these gifts and the drive of a powerful personal ambition, many have wondered why he switched off. Why, they not unreasonably asked, had he largely abandoned academia whilst seemingly at the height of his powers?

One reason, which many critics perhaps fail sufficiently to stress, was the dramatic decline in energy that came with Jack's increasingly poor health. Few people seem to realise what massive reserves of stamina are needed to generate the kind of torrents of words that historians such as Joseph Needham, Asa Briggs and Jack Plumb produced in their prime. I have been lucky enough to witness these three great scholars at work, and, having for many years shared a college staircase with Needham, having shared holidays with Briggs and having shared a house with Jack, I have seen at first hand the kind of commitment and endurance required to sustain their scholarship.

Even when apparently chairing a College Council meeting, Needham would be remorselessly compiling his great works of scholarship, using his elegant Chinese characters to disguise his real purpose from his less gifted colleagues; even when on holiday, Briggs would rise before dawn in order to complete his day's work before his guests rose for their leisurely breakfast; and Jack would maintain his output by never taking a day off from his writing wherever he might be and whatever he was doing. Over forty years ago when Jack was still at his peak of productivity I tried to explain what drove him to write. I listed *"his intellectual fascination with historical causation, and the yeast which stirs different societies to pursue their manifest destinies, and the remarkable justifications with which they seek to uphold them; his need to assuage, and to indulge, his own obsessions with the past (plus, of course, a realistic worldly concern for both his career and his pocket); but the dominant drive has always been the creative one. His need to write is such that every day which passes, whether holiday or Christmas day, without several hundred words safely down on paper in publishable form leaves him restless, fretful and miserable. He alone, among contemporary professionals that I know, is one of those few, the true creators, who write to ease the ache within."* I then added *"Fortunately he was blessed with the phenomenal energy to give that creative drive its fullest expression"*. When that phenomenal energy started to dry up, the torrent of words started to dry up with it.

But boredom also played its part. For my part, I think that much of the explanation of Plumb's decline in productivity and his apparent flight from the field of battle lies in the fact that he became increasingly bored with academia and increasingly exasperated by his colleagues. It no longer satisfied his ambition. It seemed to have less and less to offer him. It offered him neither financial reward nor intellectual excitement. Much of what it asked of him he found increasingly tedious. He had always had a healthy scepticism about many of its habits. He never believed in conferences, he scorned much of the arid scholarship which no one ever read, he had little time for the nit-picking point-scoring which kept some scholars gainfully employed for most of their lives. He hated the seemingly endless growth of time-wasting bureaucratic interference, which universities seemed to be subsiding under. Cut off from the stimulus of youth by his retirement from teaching, and with his power and influence reduced by his retirement from the Mastership, he turned more and more to new worlds to satisfy his curiosity and to fire his imagination. He continued to write – but less and less for publication.

Some of his colleagues perceptively recognised that the real reason for his declining scholarly productivity was, as Quentin Skinner put it, "that increasingly he became bored with academics and academic life. The issues weren't important enough, the people weren't interesting enough". Jack, when he took early retirement in his early sixties, left little doubt as to the reasons why. In *The Making of an Historian* he wrote "I became so bored with academic chores that, independent financially of what I was paid as a professor, I resigned early in 1974". He hated the flight of historians into ever-tinier, ever-more specialized territories. He hated the venom with which they defended these miniature personal fiefdoms from any rival academics who expressed a common interest in them. He hated the fact that they insisted that their students should follow them into these Lilliput kingdoms and, once there, worship at the altars of ever-smaller fragments of ever-more arcane archives. For a man who had been happy to speculate about the importance of the great sea-borne empires, who had engaged himself with little hesitation in the study of *The History of Human Society*, who contentedly took on such mammoth topics as sex, slavery, the family and society, and who had attempted to write the history of whole centuries and entire continents, his colleagues' preoccupations seemed parochial and piffling. "They make Monaco and San Marino and Lichtenstein seem like great empires, too grand and demanding to take on. Instead they bury themselves in the graveyards of a single village or the chronicles of a single year and call it history in microcosm. Such topics," he said, "were all very well for apprenticeship pieces but scarcely subjects with which to occupy a whole career". As he wrote despairingly of the Cambridge History Faculty in 1988, "the younger historians, hell-bent to prove the singular importance of their own piece of turf, chopped the subjects into smaller and smaller pieces or added tiny pebbles from the wilder shores of the Third World".

These were not the only reasons why he sought refuge in retirement. "If these aspects of the History Faculty fatigued me", he wrote, "the appointments which the Board made filled me with doom. How could any body of rational men pass over Simon Schama or Geoffrey Parker, or get rid of Hugh Brogan? As for professorial appointments, they filled me with disquiet and a sense of hopelessness".

He had to concede that "it would be ridiculous to give the impression that the Faculty was wholly without distinction. It was not", but the concession was hardly fulsome. He recognized that "even men most inclined to favour the second-rate could never withhold recognition from supreme talent. And this is certainly true of the Faculty", but his ultimate, much-quoted verdict was a bleak and unforgiving one, and in my view wholly unfair one: "for decades nothing exciting, nothing original, nothing creative".

That dismissive verdict on Cambridge history was to haunt his declining years and do much to damage his reputation.

22. PLUMB'S CRITIQUE OF CAMBRIDGE HISTORIANS

That infamous and wholly unfair sweeping dismissal of the work of his Cambridge colleagues did much to fuel the controversy over Jack's standing in the profession.

Privately he was even more contemptuous of his colleagues. Of the Cambridge History professors, he wrote "they look like bank clerks, they write like bank clerks, and their books read like Gas board reports". He even found fault with their wives – mocking unmercifully their clothes, their homes, their taste and their attempts at entertainment. "Is there anything dowdier than an academic's wife?" he would ask. "Is there anything less enticing than an academic dinner party? Is there anything duller?" He would then cheerfully answer his own question by shouting gleefully, "Yes, their husbands' books are even duller, even drabber, even less enticing, even more boring!" "Most of their works," he said, "amount to little more than arid, ill-written accounts of ill-digested statistics. The fact that their books are well-researched does not prevent them from being jargon-filled and unbearably boring". Such men and such books would, he was sure, kill the subject he had once loved, strangle it with statistics, stifle it in incomprehensible jargon, and bury it under a morass of arid and meaningless scholarship. He admitted that there were a few cheering exceptions to the rule, but there were not enough to stimulate him into staying. He felt in any case that the exceptions were now an endangered species.

As Jack's paranoia grew, he also felt that his own pupils were particularly endangered – many not appointed at all and those appointed systematically blocked from promotion. He urged them to emigrate to the more generous world of America. Many took his advice. Those who stayed would, he felt, only suffer from his support. It was surely time for him to leave the stage – not as he saw it, in personal defeat, but with a sense of despairing hopelessness and contemptuous boredom. Both feelings were understandably exacerbated by chronic ill health and further fuelled by all too frequent spells in hospital.

He never doubted that he had made the right decision. When he wrote his savage indictment of the Faculty in 1988, he still thought that there were historians of real promise in Cambridge. In his view the best soon left – discouraged by lack of recognition and attracted by more exciting worlds to conquer. In his last years, he was increasingly convinced that his worst predictions were being all too vividly proved true. Compared to the twenty-eight stellar names I mentioned in the first paragraph of my obituary of him, (the names which collectively made up such a golden age of achievement in the History Faculty of the 1960s), Plumb felt that, on the most generous assessment, there were a mere three or four names who could reasonably claim to be of such unchallengeable international standard by the beginning of the new millennium. He was blind to the evidence of what else Cambridge still had to offer. Had he been better informed and had he listened more attentively to his old friends such as Jo Whaley and myself, he would have realised that (even restricting himself to historians from Caius) he would have found a much more encouraging situation.

If one included the Honorary Fellows of Caius one could still find such superstars as Sir Richard Evans, Sir Noel Malcolm and Quentin Skinner (who declined a knighthood), and a significant cluster of other undoubted heavy-weight professors such as David Abulafia, Jo Whaley, Paul Binski, Peter Mandler and Vic Gatrell, all of whom shared Plumb's desire to tackle big subjects and to communicate with a wide audience. In addition seven of those eight professors were Fellows of the British Academy.

Richard Evans alone could match Jack in achieving a Knighthood, a college Mastership, an FBA, and many Honorary degrees. Even more significantly he could more than match him in royalties measured in millions and radio audiences of the same magnitude. He could also, of course, surpass him in achieving both a named Cambridge chair and then the Cambridge Regius chair, both of which to his great anguish eluded Jack. Evans's very public trouncing of Irving's notorious Holocaust denials gave him a name recognition which also more than matched Jack's. His scholarly publications make him an undoubted international superstar.

Given that Jack was lambasting Cambridge history in general, it is worth pointing out that this single college could also boast such other significant figures as Philip Grierson, Christopher Brooke, William Frend, Richard Duncan-Jones, (all Fellows of the British Academy) and, of course, most significant of all, Joseph Needham (both FBA and FRS) whose scholarly achievements dwarfed all the others put together. When Needham died six years before Jack, he was widely hailed as the greatest scholar since Aristotle and Erasmus, being described in obituaries as the greatest scholar of this or any country and the greatest scholar of this or any century. In his lifetime, he may not have matched Jack in name recognition, but he far surpassed him in national and international honours.

Not surprisingly, scholars of this stature did not react warmly to Plumb's sweeping dismissal of Cambridge historians. Younger Caian historians of great promise who were to go on to future distinction such as Annabel Brett, Stephen Tuck, Melissa Calaresu, Catherine Holmes, John Chalcraft, Maiken Umbach, Peter Stacey, Kate Retford, Sujit Sivasundaram, Berhard

Fulda and many others would not have taken kindly to having their work comprehensively dismissed.

Those twenty-six Caian names include ten FBAs, fourteen professorships and I am sure many future ones — not a bad haul for a single Cambridge College.

It is true that Cambridge let too many of these distinguished Caian historians leave. Professor Norman Stone, Professor Richard Overy,, Sir Noel Malcolm,, Professor Geoffrey Crossick, Professor Harold James, Professor John Miller, Professor Norman Houseley, Professor John Watts, Professor Sarah Foot, Professor Laurence Brockliss, Professor Orlando Figes, Professor Steven Tolliday, Professor Maiken Umbach, Professor Mark Bailey and Professor Tim Bale, to give but a select ample, all left either because they were not given jobs in the Faculty or because they were not given the promotion they deserved, but, to be fair, no college and no faculty can keep all its stars. One could also point out that many other ambitious young historians, such as Andrew Roberts, Simon Sebag-Montefiore, Helen Castor and Justin Marrozi (to offer only a small sample just from Caius) preferred the freedom to leave Cambridge to operate largely outside the constraints of academia in order to write for a wider public and to enjoy the further rewards of television and the radio. More recently the young Caian art historian, Dr James Fox, has performed so brilliantly on television that he is being heralded as the new Simon Schama.

A single college such as Caius alone provides more than enough evidence to counter Plumb's misguided dismissal of Cambridge history. His own college could do much the same. Collectively the historians in the thirty-one Cambridge colleges make it sound quite absurd.

One could also simply point out that the Cambridge History Faculty almost invariably comes top of every national league-table for both research and teaching and quite recently came top of a world league table. There may not have been the same range of charismatic stars as those who shone so brilliantly in the sixties but the plateau of competence was exceptionally high. There was also less dead wood than in the old days. In his old age there was little point in arguing this case to Jack. By then he was past caring. Listening to him lacerating the reputations of the Cambridge professors you would have thought that all that was left was a wasteland of depressing mediocrity. It was quite untrue but he thought that he was well out it.

Few things earned Jack more enemies and more lasting hostility amongst his fellow historians than this ill-advised rant and ill-deserved comprehensive criticism of their work. It is important, however, to acknowledge that he was far from alone in this kind of sweeping criticism.

When Trevor-Roper was Master of Peterhouse, he often came to dine on Caius High Table, and his contemptuous denunciation of the Peterhouse historians, who had just elected him into the Mastership, more than matched Plumb's disobliging comments on the History Faculty. In Trevor-Roper's view, there was little or no justification for what he regarded as their absurdly over-inflated reputation. In his view, it was a reputation largely self-inflated: the undeserved result of a mutual admiration society created by historians ("all ideologues in search of a dogma") whose work was "not worth reading". Having dismissed them collectively, he then dismissed them individually: "Butterfield was a Methodist tub-preacher. Cowling is a resentful inner émigré from Anglicanism. Wormald is a convert to popery. Secondly, their writing is always opaque and circular and seldom finished – which hardly matters since it has no direction. Butterfield rambles round his Methodist tub. Wormald (as Noel Annan put it) 'wrote half a book, backwards'. Cowling is writing an open-ended part-work of which vol. 1 – the only one in print – leads nowhere. Williams flounders hopelessly in an alcoholic Irish bog." He sees "the whole lot of them as a gaggle of muddle-headed muffaroos bumbling and fumbling after each other in broken circles."

Richard Cobb could be equally scathingly dismissive of Cambridge historians. In 1968, he described the Cambridge historians of the French Revolution as so idle that they "never bothered to cross the Channel". They were, he said, "too fixed in their ways, too embedded in their comfortable colleges, even frequently to make the journey to London". He named one of them as "the arch-sloth" who had stayed there doing virtually nothing for sixty years.

Some might forgive these dismissive comments on Cambridge historians by Trevor-Roper and Cobb as part of the traditional tribalism between Oxford and Cambridge. They were not after all targeting their own university colleagues as Jack had so ill-advisedly and so unfairly done.

But such an excuse would not let Trevor-Roper off the hook if one also considers his comprehensive survey of the inadequacies of the Oxford professoriat. In what has been described as "a disguised manifesto" for the Regius Chair at Oxford, he declared that "we need a summary break with the present Oxford tradition, a tradition which has continued itself, *vi inertiae*, for thirty years. During those thirty years, in which the aims and methods of historical study have been profitably re-examined abroad, and important works published and new horizons envisaged, Oxford (as it seems to me) has become a backwater left ever further behind by the intellectual tide. Can anyone point to any serious historical book, or school of thought, or set of ideas, as being typical or worthy of Oxford in those years? Our professors … seem to think it positively indecent to risk error by writing anything: for may not some plodding pedant one day discover some new document which will overturn their rash conclusions? How much safer to edit, with factual and bibliographical footnotes, some hitherto deservedly unnoticed monastic laundry-book! Given this philosophy ... it is hardly surprising if historical writing, historical thought, has dwindled to a standstill in Oxford just when it has been rising, and raising most interest, in the rest of the world."

It was a comprehensive dismissal of the Oxford School of History which more than matched Jack's dismissal of Cambridge's History Faculty.

And Trevor-Roper's detailed individual dissection of each of Oxford's named professors more than matched Plumb's sweeping denunciation of Cambridge history in general.

Lest anyone should think his condemnation of Oxford history "too radical a statement", Trevor-Roper invited the reader to "Consider the facts. Of our seven historical professors today, only one (the Chichele Professor) has written so much as one original book... Of the other six professors, two (the Professors of Military History and International Relations) have not, so far as I can see, written so much as one article between them. The Professor of Modern History has usefully edited some documents but never ventured an opinion. The retiring Regius Professor, in his full career, has edited a text and published two short treatises on the prohibitive danger of seeking to interpret any such text. The Professor of Economic History has written three articles, all more or less on the same subject of aristocratic marriage settlements in the time of Queen Anne; and I believe that, had we but world enough and time, we could find, in obscure parish journals, one or two *trivia* by the Professor of Ecclesiastical History." He adds "It mortifies me to think that this is Oxford's contribution to historical study today."

Trevor-Roper conceded that "I know that there are articles which, though short, can be of disproportionate significance and can by themselves justify a career ... but I do not think that anyone would put the few articles of our Professors in that class."

Trevor-Roper also conceded that "it can be argued that a Professor reveals his quality not merely in his own writing but in the work of his pupils, in the 'school' he creates, so that a Professor who writes nothing at all may nevertheless be important by his influence. I agree. But where is the 'school' of any present Oxford professor? There is no such thing."

The important point about this dismissal of the quality of historical writing by Trevor-Roper is that it serves to highlight the significance of the dramatic change in the direction of travel pioneered by scholars such as Plumb.

Plumb's prolific publications stand in dramatic contrast to the meagre output of the previous generation of Oxbridge historians. They also stand in stark contrast in their aim to reach out to a much wider public. They were clearly not written to be read solely by other scholars. A professorial career based on a couple of articles on the same subject (which Trevor-Roper identified as so characteristic of Oxford) would have been thought derisory by Plumb.

So Plumb would have shared and welcomed most of these negative judgments, but he would have preferred Trevor-Roper to have delivered them publicly. Whereas when Plumb wrote off the Cambridge History Faculty *en masse* he did so in print. When Trevor Roper wrote off the Oxford professors *en masse* he did so in private. His letter was drafted to be sent to Sir John Masterman, the Provost of Worcester and his former tutor, who he knew was advising his former pupil, the patronage secretary, on the choice of the new Regius professor. Perhaps his characteristically shrewd discretion helps to explain why he became Regius Professor, and Jack's typically ill-advised public indiscretions helps to explain why he did not. Perhaps his discretion (and his easy access to the patronage secretary) also helps to explain why he became Lord Dacre whilst Jack remained Sir John.

The important point here is that Jack accepted and whole-heartedly agreed with the portrait of the thirty-year drought in Oxford. He thought much the same about Cambridge as he found it when he was doing his Ph.D. in the late 1930s. This was the period when he wrote to Snow saying: "As soon as possible I shall get out of academic history into writing, journalism – life on my own terms."

It is worth remembering that Jack was not a born scholar, not an obsessive foot-noting type of academic, not one so addicted to pure scholarship that he could be satisfied with the meticulous editing of rare texts. His talents were those of the communicator, the re-interpreter, the (in the best sense of the word) populariser, but he knew that he had left substantial and lasting monuments to the history of the eighteenth century – his two volumes of Walpole and his Ford Lectures.

They were fine works of scholarship. They were also a pleasure to read.

I am not alone in ranking them as Plumb's finest work. Geoffrey Parker recently wrote to me to say: *"Political Stability* remains a remarkable work. Kenyon always considered it Jack's best work, and I agree. In 2012, I had cause to re-read it for my Global Crisis book, cited it at some length, and included the following note: "I first heard Dr Plumb (as he then was) expound his thesis in Oxford in 1965, when I attended his Ford's lectures. It was a thrill to discover, 45 years later, that it still rings true."

I, too, have always ranked *The Growth of Political Stability,* together with his two great volumes on *Sir Robert Walpole,* as his most significant works of scholarship. I am possibly biased because these were the volumes in which I was most closely concerned whilst he was writing them, but I think that the dedications in them confirm my view that that is how he rated them.

23. PLUMB'S DEDICATIONS

Dedications can be a very revealing guide to an author's assessment of his own work and Jack dedicated his best work to his teachers, his patrons and his pupils – many of whom were also his friends. Duty dictated that his first book, his best-selling *Penguin History of the Eighteenth Century*, should be dedicated to his mother; long-term friendship led others to be dedicated to the Williams, the Campaillas, Sydney Grose, John Burrow and the Nobletts; an enduring sense of gratitude led yet another to be dedicated to the Rothschilds. But he always said that his best books were dedicated to those to whom he owed the greatest debt of gratitude. So the first volume of *Walpole: The Making of a Statesman* was dedicated to the Marquess and the Marchioness of Cholmondeley whom he always rightly regarded as his most significant patrons; the second volume of *Walpole: The King's Minister* was dedicated to Bert Howard, whom he always rightly regarded as his most significant early mentor and motivator; and his Ford Lectures, published as *The Growth of Political Stability*, were dedicated to me – this was probably mainly in recognition of an enduring friendship, but back in 1967 he also had an exaggerated view of my future significance as a pupil.

Curiously he never dedicated any of his books to Snow. Snow was arguably the most important and longest-lasting influence on Jack from his schooldays right through to old age. Snow always retained the aura of the senior, more successful friend, guide and advisor. In spite of his poor track record as a skilful planner and plotter of Jack's attempt to climb the greasy pole of social and academic success, Jack remained curiously dependent on his advice. Just as he asked Snow how to get into Cambridge in the late 1920s so he continued to ask him in the 1970s for his advice about how best to attract the favourable attention of the Patronage Secretary. When it came to the successful pursuit of honours Jack regarded Snow as the acknowledged master. In this particular relationship Jack, very uncharacteristically, always seemed to accept his junior and subordinate role. Snow was always accorded the respect due to someone who had collected his C.B.E in 1948, his knighthood in 1957 and his peerage in 1964, who had become a Minister of the Crown and achieved the status of international guru – not to mention his being a highly successful novelist. Snow enjoyed dispensing advice to his juniors almost as much as Jack did, and Jack was quite willing to listen and to learn. I can recall Snow solemnly informing him about how to respond to the slightest signs of interest from the Establishment. "Jack you must accept invitations to the Palace Garden Parties for tea – they take note of refusals", "Jack, you must accept a C.B.E. if that is all they offer you at first – if you turn it down they won't give you the higher honours you want and, of course, deserve", "We must mobilise support for your knighthood – we will need letters of support from the right people. I will fix it for you". Jack would gratefully and humbly lap up the advice.

He also rallied to the cause whenever Snow asked him for his support – as when Leavis launched his ferociously polemical attack on Snow, calling him a failed scientist, a failed novelist and a failed politician. Jack took up his pen and lambasted Leavis as a literary Romantic peddling absurdly ill-informed historical nonsense, offering versions of the prelapsarian myth that bordered on historical illiteracy.

Common enemies could still inspire vigorous reassertions of old loyalties, but the Snow-Plumb relationship became increasingly ambivalent as the years past. For decades they had maintained a vigorous correspondence. In the years in which Snow was "in full blizzard" in his writing and publishing and pontificating, and when the annual harvests of Plumb's publications were at their richest and most prolific, they still found time to write to each other – frequently and at length – as the Snow archive in Texas and the Plumb archive in Cambridge amply prove. But in the later years they both grew somewhat mistrustful of the other. Both politically and socially they were moving apart, and Jack grew quite paranoid about some excessively revealing interviews given by Snow, in which he became convinced that Snow had falsely accused him of various sexual deviations. When Snow died in 1980, they were no longer very close. Their relationship had noticeably cooled since the time when Jack and Pamela Hansford Johnson and I were the only celebrants of Snow's knighthood on New Year's Eve 1956 before it was announced on 1st January 1957. They kept rather intermittently in touch but by the mid-1970s it seemed quite improbable that either would wish to dedicate one of their books to the other. By then, neither was any longer in the full flood of publishing new work. By then, neither was producing their best work. Ambivalent they may have been but ancient respect would have made them both wary of dedicating anything but their best to the other. Both, by then, were in decline as major writers. Both had begun, with anger and fury, to accept that most unwelcome truth.

24. PLUMB'S OTHER WRITING

It is important, however, that the decline in Jack's output is not exaggerated. His major scholarly output did not long outlast the 1960s and early 1970s, but the quantity of what he wrote and published held up surprisingly well. Admittedly, his best days were behind him. By the 1980s, he lacked both the desire and the rude health that would have allowed him to conduct sustained in-depth research but he certainly kept on writing. His journalism sustained him longer than his scholarship, and his output of books right up to his retirement, and even after it, would still put many scholars to shame. It is obviously a rather crude measure but the University Library Catalogue (although far from complete) includes forty-four separate publications by him and their distribution by date is not without interest: in the 1940s, nil; in the 1950s 4; in the 1960s 12; in the 1970s 12; in the 1980s 13; in the1990s 2; and for the year 2000 just one. Obviously there is an element of double counting involved in these figures, which include new editions and collected essays and such like, but such books still had to be compiled, edited and seen through the press. The figures show an almost perfect Gaussian curve, starting gently in his forties, maintaining a high plateau in his fifties, sixties and seventies, and understandably descending abruptly in his eighties. That an old man in very poor health stopped publishing significant new work in his eighties seems to me to be very forgivable. It is true that there are exceptional men, such as Joseph Needham and Philip Grierson and Asa Briggs and Owen Chadwick, who continued to publish significant scholarly works in their eighties and even nineties, but all of these great figures were blessed with exceptional good health, an obsessive commitment to scholarship and very generous support from research assistants. Jack had none of those advantages in his last decades.

He also had many other commitments. His personal papers provide ample evidence of his once prodigious energy and his once remarkable stamina. Few academics will leave such a massive personal archive as Jack Plumb. Quite apart from his books and in spite of earnest filleting by his executors, there are nearly 150 feet of shelf-space in the Cambridge University Library dedicated to his personal diaries and his personal correspondence. Bill Noblett has read the first nine thousand of his letters and has only got to the letter P in the alphabetically arranged collection in the University Library. The shifting nature of Jack's preoccupations can be traced in the great swathes of these letters, ranging from those to Namier and Snow in his earnest youth to those

171

to his royal chums in his old age. His wine diaries alone contain millions of words. In addition to his archive in the University Library in Cambridge, there are substantial satellite collections of his letters elsewhere. Snow's side of the Plumb-Snow correspondence was sold by Snow, along with the rest of his literary archive, to the University of Texas at Austin. All of the massive Plumb-McKendrick correspondence (written over a fifty year period) is safely stored in my rooms in Caius.

Compared with the monumental archives of Asa and Susan Briggs, Jack's papers are, admittedly, mere Alps lurking in the shadow of two towering Himalayas, but when compared with the modest little Gog and Magog hills that most Cambridge academics produce, Jack's Alps look seriously mountainous and truly impressive. If Asa Briggs was a Gladstone in his production of personal papers, Jack was at least a Walpole and what could be more appropriate than that.

His papers show that there was far more to Jack's life than his academic concerns alone.

25. PLUMB'S OTHER PUPILS AND PLUMB THE NOVELIST MANQUÉ

It is worth remembering that Jack taught many successful pupils who did not follow him into the historical profession, and many of those who did become historians did not follow him into his chosen area of specialisation.

Jack had no desire to create a narrowly based Plumb school of history. He had no desire to see his pupils all beavering away on the history of early eighteenth-century politics. At a time in Cambridge when some historians were cruising the streets in search of research students who would all work with them in the same concentrated field, Jack positively encouraged us to seek our own fields to conquer.

He took as much delight in those of his pupils who left history altogether to go and seek success in politics, journalism, business, industry and even the Church. He took legitimate pride in his bishops, such as Michael Manktelow, once Chaplain at Christ's and later Bishop of Basingstoke, and John Taylor, Bishop of St. Albans, not to mention the Rev Dr Gary Bennett, who was Dean of New College, Oxford; his academic administrators, such as Professor Sir Lawrence Martin, Vice-Chancellor of Newcastle University and later head of Chatham House and Professor Maurice Kogan, acting Vice-Chancellor of Brunel and Director of the Centre for the Evaluation of Public Policy; his politicians, such as John Schofield Allen, John Lee, M.P., and his only peer, Norman Hunt; his ambassadors, such as Sir Roderick Braithwaite and John Gay; his businessmen, such as Ian Strachan, once head of BTR; his journalists such as Michael Ratcliffe and Peter Oborne; his librarians, such as William Noblett of the Cambridge University Library; his museum directors, such as John Jacob, head of the Walker Gallery in Liverpool and Kenwood House, and Charles Saumarez Smith, head of the National Portrait Gallery; his writers, such as Andrew Wheatcroft; his civil servants, such as Sir Clive Whitmore, Sir Robert Culpin and Alistair Breeze; and his renegade historians, such as Ian Lister who switched subjects and became Professor of Education at York. All of these he taught and supported en route to their successful careers. The list could be effortlessly extended. The Plumb diaspora is in many ways more impressive in its outer reaches than those who have remained in Cambridge as historians.

Jack did briefly run a successful graduate seminar. It was a dazzling one at that (including John Brewer, Roy Porter, Simon Schama, Keith Wrightson, Linda Colley, Richard Tuck, Derek Hirst, John Miller et al.) but what is striking is how so many of these outstanding historians have scattered their interests over a wide range of countries, cultures and centuries. They include social, economic, political and cultural historians. They include historians of Holland, Spain, Portugal and England. They include historians of science and medicine and madness, historians of art and culture and historians of consumption; not to mention military historians, demographic historians and even constitutional and intellectual historians. He was never seeking to produce a school of co-workers after the Germanic Eltonian model. The temperaments of those he chose did not lend themselves to the worker-bee approach. They would not have been content to buzz away together in a restrictive historical hive designed by Jack Plumb. A single approach to a single issue was neither their style nor that of their mentor. As Jack once wrote, "My delight in their success has been strengthened greatly because their field of work has been distinct from my own. I have never regarded research students or bright undergraduates as fodder for my own researches. They are all independent scholars in their own right, owing nothing to me but talk and encouragement".

One has to remember, too, that in some ways Jack Plumb was a frustrated novelist. The novel he wrote in his youth (revealingly entitled *Mutual Torment*) got very close to publication. Its rejection probably saved him for History, but for all his undoubted public success as an historian he always had regrets that he had not become a novelist. He found the company of novelists much more exciting than the company of academics; and the praise for his written work that he most treasured was the whole page review by Grahame Greene in *The Evening Standard* welcoming an historian who could really write. It is, perhaps, not without significance that when I reached for further tributes to his distinctive skills as an historian, I found them most readily available in the generous words of Lord Snow and Sir Angus Wilson – both novelists of distinction who could readily respond to his human insights and his memorable prose.

He frequently bewailed the fact that an historian needs archives. How he would have loved, he said, to travel with only his imagination as holiday baggage. In old age he tried to write short stories but found that his imaginative spark had gone. Anyone who has spent much time with him will recall how he could never resist imagining the life stories of even complete strangers. Sit with Jack at a Parisian pavement cafe or in a pub in East Anglia or the Ritz in London or the Carlyle in New York and he would draw your attention to someone at a nearby table and start to weave a rich and plausible life story about them. Sexual prurience (always of a heterosexual kind) always played a large part in these fantasies, as did imaginings about the frustrations that dogged their lives, the compulsions that drove them into unfortunate relationships, and the compromises and disappointments they had learned to live with. Sometimes in French cafés, thinking that speaking in English made him somehow un-hearable or at least incomprehensible, he would fail to lower his voice and would be in full flow imagining the golden thighs of the past that had once lurked under the ample skirts and even more ample flesh of the present. "Just imagine what her pert young bottom and breasts must have been like", he would loudly declare only for the unfortunate subject of his musings to leap to her feet and leave saying in perfect English "I can't stand any more of that appalling dirty old man!" He never seemed to learn and the incident was repeated in my presence on more than one occasion.

To the end he never really gave up being a novelist manqué.

26. PLUMB'S CHANGING POLITICAL BELIEFS AND THE BLUNT AFFAIR: FROM COMMUNIST SYMPATHISER TO COMBATIVE TORY

Jack liked to shock and he never ceased to surprise. After half a century as a passionate Socialist, he suddenly embraced Thatcherism with an ardour that astonished his friends. It was no gentle drift to the Right. He never lingered in the centre ground. He now quoted with approval one of his new heroine's better known sayings, "Stand in the middle of the road and you get run over in both directions", and in consequence moved decisively away from his ardent socialist convictions.

As he moved ever further to the Right, he met the appalled response of his old liberal friends with the smug retort "There's no rage like the rage of the convert". Many of his friends had, with age and maturity, moved to the Right with him, but for many very old friends, it seemed an unforgivable betrayal of their youthful enthusiasms. For the socialist and republican Jack (with whom they had once caroused in provincial pubs) now to be a familiar of the Royal Family and to sing the praises of Lady Thatcher and Lord Tebbitt was, to them, as much an outrage as for their once adored Brigitte Bardot now to sing the praises of the right-wing populist Le Pen. It seemed like an unacceptable affront and a betrayal of old loyalties. To old friends such as Cecil Howard and Gordon Winterton, it seemed to spell the end of the youthful dreams of social justice that they had once so ardently shared. It also spelt the end of their years of close friendship. They simply could not forgive what they saw as treachery.

Gordon Winterton, for instance, never wavered in his fervent socialist beliefs and was understandably delighted when his daughter Rosie grew up to share his political views and was elected as the Labour member for Doncaster. The stark divergence between the political trajectories in later life of Jack and the Wintertons is vividly illustrated by the fact that whilst he had moved well to the right of Margaret Thatcher, Winterton's daughter is now the Right Honourable Dame Rosie Winterton, M.P., DBE, P.C., former Shadow Chief Whip and currently Deputy Speaker of the House of Commons. Jack in his old age was light years away from the political aims that he and Winterton had once so fiercely espoused and so fervently shared. Winterton had stayed faithfully true to his convictions whilst Jack had completely abandoned his and took great pleasure in saying so. Together with his affairs with the wives of several old friends, it was yet another reason for the unforgiving and permanent end of many of his early close friendships. When William Noblett rang up Gordon Winterton to tell him of Plumb's death, he was met with such a violent denunciation of his old friend, now such a committed Tory, that Noblett had to ring off.

In an answer to a question after his Lady Margaret lecture at Christ's, David Cannadine gave a very charitable explanation for Jack's dramatic change of political allegiance. He said that he thought that it was Jack's instinctive sympathy for the self-made, upwardly mobile provincial girl from Grantham that drew him to support Thatcher. It was a charmingly sweet explanation – Jack feeling sorry for the way the metropolitan élite made fun of her voice and her elocution lessons and her earnest efforts at self-improvement. There is probably a considerable element of truth in it. It chimes well with Geoffrey Parker's observation to me that "although Jack was solicitous for all his students, I believe he looked out with especial care for those of us who came from the Midlands: me from Nottingham as well as you from Leicester, of course – but also Bill Noblett, Peter Musgrave and others". Like Thatcher, the daughter of a grocer who was the product of Grantham Girls Grammar School, those whom Parker picked out as receiving especially sympathetic treatment from Plumb were all the humbly-born, modestly-financed, upwardly-mobile products mainly from Midland grammar schools, often regarded with some condescension in the prevailing public school ethos in much of Cambridge.

Jack, himself, offered a more brutal explanation for his change of political allegiance. His answer was on the lines of the reply from the bank-robber when asked why he robbed banks: "Because that's where the money is, stupid!" Jack said he switched to the Tories "because that's where the power is, stupid!" There were plenty of provincial, self-made politicians in the Labour party to empathise with, but they no longer had the power and the patronage that interested Jack. There were, of course, other motives and other reasons. As the Labour Party, in his eyes, seemed set on self-destruction, choosing the wrong leaders and allowing the Trade Unions seemingly unfettered powers which they were only too happy to abuse, he felt that it had become as unelectable as it was to him now so very unattractive. So like many radicals of the Left, he became a radical of the Right – devoted to breaking the power of the Union Barons and devoted to restoring the Grammar School system to which he not unreasonably gave most of the credit for allowing humbly born boys like Snow and him and me the chance of a university education. As his income continued to grow, a low-tax party seemed increasingly attractive. As he moved in ever smarter social circles, their traditional conservative views seemed to grow ever more appealing. But since the Labour party, which in the 1960s he thought was set for office throughout his lifetime, had not delivered the honours that he felt his support and achievements deserved, he decided, as he put it, "to try the other side". He received his knighthood in 1982 under a Conservative government run by Mrs Thatcher.

Just how left-wing Jack was in his early days in Cambridge is difficult now to assess. Rumour (and reports from some of his surviving friends) suggests that J. D. Bernal propositioned both him and Snow to join the Communist Party. They were certainly sympathisers in the 1930s. Some say that at least one of them accepted the invitation to join, they certainly discussed doing so, but the majority vote seems to be that they refused. Some claim that Jack was certainly an active and card-carrying member and some Cambridge contemporaries of his claimed that he boasted to them that he had formally joined the party. He may well have done so but I have found no wholly convincing evidence of this, and in later life he resolutely denied that this was true. He and Snow were certainly passionately anti-Nazi and anti-Fascist. They were outraged by Munich and appalled by Neville Chamberlain. They certainly discussed leaving England before the war in the expectation that an ill-prepared country would lose any forthcoming conflict.

It is, perhaps, worth recording one old friend's mature judgment that Jack would have been ripe for seduction if Anthony Blunt had propositioned him. In his view "socially, politically, aesthetically and even sexually Blunt held all the cards and had he cared to play them Jack would have found the invitation to join that private world quite irresistible". I think that this is a very perceptive view. The record certainly suggests that Blunt's world would have appealed very strongly to Jack's youthful ambitions. In that world he would be an outsider who was also an insider. He would be radical but smart. Above all, it would signal that he was accepted in Cambridge. For there can be no doubt that in the 1930s, he longed to join the Cambridge "smart set". He longed to be invited to join the Apostles – the semi-secret intellectual society, famous for its distinguished members and later notorious for including three of the five Cambridge spies. He always used to say in later life that the key to the inner world of King's was through the "homintern" and the key to acceptance in Trinity was through the "commintern". Alas, from his point of view the keys were never offered to him. According to his own account, he was invited once to Blunt's exquisite rooms in Trinity, but the invitation was never repeated. As he put it, rather coarsely, "I don't think he liked my smell".

One needs to remember that in the anti-fascist days of Cambridge in the 1930s, communist sympathies were part of the common currency of much academic life. Jack certainly shared those sympathies as did many others known to me. In my own college, Joseph Needham (later Master of Caius) and Philip Grierson (later President of Caius) both loudly professed their support for the Communist party, but as Philip Grierson explained to me he was never an actual member because he "wasn't much of a joiner".

In those days Jack was certainly an ardent socialist. His first published work *The History of Equity Shoemaking* which came out when he was twenty-four was doctrinaire to an extreme degree. It was vehemently anti-capitalist in tone and looked forward to revolutionary social and political change with undisguised approval. His close friends were equally ardent in their political opinions. I can remember him often quoting with approval the words of Bert Howard, who, whenever he saw the rolling green pastureland of English country houses, used to growl "the sooner that lot is ploughed up for the benefit of the workers the better". In those days, Jack was all for punitive tax rates and swingeing death duties. Super-tax was seen as an unambiguously good thing. When he was faced with such taxes himself, he took a rather less progressive view.

His reactions to those in the thirties who allowed their left-wing sympathies to lead them into spying for Russia changed dramatically over time. I can recall him explaining how easily anti-fascism and anti-Nazi feelings could make Russia and communism seem the only answer in pre-war Britain. I can recall his robust reaction to some Oxford put-downs of Cambridge as the breeding ground of spies – "When Oxford was playing at being *Brideshead Revisited,* Cambridge was changing the world". On the other hand, I can recall in the 1980s his threat to resign from the British Academy if it failed to expel the self-confessed traitor, Sir Anthony Blunt. As was so often the case with Jack, his views were not always consistent, and they certainly changed with age and his new political allegiances.

Plumb played a major role in the battle over whether or not to expel Blunt from the Academy after Margaret Thatcher had revealed his clandestine career as a Soviet spy who had passed on to the Russians the knowledge of how Bletchley was able to decipher the German wartime codes. Blunt had been unmasked as early as 1963, but had confessed in return for a promise of immunity from prosecution. MI5 had agreed to keep the matter secret for fifteen years and on the 5th of November 1979 Mrs Thatcher announced his guilt to the House of Commons. Jack Plumb was infuriated that Sir Anthony Blunt, Knight of the Realm, Surveyor of the Queen's pictures, Fellow of the

British Academy and Honorary Fellow of Trinity College, Cambridge had been able to enjoy these honours for so many years as an unmasked traitor.

He thought that all these honours should be promptly and publicly stripped away and did his best to encourage others to join him in making sure that they were. His own efforts were characteristically robust.

On the 16th of November 1979, he wrote to Sir Kenneth Dover the President of the British Academy:

"Dear Dover,

I hope that immediate action will be taken to expel Anthony Blunt from the Academy. I do not think that we should harbour traitors."

Yours sincerely,

Jack Plumb

If he had hoped that by showing quick and decisive leadership, he would impress the Academy, he was to prove to be sadly mistaken. His initiative was to ignite a ferocious and long running feud

Initially Dover's reply was to point out that, whilst he shared "your sentiments about traitors", immediate action was not procedurally possible. He went on to warn Plumb that "You may find that many Fellows will be sympathetic (as I am not) to E.M. Forster's declaration, 'If I were ever forced to choose whether to betray a friend or to betray my country, I hope I would have the guts to betray my country'. His warning that expelling Blunt might not be straightforward proved to be only too true.

Poor Dover was caught between warring factions and he knew all too well that there was no way that he could please both. It was not that he was shy of controversy. His famous book on *Greek Homosexuality*, which came out in 1978, was noted for its unprecedented openness and it use of explicit sexual evidence. His later autobiography shocked Oxford even more. First with its revelations about Dover and his wife's sex life in their sixties, and then with its open admission that, when he was President of Corpus Christi, his reaction to a troublesome history don (Trevor Aston) was to think "long and hard how to murder him" and to wonder "how to kill him without getting into trouble". When Aston committed suicide he then admitted to "immense relief".

As President of the Academy, his attempts at impartiality in the Blunt affair seemed to infuriate both sides.

Led by Plumb on one side and A.J.P.Taylor on the other, there ensued a bitter battle between those who agreed with Plumb and those who thought that the only legitimate justification for removing an honour awarded entirely for scholarly distinction would be academic misconduct, such as stealing someone else's work. Expulsion for reasons, however reprehensible, which had nothing to do with the criteria that had led to the election, could only it was argued bring the Academy into disrepute.

Plumb narrowly won the first round of the battle when the Council of the Academy voted by nine votes to eight to bring a motion for Blunt's expulsion before the annual general meeting of the Fellows. At that meeting he decisively lost the battle when the Fellows voted by 42 votes to 20, with 25 abstentions, to move to the next business. Plumb did not give up and campaigned vigorously to reverse the decision, further angering such heavyweights as Trevor-Roper, Eric Hobsbawn and A.J.P. Taylor. Eventually Blunt was asked to consider resignation and dutifully fell on his sword. He was also stripped of his knighthood and his Honorary Fellowship of Trinity (resigning from Trinity at the last minute after being tipped off that he was just about to be expelled). Plumb had eventually succeeded in his campaign but it was something of a hollow victory. He acquired some staunch allies, but it also served to win him a great many new and unforgiving enemies in the academic world and especially in the Academy. When Dover stood down, Plumb's eternal nemesis, Owen Chadwick was elected as President.

The battle was fought in the press and in private. It was still going strong in early 1981 when Taylor wrote a piece for *Encounter* that ended with a damning and, as it turned out, defamatory last paragraph attacking Jack Plumb and Robert Blake in the following terms:

"I grudgingly admire the persistence of the witch hunters, so much more determined than that of the defenders of intellectual liberty. The cause of the minority has perhaps more conviction about it as obscurancy often has. They were also men of power. Lord Blake was Provost of Queens College, Oxford; Professor Plumb, Master of Christ's College, Cambridge. This suggests a variation of Connolly's Law ("Inside every fat man there is a thin man struggling to get out") – inside some heads of Colleges Senator McCarthy is struggling to get out. In this case the Senator succeeded."

To be likened to the infamous Senator Joseph McCarthy and his Communist witch-hunting was about as offensive as one could go in the academic world. It was intended to be provocative and it certainly provoked its two main targets.

Blake wrote to Plumb saying: "Many thanks for your letter. I have seen AJPT's diatribe ... I thought of legal action or the threat of it for I agree with you that to call people like ourselves 'McCarthyites' must be defamatory ... I had not thought of telling Lasky (the editor of *Encounter*) to consult his lawyers. That was a very good idea on your part". The good idea seemed to have worked because Blake's next letter said: "Your veiled menace seems to have been very effective ... I was a bit feeble in merely replying to AJPT and demanding a withdrawal which, I am now sure would never have been forthcoming".

Plumb's victory proved to be something of a pyrrhic one, because although Blunt's resignation was welcomed by much of the press and although Plumb received many letters of congratulation for leading the charge against him, his success simply confirmed him as a controversial figure who was firmly in a minority of the Fellows of the Academy.

In the highly charged moral debate which took place in the public press, some such as Robert Blake, Ian Christie, John Ehrman and Norman Gash had steadfastly supported him in arguing that the failure of the Fellows to expel Blunt was "deplorable, damaging, discreditable and morally dubious", but on balance he made far more enemies than allies and many major figures never forgave him.

By the time that Alan Bennett's brilliant *A Question of Attribution* appeared on stage in 1988 and then appeared on television in 1991, much more was known about Blunt's twenty-five year career as a Soviet spy. Bennett used a question of whether or not a favourite Titian in the Royal collection was a forgery as an inspired theatrical metaphor for what constitutes a fake and what were the arguments for exposing it or not. Bennett's artful use of the Queen as an apparently innocent enquirer into what secrets could be concealed behind the appealing surface of a well-known and highly respected image gave a particular poignancy to the debate about the unmasking of a trusted servant of the Crown.

By then the heat had gone out of the Academy's debate over the Blunt scandal, but by then Plumb's decisive move to the Right in his political sympathies was so well established that it made little difference to how he was regarded.

To justify his new political sympathies, he often quoted with approval the famous question by Maynard Keynes "When my information changes, I alter my conclusions. What do you do?" This glib justification cut little ice with many old friends and admirers. His dramatic move to the Right probably earned him as many unforgiving critics as did his unwise dismissal of the state of Cambridge history, because the Left never forgave him and the Right never really believed him.

A typical example of how dramatically left wing historians reacted to his political conversion is to be found in Sir Richard Evans' magisterial study of Eric Hobsbawm, who in later life was one of the most famous historians in the world. Professor Evans records that in his Cambridge days at King's, Hobsbawm did not get on well with the other dons or indeed with those in the History Faculty "which was still at the time notably conservative both politically and methodologically. One exception was … J.H. (Jack) Plumb, a brilliant historian of eighteenth-century English politics who was still at this time on the political left. 'He was a man of great abilities', Eric remembered later, 'and I liked talking to him in the 50's, though I never had close contact with him after he stopped being a 1930's Red.' Hobsbawn "could never understand how he came to end up such a political reactionary" and, in consequence, was later brutally dismissive of his old friend and colleague. After a party thrown by George Weidenfeld in New York, he wrote: "I said hello at the bar to Jack (Sir John) Plumb, who once commissioned Christopher (Hill) and myself to write books for Penguin (*Industry and Empire*) and is now a rich unhappy old reactionary and lonely gay."

What makes that description particularly sad, was that, although their political commitments had diverged so dramatically, they had also once been and still were two distinguished historians committed in Professor Evans's words "to writing serious history for a readership beyond the limits of academia" and sharing this aim at a time when doing this "while pursuing an academic career was by no means easy".

Hobsbawm's description of academic history, before academics such as J.H. Plumb and A.J.P. Taylor and himself transformed it in the middle of the twentieth century, might have been written word for word by Plumb: "there was a time when British academic historians would have been shocked to think of themselves as potential paperback writers, i.e. writers for a broad public. Between the world wars hardly any historians of standing did, other than G.M. Trevelyan. Many of them even shied away from writing books of any kind, hoping to make their reputations with learned articles in specialist journals and savage reviews of other colleagues unwise enough to bare themselves between hard covers."

They both shared the view that "obsolescence is the unavoidable fate of the historian". They both believed that the only ones whose work was likely to survive were those whose writing "attained the status of literature". They both ranked the work of Gibbon, and Macaulay and Trevelyan as far more significant in the long term as those learned scholars who wrote only for fellow academics. They had both helped massively to change the direction of travel of academic history.

Yet in their more mature years they had diverged to an unbridgeable degree. Where once there had been friendship, mutual admiration and common academic goals, there was now a yawning gulf – largely the result of their political differences. Just as Plumb and A.J.P. Taylor had irrevocably split over the Blunt and the British Academy affair, so Hobsbawn and Plumb had irrevocably split over Plumb's political lurch to the Right.

27. PLUMB'S GENEROSITY TO HIS STAFF, HIS FRIENDS AND HIMSELF

In both his socialist and his Thatcherite guises, Plumb had a very ambivalent relationship with those who looked after him – whether it was his secretaries, his drivers or those who cooked for him and waited on him. Indeed one of the things he was most criticised for by his enemies and most praised for by himself was his treatment of the college staff. He used the same mixture that he used on his pupils – a combination of extravagant praise and excoriating blame. He often mixed extreme financial generosity with unspeakable verbal mean-ness. This, he claimed was the way to treat staff – the financial generosity showed that he appreciated excellent service, the harsh rebukes showed that he would not tolerate inadequate service. He thought that, as a result, he was brilliant at handling both the college servants and his own staff.

Others were much more doubtful. I recall being astonished by the violence of his language when he was discussing those who looked after him: of his bed-maker who looked after him for many years on O staircase in Christs', he wrote: "She's really a frightful bloody slut. My rooms were a shambles when I got back. She's just a dirty Irish peasant." As she had looked after me for five years on the same staircase, I knew how outrageously unfair this judgement was. There were, alas, many other such unjustified reactions. Those members of his staff who were kindest to him often suffered the worst. Many of us were very severely embarrassed, for instance, by the fact that he never gave his last secretary, Mrs Lily Volans, a raise in her wages over the course of thirteen years and left her nothing in his will, although she had maintained a stoic and saintly calm and served him faithfully in the face of appalling rudeness in his later years. On the other hand, others such as Paul Davies, the current college butler at Christ's, received £5,000; Robert Robb, his chauffeur received £2,000; and the sum of £1,500 was left to pay for three parties – one for the Porters, one for the Maintenance staff and one for the Kitchen staff. That he could be financially generous – both before and after his death – to some of those who looked after him is not in doubt, but for many that could not justify the peremptory rudeness to which they were often publicly subjected.

Many tolerantly forgave him and indeed became quite fond of "the old bastard" as many of them called him. Cambridge can be a breeding house for eccentric and colourful characters and I suspect that many simply put "Sir John" into that useful category. As one of them said to me, "It's rarely boring when Sir John is around!" Not everyone could be quite so forgiving. Many of his old friends must have allowed themselves a wry smile when they read an editorial in the *Cambridge Daily News* and a piece in *The Times* Diary praising a don who really knew how to show his gratitude to those who looked after him. As so often was the case with Jack, this part of his make-up was as full of contradictions as were the sexual, political and social aspects of his complicated life.

Such a complex personality inevitably subjected some of Jack's friendships to strain. Not all of them survived, but most of his friends eventually accepted the fact that, as one of them put it, "the stimulation was worth the aggravation, the fun was worth the fury". Over the years, most of us came to realise that he saw it as his self-appointed task to set the academic and career standards we were supposed to live up to. In doing so, he amused and outraged us, encouraged and deflated us, flattered and denounced us, cajoled and contradicted us, informed and corrected us, entranced and enraged us, inspired and provoked us – all with the intent (sometimes with the insistence) of exhorting and educating us to the levels he aspired to on our behalf. If we did not always achieve the levels he set for us, it could be fun trying to do so. And when it wasn't fun, it was always memorable. Jack Plumb made good copy. His turn of phrase made him eminently quotable. His trenchant judgements made good stories – and, sometimes, unforgiving enemies. His material generosity made him a splendid host. His generosity of spirit made him a splendid exemplar. His encyclopaedic knowledge made him a splendid teacher.

He will, of course, be remembered best by historians for the impact of his work on what is known as "Plumb's century", but in London, New York and Cambridge (and in much of academia at large) he will, perhaps, be remembered even more for his ebullient personality which expressed itself in not only his erudition but in his enthusiasm and his enjoyment of the good things of life. For he played as hard as he worked. In his later years, he was increasingly seen by many simply as an entrepreneur, a bon viveur and a bon vivant, a connoisseur of food and wine, and a collector of fine silver and porcelain. Not for Plumb the life of the cloistered and ascetic scholar, not for Plumb the life of the remote and ineffectual don. He lived his life to the full. More dined against than dining, more wined against than wining, more partied against that partying, he almost always gave more than he received. He had little time for what he called "the quiet rich", he abhorred meanness, and he spent his money with as much gusto as he earned it.

A revealing vignette of his characteristic attitude to life emerged during the making of *Royal Heritage*. Plumb wanted to present an image of George IV on his deathbed in April 1830, when the King called for his breakfast and consumed two pigeons, three beefsteaks, three parts of a bottle of Moselle, a glass of champagne, two of port and one of brandy. To Plumb's great regret he was overruled, but he noted, wistfully and admiringly, "what a marvellous appetite for life that man had". He was equally sympathetic to the appetites (sexual and otherwise) of Edward VII, also popularly known as "Edward the Caresser".

Once having achieved the necessary prosperity, he too gloried in his luxurious lifestyle.

His college rooms were far more opulent than those of most dons. Fine paintings adorned the walls, fine claret and champagne flowed with abandon and up to 1990 his collection of Vincennes and Sèvres was far superior to many museum collections. His cellar remained the finest in Cambridge for most of his life, until he realized that he could never (even with the most enthusiastic help of his friends) drink his way through it, and decided to let most of it go.

In old age, his property interests dramatically shrank. The Old Rectory in Westhorpe had gone; Le Moulin de la Ressence at Plan de la Tour (in which he had negotiated a time-share with its owner Michael Behrens) had gone; and he no longer even rented Quinta Rebecca on the Algarve or borrowed La Jalousie near the twin Pitons on St Lucia. He retained a non-financial interest in his pied-a-terre twenty-two stories up in the Carlyle in New York where he was still known as Sir Plumb by the porters, but increasingly he shrank back like a tortoise into its shell and rarely ventured out from his fine but increasingly shabby rooms in Christ's. At least, the carpets and chairs were shabby. Even after the great sales of the 1990s, the vitrines were still full of everyday Sèvres; the mantelpiece still supported early Chelsea and fine faience; the Schofield candlesticks still gleamed; and the glow from the enchanting Cuyp of the young girl clutching her dog's lead in one hand and a pretzel in the other was matched by a splendid supporting cast consisting, amongst many other distinguished paintings, of the Jacob van Hulsdonck still life (which he often plausibly attributed to grander artists), the Waterloo landscape, and the portrait of George IV by Sir Thomas Lawrence. Obviously there is shabby and there is opulent shabby.

An unusually generous college allowed him to occupy three sets of rooms. He finally occupied almost the whole of O Staircase in Christ's First Court where he had lived since 1946, but although his college empire never shrank he recognised extreme old age by starting to shed more and more of his possessions. He sold the best of his French porcelain for a million dollars (much of it to his friend Robert Pirie); he sold his best silver for a six-figure sum; he even sold a quarter of million pounds worth of his wine at Christies; and much else was discreetly sold or given away.

When his will was published, some of his colleagues expressed surprise that he had left only £1.3 million, but allowance should be made for what he had already given away and what he spent during his lifetime. For many decades he lived a very extravagant lifestyle – flying on Concorde, hiring hugely expensive villas abroad, hosting large and opulent dinner parties for his grand London friends, serving wines of the finest quality and often breathtaking value, driving extremely expensive cars and eating in the most expensive restaurants in London, New York and the whole of France, serving meals on solid silver, giving at times very expensive presents and hiring a chauffeur not only for himself but often also for his visiting guests as well.

His charitable giving matched his self-indulgence. Substantial lifetime gifts to Christ's, a steady trickle of generous annual grants to young historians from the Sir John Plumb Charitable trust, and many personal gifts had significantly eroded his personal fortune. He was, for instance, extremely generous to those he called his anti-God children or his pseudo-adopted grandchildren. I know of several who received gifts of £20,000, and this was at a time when such a sum could be of life-altering significance in providing a deposit on a first house or flat.

Some random gifts could be of breath-taking generosity, such as the "loan" he gave to one of my daughter's boyfriends who had casually admitted that it was his ambition to fly around the world to compete in kayak races in New Zealand. It was first offered as a gift but, when this was rejected as being impossibly generous, Jack said "Well regard it as a loan but don't hurry to think of paying it back". That young man is now a headmaster in New Zealand. The loan was never called in by Jack.

Some of his individual gifts to his friends could also be of breath-taking generosity. When Melveena and I married in 1967 he gave us, as a wedding present, Graham Sutherland's beautiful painting of "The Crucifixion" painted in 1964. Later he gave to Melveena a portrait of me by Steven Hubbard to mark my fiftieth birthday, and then gave a portrait of Melveena by John Ward to me to mark my sixtieth birthday. Other presents, as we shall see, were part of a more complex web of gift exchange.

Some gifts were more Machiavellian in intent. When my wife and I (partly on grounds of egalitarian principle but probably more on grounds of lack of financial affordability) were planning to send our daughters to an admittedly less than outstanding state primary school, Jack exploded with rage. We, as academics professionally devoted to educational excellence for our pupils in Cambridge, should surely insist on the same for our own children. If we were too mean to pay the modest school fees for one of the outstanding schools in Cambridge, he would insist on doing so and he sent a cheque to cover the fees. Browbeaten (and a bit guilt ridden) we gave in and sent the girls to

Byron House (the infant part of St. John's School). Once they were settled in and thriving, Jack promptly withdrew his financial support in the certain knowledge that we would not now withdraw them and would somehow find the money. Of course he was right. They continued their education at the fee-paying Perse Girls School. He was much amused by the success of his cunning plan and continued for many years to take full credit for their educational success – for one a place to read Law at Oxford and for the other a top First in English at Aberdeen and a Distinction in Law School at Guildford. "They would never have become corporate finance lawyers at "magic circle" firms in London (Olivia, a partner at Linklaters, and Cornelia at Slaughter and May) if I had not set them off on the right track in their infancy in Cambridge", he used contentedly to boast. Clearly it was not possible to prove that he was wrong. In the face of such happy certainty, it would have been pointless to try.

Although he could be very generous in a whole host of ways, his attitude to both giving and receiving presents was not without its eccentricities. His giving often involved his own form of recycling.

Indeed it became something of a joke amongst his older friends as they saw presents they had given to him being redistributed to other friends often with a highly coloured and completely erroneous new provenance. They also got used to presents from Jack being reclaimed by him on the grounds that they had had them for years or even decades merely on a loan basis. Their reactions, when they saw them proudly displayed by other friends who were currently more in favour, were fascinating to behold – and sometimes painful to experience. A charming Sidney Nolan painting on glass did the rounds amongst his old friends (my wife and I enjoyed it for many years as a very much appreciated gift before it was reclaimed and passed on to Leslie and Terry Green). We were equally sorry to say goodbye to some lovely Georgian silver, which had graced our dining room for a decade or so, before it was physically reclaimed and removed by the erstwhile giver (on the spurious grounds that it had always been intended as a loan not a gift), when we were temporarily out of favour.

It could be a hazardous business showing Jack around your house – you never quite knew what much-prized gift might be reclaimed when he was in need of a suitable present for someone else. Some said that it was rather like being visited by the kleptomaniac Queen Mary – indeed, some said that it was worse because Jack was demanding back a present that he had already given away, but that never seemed to trouble him when he demanded that he leave with some much coveted gift. Some of his friends took to concealing old presents from Jack whenever he came to stay to make sure that they did not leave with him when he left. If a mutual friend was about to get married or was approaching a significant birthday, the warning words would be passed round the Plumb circle, "Jack is on the look-out for a wedding present, so lock up your gifts, conceal all prominently and proudly displayed presents you have received from him in the past." If, on the other hand, there was a gift from him that you had never much liked, but were too embarrassed to disown, then a weekend visit from Jack could be the very moment to display it very prominently indeed. With any luck, it would depart with a beaming Plumb.

Sometimes Jack speeded up his present reclamation scheme by never actually handing them over. At his final sale at Cheffins, both Bill Noblett and my wife had the mildly galling experience of seeing gifts that had been "given" to them listed for public sale. Bill claimed to be the greater sufferer of the two because the fiftieth birthday "present" he had been given was a fine Georgian silver tankard: Melveena claimed to be able to trump his experience because she had been given the same charming Duc d'Angouleme patterned Paris porcelain bowl on three successive birthdays, but had been asked each time not to take it away until it had been properly wrapped. Both managed to buy back their "presents" at the auction.

His friends were often asked why they put up with such eccentric behaviour. Most of them thought given his extraordinarily generous habit of present giving, letting him take back the odd one when he needed it for some other friend was a small price to pay. And anyway they might well be the beneficiary next time. As one of them said to me "What goes around, often comes around". It all added to the colourful character of our old friend.

In any case, gift exchange with Jack Plumb in his later years took on a ritual rather than a personal flavour. He would accept my daughters' carefully chosen and exquisitely wrapped Christmas presents but would then display no sign of opening them. They would be taken home and promptly recycled. Having sometimes received them back themselves, Olivia and Cornelia were very keen to make sure that their presents were at least opened in their presence and seen by Jack, before they were recycled. So they offered to open them for him on Christmas morning. "You may remove the greetings cards attached", he would say, "but I don't want the beautiful wrapping disturbed. Then I won't have to have them rewrapped when I give them away". When they looked dismayed, he would contentedly (and quite rationally) point out that at his age he was in the process of clearing the decks of unnecessary clutter. He had everything he wanted and so, although he expected appropriate gifts to be respectfully given on all festive occasions, no one should expect them to be cherished or even kept. Although such reactions sound shameless, they were to Jack the logical response of a man in his eighties who was trying to avoid acquiring any more cumbersome possessions. Accepting them and then promptly giving them away seemed a very rational response, and since I have always worked on the principle of giving to others presents that I really coveted myself, I was very content with the Plumb system of gift exchange. I was always delighted to be given back presents that I had given to him. Admittedly, I sometimes had to bite my lip when I heard his colourful account of his serendipitous "discovery" of the present in question and its "expensive provenance".

In the 1990s, he began a systematic clearance of his rooms to make sure that anything surplus to his needs was discarded.

28. PLUMB AND HIS WINE

Even Jack's cellars were to undergo a dramatic clear-out. He always said that his wines were a better investment than anything else he ever owned. Nothing symbolized more poignantly his recognition of declining appetites and failing senses than his great wine sales. Wine had been a central thread in his social life for over half a century. His wine diaries were maintained over all those years in great and discerning detail. They were woven through with tales of his private life, but wine bulks far larger than either sex or emotion. He was no more a forgiving critic of wine than he was of historians. When at my first dinner as host of the Bordeaux Club I anxiously put on my best clarets including Cheval Blanc '47, Lafite '45 and Latour '28 (arguably three of the best clarets of the century), I was rewarded with the scathing comment, "Anyone can put on obvious wines, Neil. At this club we expect claret to be interesting and challenging, not just obviously good!" As Hugh Johnson wrote in his own brilliant memoirs *Wine: A Life Uncorked*: "When Jack doesn't like something he makes a point of saying so".

He was ferociously protective about his own claret – anyone (apart from a very special few highly cherished exceptions, such as Princess Margaret) who left his fine wine in their glass could expect to be struck off his future guest list, anyone who failed to recognise its quality and say so could expect to be denounced for their failure, anyone who smoked in his dining room could expect a fierce rebuke. Princess Margaret apart, his guests were expected to be well-informed and eloquently responsive connoisseurs. Not only smoking but perfume and after-shave were also strictly forbidden.

The fate that befell the college cat, which sprayed the legs of Jack's dining room table before a Bordeaux Club dinner, shows how severe his displeasure could be when alien scents threatened his claret. The college cat (a large and over-fed Tom) used to perambulate slowly through the courts of Christ's on stately milk-drinking tours. Undergraduates kept it well supplied with milk, but when it dropped in on O staircase Jack characteristically gave it double cream, so not surprisingly it gave him high priority on its visits. In Jack's view, this showed that it was a most discriminating and intelligent cat and so he spoiled it even more. But on the fateful day when his dining room was being prepared for an especially important claret-fest, the door was left open and the cat took the opportunity to mark its territory. The effects were hugely offensive to Jack's nose. His cat-loving secretary was summoned to find and remove the offending scent, but her success was only partial. "I'll have that bloody cat put down", thundered Jack. Whether or not he did so I never discovered. I suspect and hope that some cat-loving member of the college came to its rescue and smuggled it to safety, but suffice it to say that the cat was never seen again. Clearly the penalty for spoiling a Bordeaux Club dinner could be very severe indeed.

He belonged, of course, to both the Saintsbury Club and the Bordeaux Club, the two most prestigious wine clubs in England, but he finally retired from both.

He had founded the Bordeaux Club with Harry Waugh back in the 1940s. It was designed to be a club of six so that each of the bottles could be tasted and judged by each of the members. The six members were supposed to consist of two dons from Cambridge, two dons from Oxford and two London wine merchants. Jack represented Cambridge for fifty years, as have I, but others such as Carl Winter, the Director of the Fitzwilliam Museum, and Denis Mack Smith, the brilliant historian of Italy, showed less stamina and less well stocked cellars and reluctantly resigned. Oxford did even less well. After the death of the former Principal of Brasenose, Maurice Platnauer, Oxford's involvement never really recovered.

Almost all the members of the Bordeaux Club not only had enviable cellars, but also enviable settings in which to display and drink their wine. Hugh Johnson had his beautiful seventeenth-century home at Saling Hall, John Jenkins had his magnificent sixteenth-century home at Childerley Hall, I had the fourteenth century panelled room in Caius and later the Master's Lodge, Michael Broadbent had the Board Room at Christies, Simon Berry had the Board Room at Berry Brothers in St James's Street, Maurice Platnauer had the view from his bachelor rooms in Brasenose overlooking the Radcliffe Camera. Perhaps not surprisingly, when prospective members were invited as guests and faced the formidable wine lists presented in these glamorous surroundings, they very often felt that membership would be more challenging than they would feel comfortable with.

Alas with the declining quality of Oxbridge dons' cellars, I am currently the only surviving academic. Wine experts of the outstanding quality of Harry Waugh, Michael Broadbent, Hugh Johnson, John Jenkins, John Avery and Simon Berry had the superb cellars and the exceptional knowledge that few, if any, dons could aspire to. They understandably and perhaps inevitably came to dominate the membership. Jack Plumb and I clung on with increasing difficulty as the representatives of Oxbridge, but he gave up in 1999 and I am giving up in 2019. I have kept the records of the club for the last thirty years but I was hugely indebted to the magisterial knowledge of Michael Broadbent, the superb prose of Hugh Johnson and the unrivalled generosity and unrivalled cellars of John Avery and Simon Berry, to compile the detailed judgements on the unrivalled wines we drank. Two great champagnes, a great dry White Bordeaux, up to six or seven really great clarets, and a magnificent Sauternes was the usual wine list for each dinner. When one reveals that John Avery might offer seven of the greatest bottles of Petrus or six of the greatest vintages of Cheval Blanc followed by say a 1921 Yquem, that Hugh Johnson might open with a 1911 champagne and follow it up with eight great Latours, or that Simon Berry might offer us a flight of six 1947 clarets, it is easy to see why very few academics could compete. I had the advantage of having bought a cellar of fine clarets when a foolish new Senior Bursar at Caius insisted that the college should sell off its best wine in a misguided moment of rigid and false economy and equally mistimed austerity, and I was the happy recipient of under-priced Latour '28 and Lafite '45 (sold to me for £1 a bottle in 1958) and a marvellous collection of the best claret vintages between 1945 and 1961, including such personal favourites as the 1953s and the 1959s.. As chairman of the Caius Wine committee for nearly half a century I continued to buy fine claret up to my favourite vintage of 1990 when colleges largely gave up buying First growths. After that I found it very difficult to compete. Jack Plumb could, of course, very easily compete and did so very combatively. He had the advantage of having built up a fine cellar of clarets from the 1920s and, having written off the 1930s completely, gone on to buy very judiciously the '45s, '47s, '48s, '49s, '53s, '59s, and '61s, so he could produce a choice selection of first growths starting with say a 1920, a '24, a '26 a '28 and a '29, which very few could equal.

Unlike the Saintsbury Club where the food was at times so undistinguished that members had been known to ask impertinently if they could bring sandwiches, the food at the Bordeaux Club often matched the wine. In consequence these dinners must sound alarmingly indulgent, even decadently and dangerously so, but, of the four longest lasting members, Harry Waugh lived to be 95 (having fathered twins when he was 70), Jack Plumb lived to be 90, Michael Broadbent is still going strong aged 93, and I am still going at 84. Admittedly Jack retired early when he was only 87.

His departure from the Bordeaux Club in February 1999 was a particularly memorable and moving occasion. We met, as usual when he was the host, in his panelled dining room in Christ's, with the portrait of the claret-loving Sir Robert Walpole appropriately presiding over the table, the poignant young Jewish couple (or so he claimed) painted by Lotte Laserstein presiding over the Georgian sideboard, the magnificent Matthew Boulton candelabra (which had once been mine) dominating the dining table, the splendid rich flowers decorating the early Iznik platter glowing on the sideboard, and of course, Jack presiding anxiously over a glittering array of glasses and decanters and silver. Michael Broadbent was there, Hugh Johnson was there, as was John

Jenkins, and although Harry Waugh had had to cry off at the last minute, Jack had characteristically chosen to replace the ninety-five year old Harry with a brilliant young historian, Paul Readman, who had just started to build up his own cellar in his mid-twenties.

In the middle of this final dinner (given to mark the completion of fifty years of fine wine drinking since he founded the Bordeaux Club with Harry Waugh and Alan Sichel in 1949), Jack suddenly stood up, announced that he could go on no longer, thanked us for all our friendship and good fellowship over the years, and left saying that he was retiring for the night – and forever. For some it was almost intolerably sad. All the members were visibly moved. As John Jenkins wrote, "It was a moment of intense emotion and many of us could not hide our feelings". I was persuaded to take him a glass of the Latour 1924, which we were just about to drink, to his bedside. He tasted it, said "Not a bad wine to go out on", turned off the light and never returned.

29. PLUMB AND PHILANTHROPY

Much else was also discarded but Jack approached his nineties full of plans for the Millennium, still encouraging and exhorting the gifted young, still planning further trips to the States, still plotting the outcome of his munificent charities. He continued to do much good by stealth – offering discreet financial assistance to the needy with no hope of either recognition or reward. In old age, he claimed that he had voluntarily tithed his income throughout his whole career. I know for certain that this was not true (and that is hardly surprising given the extortionate rate of taxation in his high earning years) but I am equally certain that he very much more than tithed his income in old age. He was formidably generous during the last quarter of his life – mainly to his College but also to many others.

In his later years, he proved to be just as good at raising money from other people as he was at giving his own away. By his seventies and eighties he had become a quite formidable fund-raiser. He did not scruple to flatter or cajole or bully his friends into stumping up for the charities he believed in. He once sent back a cheque to me by return of post with the words "Returned – insufficiently generous" written across it, and accompanied by a letter which read "I know you are not a rich man, Neil, but I would not like you to seem that poor, or, even worse, that mean. Please add a nought and return it to me at once". Amazingly I did so, and turned a £100 gift into a £1000 one, in support of the Dr. E.N. Williams' Fund at Dulwich School. I learned later that I was not alone in receiving the insistence that I give more, and not alone in coughing up more generously for such a deserving fund.

As a result of such measures and such pressures, he claimed to have raised over £3 million for Christ's alone· About a third of that came from his own pocket. His not inconsiderable fortune eventually went largely to promote the two things that dominated his life – Christ's College, Cambridge and the study of History. The £100,000 he gave and the £300,000 he raised for the Plumb Auditorium, and the £2,000,000 Plumb-Levy Trust, were all given solely for the benefit of Christ's. Most of his giving through the Sir John Plumb Charitable Trust (currently worth about £100,000) is used mainly to support history students; the £65,000 he personally raised to boost the Robert Owen Bishop Fund to £250,000 produced the most generous postgraduate studentship in Cambridge for Christ's historians; the £20,000 he raised for the E.N. Williams›s Fund was for a History Prize at Dulwich; the Sir John Plumb prize he endowed at the University of Leicester was for the best First awarded in History; and the Christopher and Helen Morris Prize at King's, which was funded by Jack alone, was set up solely for his recognition of King's historians. How apt it was that when the American Capitol flew its country's flag in his honour, the citation stressed that it was flown in recognition of what he had taught the American people about its past. It ends with the words "for that has been his life – teaching – and we have learned from him as from no other British historian.

30. PLUMB'S VERY PRIVATE LOVE LIFE: SEX, SECRETS AND SUBTERFUGE

There was, of course, more to his life than writing and teaching. Although he remained unmarried, he was twice engaged and he would have been very mortified to learn how amazed many have been to learn even of those modest emotional milestones in his love life. "What woman would ever have contemplated marrying Jack?" asked several of his more sceptical colleagues when they read in my *Guardian* obituary of his two engagements. I confess that I was surprised by their surprise. Indeed for a man of Jack's ebullient nature and hearty appetites, a couple of engagements would be a surprisingly meagre record. And if Jack were to be believed, there was much more to tell.

Some of it was much more straightforward than many might think. The standard assumptions about life-long bachelors do not all apply. Celibacy was certainly not the answer and he was not, like his old bachelor mentor, Bert Howard, a notorious whore-monger. Indeed Jack said that he never paid for sex in his life. Unlike Howard, too, who later disastrously moved from prostitutes to an early adolescent boy, he was not interested in that option either. Yet according to his account he lived a very full life, both emotionally and sexually. His diaries certainly reveal some surprising details. There are appreciative accounts of brief adulterous affairs and other stories of delightful sexual dalliance – one apparently extremely successful event improbably taking place on the back seat of his car. Much of this detail is, perhaps, best reserved for later publication when those involved are no longer here to be embarrassed, but there were times when he lovingly recalled the names and the circumstances of past conquests.

I remember one remarkable evening in the South of France when my family and a group of his friends were sitting on the terrace after dinner listening open-mouthed and goggle-eyed to Jack's contented rehearsal of a remarkable series of lovers. He enthusiastically re-lived, in excessively graphic detail, the many sexual exploits of his youth and early middle age. A rather relaxed, not to say promiscuous, attitude with regard to borrowing the partners of his friends seems to have accounted for his collection of an impressive number of unforgiving ex-friends.

Consoling bored and disaffected wives bulked larger in his life than many would suspect. "My pan-amorous period" was the perhaps not inappropriate phrase that he used to describe his early decades as he recounted them that night. Two of the more improbable highlights which everyone who was there seems to remember were the story of the hennaed pubic hair of one of his female conquests and the story of the war-time rationed sugar which, when melted, acted as a depilatory to remove it. Tame and simple stuff you may think by present day standards but coming from the lips of our ancient learned academic bachelor friend, it produced in his audience one of the few reactions which I think one might properly call "gob smacked".

But the biggest surprise came from the names and the numbers involved. How much was true one can only guess at. Jack was much given to vivid fantasies about his own life and the lives of others. He was blessed with a fertile imagination and great story-telling skills, and the tale we heard that night might well have benefited from nostalgic over-elaboration. Much may have been pure invention. It was certainly an arresting narrative, but the level of scepticism of those who listened might best be judged by the dignified comment of "It's impressive, if true" from one of his older friends, and the less dignified singing of *"Mille e tre"* from Don Giovanni by some of the younger members of the party. In defence of both spokesman and his audience, it has to be said that the whole party had dined well and were all suitably exalted by wine. Jack's staff poured out the stiffest pre-dinner drinks I have known outside Washington and our host had ensured that the wine had flowed generously throughout dinner and afterwards.

The two fiancées do, however, seem to be well bedded in fact as well as in Jack's fond recollection.

Not many can now recall the Leicester girl to whom he impulsively proposed (solely in order to get her into bed he claimed). Having accepted his proposal and succumbed to his advances, she promptly dumped him for the superior attractions of Tom, a local Leicester policeman. The "Dear John" letter, signed Kathleen, written in pencil on Christmas Eve 1933 with a request for it to be destroyed because of the indiscretions it contained, is still faithfully preserved in his archive. Rather touchingly, she wrote three days later to say "you are a very learned and particular person, and I am just very ordinary, in fact had I not a decent face, I do not believe you would have noticed me at all". Her maiden name was Kathleen Goodman. Once again, she asked him to destroy this letter, but Jack, of course, promptly filed it away in his youthful archive. Some forty-four years later she wrote again, under her married name of Kathleen Gray, to congratulate him on the success of *Royal Heritage* and to express the hope that "you have found happiness in your chosen career and that life has been kind to you". Inevitably Jack, historian to the last, neatly filed away the letter with the words "the girl I was briefly engaged to in 1932/33" written on the envelope.

Very few can remember the other claimed fiancée, the blonde, blue-eyed Nina from Cheshire who beguiled him during the war years when they worked together at Bletchley. In Jack's version of events, peace and his return to Cambridge saved him from marriage.

He always argued that marriage would have stifled his career, stunted his creativity and forced him to settle for staid domesticity. He routinely challenged his friends to name a single successful marriage that they knew of and routinely rubbished the examples they put forward. The model he offered as a workable alternative was a life of serial monogamy as long as the monogamous relationships were of an "open" character that offered one plenty of scope to travel alone, dally elsewhere and did not impinge on one's own space, one's own work or one's own ambitions. Commitment was not high on his agenda. Having decided that a wife and children were not for him, he loved nothing more than to mock marriage both in general and in particular.

Such views, together with his publicly expressed hope in the 1960s that he would love to live long enough to see gay couples walking hand in hand through the streets of London, led to much prurient speculation in Cambridge about the nature of his sexual preferences. My own view is that he would have been heterosexual by choice but that circumstances led him to lead a bisexual life. At school and at university in Leicester, he seems to have been consistently straight; in Cambridge in the thirties (when King's had a reputation for "acute homosexuality"), he seems to have been largely but not exclusively gay; at Bletchley in the war, he seems to have been predominantly but not exclusively straight. When he returned to Cambridge, he adopted a bi-sexual life, veering from gay to straight and back again as the opportunities to do so offered themselves.

Such a pattern suggests that his choices hinged largely on opportunism based on availability. In provincial Leicester, girls were available and heterosexuality was the prevailing ethos; in Cambridge in the thirties, young women were very scarce and homosexuality was the dominant academic lifestyle; at Bletchley, there was a gay set but there were thousands of lonely young women in search of distraction and the dominant culture was heterosexual; back in post-war Cambridge, the ratio of men to women was rather worse than ten to one. Lacking the looks, wealth, background or irresistible charm which might have allowed him an ample choice of female partners in the face of such odds, Plumb seems to have led a rather opportunistic sex life. As he grew richer, more established and better known, more bedroom doors seem to have opened to him and to judge from his own (and, to many people's minds, hugely exaggerated) claims, he enjoyed a surprisingly full and very varied private life thereafter. One should stress its private nature because for a variety of reasons, ranging from the law to the prospect of outraged husbands, much of what his diaries describe had to be enjoyed very discreetly.

Bill Noblett has also recently discovered that some of his sexual liaisons were so discreetly concealed, even in his own private diaries, that it required considerable archival detective work to unravel the truth. A small diary dated "Jan 1937", entitled "Reflections on Olive", seems at first sight a straightforward account of a rather exasperating relationship with a young woman called Olive. A typical entry for 17 Jan 1938 reads as follows: "Olive. We've been to Brittany, to Biarritz, to the South of France. We've lived together for long long weeks – alone. I've had to give up a great deal for her. Friends of long standing like Snow and long hours which could have been spent writing." When Bill drew my attention to what he called "the mysterious Olive", the mystery stemmed from the fact that neither he nor I had ever heard mention of her before. Other friends were equally baffled by the emergence of this previously unknown female lover.

Suitably intrigued, Bill wrote to me "I might be able to identify her when I get round to sorting out the pre-1939 correspondence." A week later, he wrote triumphantly of his successful and very surprising identification. It was a tribute to his unrivalled knowledge of the Plumb archive and a marvellous example of the intricacies of trying to understand the tangled web of Jack's private life, and a marvellous example of Bill's skill in untangling that web. He wrote as follows: "I have worked out that Olive is none other than Roy Gladwell. I was alerted to this by an envelope in the Michael Ramsbotham box of correspondence addressed thus: Miss Olive Gladwell, Trafalgar Road, Cambridge. Inside the envelope was a long letter from Michael to Jack describing a fraught meeting he had with his mother in which he obviously told her that he was having an affair with Jack. He stated twice that Jack should not worry as he had WON! The letter concluded with the words "She will be returning soon. I'll give this to you in an envelope when you come, because she's bound to be here. The envelope will be addressed to Roy Gladwell – NO – Olive Gladwell. I hope you interpret the wink & don't go searching for that weird creature. All my love. Don't worry please. I know my own mind now".

Noblett's first reaction was "I was very surprised and not entirely convinced. Throughout the diary to Olive, he constantly referred to 'She' and the pretence never slipped. Did this mean that Roy had an unknown sister? The Leicester directory for that time told me nothing. So I went to the Gladwell correspondence and there was proof that Olive and Roy are one and the same person. In the box, there are three undated letters signed Olive and one signed O. There are also four letters dated 6 & 28 April and 2 & 4 May signed Olive. The one for 28 April ends: "I send my kisses and embraces, Olive". The handwriting in these letters is Roy's and the address at the top "2 Ashleigh Road" is where he lived. I do think that all this settles the matter. I must admit that the whole episode has completely baffled me as it seems so out of Jack's character. In death as in life he never ceases to amaze".

I shared Bill's amazement because I had never heard any of Jack's friends, from the 1930s or since, mention anyone called Olive and I had never known Jack try to conceal the names of his past lovers from his close friends. I suppose one has to recognise that much of Jack's early private life was, in the eyes of the law, regarded as criminal and jailable, but this episode seems to be, as far as I know, an atypical and uncharacteristically convoluted attempt at concealment. In the 1930s, however, he still had his career to make and he doubtless felt that his humble social background and his modest educational origins were quite enough of a burden in the Cambridge of those days without making more potential enemies by revealing his less than conventional sexual activities. Later in life, his letters and diaries often use initials with which to identify his lovers but not code names or pseudonyms, and certainly nothing as elaborate as the "mysterious Olive" diary of the late 1930s. Perhaps Roy Gladwell insisted on the pseudonym for his own reasons. Clearly it amused Michael Ramsbotham.

Ramsbotham was a strikingly handsome, well-connected novelist, passionate gardener and intelligence analyst, who lived much of his life out of the closet. He became the muse of the poet Henry Reed and conducted an illicit affair with him whilst working at Bletchley in the war, and afterward lived for 67 years with Barry Gray. He died aged 96, and despite his being related to Vernon Kell, the wartime head of MI5, and Hugh Trevor-Roper, who was also in the secrecy world, his obituary in *The Times* recorded his belief that it was Jack Plumb who got him into Bletchley. He wrote successful novels, such as *The Remains of a Father* and *The Parish of Long Trister,* but seems to have been one of the rare novelists, who knew Jack well and kept in touch with him after his youthful affair, who made no use of him as an easily recognised character.

In later life Plumb seemed more likely to expatiate on his early lovers and name an impressive number of them, but the limits he placed on the use of his archives dictate that most of it must for now remain private. A list of those he claimed to have slept with would be surprisingly long, but printing it would be the cause not only of great surprise but also of considerable embarrassment. It would create a lot of unnecessary hurt. Many of Plumb's most lasting enmities stemmed from the revelation of the sexual indiscretions of his youth. There seems little point in stirring up any further enmity now.

In my view, Jack mainly fell in lust with women, and in fascinated and sometimes obsessive preoccupation with young men. There seems little evidence that, after the 1930s, he very often fell in love with either.

The nineteen-thirties seem to have been the peak decade for intense infatuation with young men. The ardent nature of those infatuations can be illustrated from a single letter to Roy Gladwell (later less flatteringly known as "the mysterious Olive" whose company he seemed to be finding rather tiresome when he recorded it in his secret diary).

In an undated letter he wrote:

Darling,

Your letters keep coming and its not possible for me to reply; how tired you must be of writing letters that are never answered. Believe me, though, darling, they are life itself to me. Today I have been unhappy all of the day because I wanted to be with you all the time. Tonight I remembered where you would be and, I'm sorry, but I was jealous, thinking perhaps, that you might be unfaithful. I'm jealous, much more than you imagine. I want you to stop going to Gordon's, although I know that is absurd of me. Please, please be faithful.

Roy, my dear, I often wonder if you believe me when I say that I love you, and if you don't, how I can convince you by some deed, by some new expression.

I do; I cannot say more than that. Each day I think of you, think of you, not as an object of delight, but as someone who has completely captured my whole life, each corner, each moment. Yes, I think of your beauty, the way that soft, saffron hair falls across your forehead, pencilled with faint wrinkles which give an air of sadness and knowledge; and of your pink nostrils, big mouth and the cold serpent. I remember teasing you cruelly and hating myself for hurting you even in play.

My life? I have done nothing, just nothing at all but work hard at my history book and teach my pupils who are very plain and very dull.

A week has gone, just a week, and it seems an age and there is another to live through before I hold you in my arms again. It seems mad this love of ours, and I'm sure if you were sensible you would send me packing. At times, I feel many silly, desperate things but mustn't say them. Good night, my love."

Alas, but characteristically for Plumb, this relationship did not mature into a lasting one. It was just another of the briefly passionate affairs (such as the one with the anonymous "flame-haired older women" in Paris) which he enjoyed and suffered in his twenties. In the ten years before the outbreak of war he was engaged and disengaged to Kathleen Goodman in Leicester, he seduced and broke up with Marjorie Howard also in Leicester, and had brief love affairs in Cambridge with Roy Gladwell, Michael Ramsbotham, and Graham Wright. He always claimed that Graham, who committed suicide after an explosive break up with Plumb, was the love of his life.

Much as he enjoyed his war years at Bletchley and his engagement with "Nina from Cheshire", he always said that he never after the 1930s experienced such a fraught and passionate love-life as he did in his twenties. This was just as well because it is difficult to see how he could have combined the anguish he seems to have felt in the nineteen-thirties with the hyper-productive years of prolific publications he lived in the nineteen-fifties, sixties and seventies.

Those who have pondered over the reasons for his low levels of productivity in the 1980s and 1990s, when compared with his prolific output between in the 1950s, 1960s and 1970s, rarely comment on his even lower levels of productivity in the 1930s and 1940s. The reasons were complex but very different. Boredom with academia and ill-health in his more mature years, and over excitement in his private life and the war in his younger years, seem to have been overlooked.

Yet it is not perhaps surprising that, in the turbulent and emotionally fraught nineteen-thirties with dramatic changes of sexual partners, he published only a single unremarkable article and a pedestrian history of the shoemaking firm his father worked at. His years of significant quality publications seem to have coincided with a less time-consuming and less melodramatic private life.

A life of many friendships with men and women, sometimes friendships with benefits, seems to have been his chosen lifestyle in his more mature years.

When I was an undergraduate at Christ's, and a young Fellow there and later at Caius in the late 1950s, Jack was enjoying an intense but intermittent affair with the wife of one of his long-term friends. When Jack was otherwise engaged I was often summoned to help entertain her, which I was delighted to do, and she made no secret of their relationship. It was serious enough for Bert Howard to warn Plumb of the dangers of "stealing her away from her husband". Perhaps fortunately she broke off the affair after a number of years.

There were other wives of other friends with whom Jack enjoyed relatively short-lived dalliances, but I do not know of any affairs with any unattached women after his years in Leicester and his time at Bletchley. In his view, affairs with married women greatly reduced the danger of his being "sucked into marriage".

What is most striking about his private life is the change from the anguished, turbulent and at times melodramatic affairs of his pre-war years, when the young women he fell in lust with were all wholly unsuitable and the young men he fell in love with were all gay, to the calmer post war years when he mainly seemed to search for companionship with young men who were all straight. In the post-war years the friendships he sought were almost all with historians and the role they played was usually that of favourite protégée, part-time research assistant and occasional travelling companion for a few years before they moved on to get married. And he certainly sought the company and friendship of far more young men than women. Given that his ideal relationship was a didactic and Socratic one – teaching, instructing and training the young – it is hardly surprising that he spent so much of his life with pupils much younger than himself. What he called his "life of serial friendship" owed much to the fact that he was always seeking new un-travelled youngsters to pass his worldly wisdom on to. A steady supply of fresh new undergraduates to sit at his feet, accept his instruction and listen to his stories suited him very well and for most of his working life in Cambridge the great majority of undergraduates were male. I suspect that a desire to instruct came well ahead of any desire to seduce.

The true nature of his sexuality may remain a mystery. He never lost the capacity to surprise one and this part of his life was no exception. If his diaries are to be believed his private life was often very complicated indeed, which may explain why his sexual relationships were on the whole pretty short-lived. I remember very well the evening I was invited to share a bottle or two of champagne with Plumb and Snow to celebrate the birth of my first child. The two old men turned the evening into a celebration of their one-night stands when on lecture tours in America. They complacently explained to me "the sexual powers of celebrity", by which they meant the added attraction to the opposite sex bestowed by success and public standing. It was a very odd way to celebrate the birth of my daughter, but a very revealing explanation of how two old men never blessed with beauty could, according to their version of events, enjoy a very rich private life. They would have thought that the famous Kissinger quote smugly singing the aphrodisiac effects of fame and power and wealth very aptly referred to them. I have little idea how much of it was true.

There were those amongst his friends and colleagues who thought that Jack's sexual preoccupations were lived out more extensively in his head than in his bed. He certainly talked a lot about sex in all its various forms. He was fascinated by its literature. He talked with equal excitement about the gritty realism and detailed statistics of the Kinsey report or about the fictional fantasies of Fanny Hill. He made a point of visiting the Kinsey Institute and was delighted to explore its archival and pictorial riches, reporting with glee how every technical advance in human history seemed to have been exploited for sexual purposes. For all his fascination with sexual history and sexual statistics, however, I suspect that, for most of his life, friendship was more important to him than love, companionship more important than sex. That companionship and those friendships were unquestionably predominantly male. After the break-up of one of his longer-term male friendships, I once found scribbled on his blotting pad the words "Loyalty is more dangerous than love – and when the loyalty of a friend is lost it can be even more painful than the loss of a lover". It was a sad but I suspect true conclusion to many periods of Jack's life. I have no doubt that for much of his life his male friends and his pupils and their children were much the most important part of his emotional life. Certainly he always claimed to have lived his life on the basis of what he called "serial friendship" and most of those friends were male.

31. PLUMB AND FRIENDSHIP

The list of those close friends who made a significant difference to Jack's life is a long one. It included Bert and Cecil Howard, the schoolmaster brothers, both historians and both now deceased; C.P. Snow, later Lord Snow, the novelist, now deceased, and his wife, the novelist Pamela Hansford-Johnson, also deceased; Gordon and Valerie Winterton, both of whom taught and are now deceased; Graham Wright, now deceased; Roy Gladwell, an actor, now deceased; Michael Ramsbottom, a novelist of independent means, now deceased; Professor Leslie Green, C.B.E., nuclear physicist, who was head of Daresbury, and his wife Dr Teresa Green, a consultant pathologist, both now deceased; Dr E.N. (Taffy) Williams, Head of History at Dulwich College, and his artist wife Joyce, both now deceased; Christopher Ragg, businessman, now deceased; Dante Campailla, solicitor, former Senior Partner of Davenport Lyons, and his wives Selina and Jan; Neil McKendrick, historian and former Master of Caius College, Cambridge, and my wife Professor Melveena McKendrick, a distinguished hispanist; Craig Barlow, an openly gay history master, now deceased; Sir Simon Schama, F.B.A., Professor of History, formerly at Harvard and now at Columbia, and his wife, the distinguished scientist, Virginia Papaioannou; William Noblett, librarian at Cambridge University Library, and his librarian wife Leslie Noblett; Professor Joachim Whaley, F.B.A., German historian and former Senior Tutor at Caius College, and his wife Alice Whaley, once a fund-raiser for Caius; Peter Oborne, journalist and political biographer; Dr Simon Smith, historian at the University of York and later Senior Tutor at Brasenose College, Oxford; David Evans, Q.C., barrister, and his wife Caroline Evans, also a barrister; and Andrew Lawrence, an engineer with Arup Associates. Obviously their importance in Jack's life differed, but many of the more junior ones acted in turn as Jack's pupils or protégés or travelling companions (often doubling up as research assistants) for a number of years before moving on.

Many people have said to me that, in many ways, they regret that Jack Plumb did not die when he reached the age of 80 when his friendships were mainly still in good repair as the many celebrations of his 80th birthday demonstrated. He was 80 when the President of the United States paid tribute to him; he was 80 when Princess Margaret organised such a splendid birthday party in Kensington Palace for him; he was 80 when his pupils organised a birthday feast in Christ's for him; he was 80 when his New York friends so generously marked that milestone; he was 80 when I organised the superb lunch for his closest friends at Raymond Blanc's *Le Manoir aux Quat'Saisons*; and so on for all eight of his eightieth birthday celebrations. It was to prove to be a very different reaction when he reached 90, as we shall see.

I have recently learned, however, that unbeknownst to me he was still acquiring new young friends and new young protégées in his late eighties.

In my tribute written in 1974, I highlighted the very different responses that Jack Plumb inspired from the young and the old and quoted the colleague who said "the difficulty with Jack is that he gets on indifferently with his seniors, adequately with his contemporaries, and superbly with those junior to him." Indeed, when I approached senior members for information and help in preparing that tribute, all too often the reply was "Mm, difficult, very difficult", and it was by no means clear whether they meant my task or my subject. In splendid contrast the response of the young was a chorus of praise and appreciation. "The marvellous thing about Jack", "The wonderful thing about Jack", was the way their replies began. They spoke with one voice of his generosity, his enthusiasm, the prodigality of his ideas for research, his unabashed pleasure in their success, his remarkable lack of envy. Their gratitude is both justified and readily evidenced, as the prefaces of so many monographs on seventeenth- and eighteenth-century English history indicate.

In 1974 the generous acclaim of the young was in stark contrast to the coolness of their elders.

It now seems that this pattern of response was still being played out a quarter of a century later.

I have recently learned that the acclaim and appreciation of the young was still evident when Plumb was in his late eighties when he was managing to fall out with many of his old friends.

I learned this from a letter which arrived out of the blue from Matthew Richards, a Christ's historian from the late 1990s, who described himself as Jack's "last protégé – if not, then certainly one of the last". He wrote of Jack. "He wined and dined me and a few others, read my Part II essays and arranged for me to go to the Levy Economics Institute in New York, where I met my wife. We kept in touch. Please do let me know if I can be of any help with your treatment of the octogenarian Plumb."

Matthew Richards explained that he had published an article in the *Christ's College Magazine* in 1998, based on an interview with Jack Plumb, which recorded amongst other things Jack's belief in the "wonderful difference" that the admission of women had made to the college, the fact he had enjoyed life most "when I had a wonderful collection of young historians in the fifties and sixties", and his admission that of all the college's many treasures the one he loved the most was First Court, and the one he disliked the most was the Lasdun Building, better known as the Typewriter, which he felt was "an appalling building – cheap, vulgar, crumbling, very badly designed".

"Having read the profile", wrote Richards, *"Jack took me under his wing. He added me to his small circle of friends and protégées among the undergraduate and graduate students, most but not all were historians. For reasons I don't understand they were all men – though he befriended my sister Helen, whom he called 'your beautiful sister', and invited her to a dinner party only after I mentioned in a letter to him that she had got a First in Part I.*

So far as I know, Jack never stopped being a friend and mentor to students. In my case he encouraged me as a writer, told me some wonderful stories, gave me some fine food and wine as well as trips to Pizza Express, and read my weekly essays. He also arranged financial assistance when my father stopped work on health grounds in the middle of my second year. Crucially, he arranged for me to go to the Levy Economics Institute at Bard College, set up by his friend Leon Levy, a self-made Wall Street billionaire. There I met my wife, who was an undergraduate from China on a scholarship. Jack and I kept up a correspondence across the Atlantic during my two years there.

Jack was gloriously uninhibited. He said 'I prefer older women, even now', and added that was the reason that nothing romantic happened between him and Princess Margaret, with whom he was very friendly. He brought her for an annual dinner with Christ's students in the 1990s, until her health made it impossible. Jack's reminiscences included a graphic description of a flame-haired lover in Paris in the 1930s – I think she was one or more decades his senior. He was often irascible, and would bang his walking stick hard on the floor when he heard the choir rehearsing in the chapel below his rooms. He once bid goodbye to a group of students at the end of a dinner party in his rooms with the words: "You're all on the road to death".

The friends of Jack's I remember were Francis Percival, Lachlan Goudie and Paul Redman. Francis shared Jack's love of fine food and wine, and has published a book on cheese called Reinventing the Wheel – he and his wife were described by the Evening Standard as 'the first couple of fromage'. Lachlan is an artist who has presented television documentaries – his career started when he received the Levy-Plumb scholarship, a year-long painting residence at Christ's that I think was set up specifically with Lachlan in mind. Paul is a professor of history at King's College, London.

Jack would probably be mildly disappointed with me today, though he would say he saw it coming when I was 21. He would be appalled by my regular church attendances (he used to use "pious" as a pejorative term) and disappointed that I am working as a fund manager for a charity investment boutique owned by the Methodist church. He might see some mitigating circumstances on the grounds that I was a journalist on the Financial Times for several years until the first of my three children was born, and in my spare time I am writing a historical novel about the Irish war of independence."

Such a letter could well have been written about Jack in any decade from the 1950s onwards, but it was good to be reminded that his capacity to inspire and encourage and promote the young (and if necessary help to finance them), which was always one of his most endearing qualities, had survived so well into his late eighties, when his relationships with his old friends seemed so often to be declining.

What Matthew Richards set out in detail was often confirmed by other alumni of his generation. My daughters frequently reported back to me the glowing tributes to Jack Plumb, both as Master and in his retirement, from young men and women they met who had been at Christ's in his later decades. What they admired most was the way he played the traditional role of the Cambridge bachelor don in entertaining them, in encouraging them, in setting goals for them to achieve and in educating them. He played that role they said through the medium of fine food and fine wine, through robust argument and racy conversation. It was a role that Jack had always excelled in. It would seem that his genius for inspiring the young with hope and ambition and aspiration survived almost to the end of his life.

Young historians, whom he felt still needed his support (whether that support was social, educational or financial), still attracted his friendship. Older historians, whom he felt had become too independent to need his backing, seemed increasingly in his old age to inspire little more than irritation and at worst open hostility.

One of the reasons that he retained the affection of the younger generation was a side of his personality that is rarely recognised. That was his capacity for expressing his sympathy and compassion and encouragement when their lives experienced painful setbacks. Many of his pupils have told me how he comforted them in times of disappointment and helped to restore their confidence with warm and encouraging letters of sympathy and understanding.

My younger daughter recently showed me a perfect example of such heartfelt compassion. It was a letter that Jack wrote to her in 1990 after she had been rejected by Oxford. It read:

"Dearest Cornelia,

I am sorry – very. I know what it is like to be rejected – I was by Cambridge when I was 18 and it hurt and hurt and hurt. But it made me more resolute to be myself and not compromise. Remember that the academic world is not the only world. Some of the ablest and most successful people I know would have nothing to do with it. Don't jump to a decision. Take a long hard think about yourself & then when you have made up your mind stick to it & work like a she-devil at whatever you decide to do.

And whatever you decide, you will always have my love and admiration. You have a wonderful personality, great strength & I'm sure talent.

Fight back

Love

Jack

She seemed to take heed of his advice since, after taking the top First in English at Aberdeen and being offered the opportunity to read for a Ph.D. at Peterhouse in Cambridge, she turned her back on academia, took a distinction at Law School and joined Slaughter & May, the highest paying law firm in London. Jack, of course, was understandably delighted that his belief in her (so eloquently expressed in his letter of sympathy) was so fully vindicated by her subsequent success.

Not surprisingly Cornelia still cherishes this letter and indeed the further loving correspondence that she received from him right up to his death, full of concern and encouragement for her, and, alas, a growing sense of loneliness, sadness and defeat for himself.

Cornelia always regarded him as her surrogate grandfather and he usually responded like an affectionate if intimately involved one. He worried about her boyfriends ("Why do you tire of your men so quickly"), he worried about her work ("I hope that you are settling down to you new work and not being too bored by it"), and he worried about her safety ("Be careful in Clapham. Have you bought a spray yet?). He loved her letters ("Thank you for your delightful letter", "You do write a staggeringly good letter", "Thank you for your letter. It was the only bit of sunshine in my day"); he loved hearing about her life (whether it be a weekend in Prague, a secondment in Hong Kong, a trip around the world or just London); but most of all he loved her visits ("Do come and see me. I love visits. I lead a lonely life, and will not have a long way to go – '99 or 2000, who knows but it can't be far off". "I am confined to my rooms in Xts & I rarely see anyone. Usually I am staring at white walls. Come and talk to me when you can."

Increasingly his letters to her were a sad catalogue of age and its ailments: "I decay steadily – a bone, marrow, flesh, it is all starting to crumble and at times the pain is almost unbearable"; "there is very little to be said for old age"; "I get older, more tired and want some one to look after me".

Throughout their considerable correspondence, however, he liked to fondly reminisce about her past and to express his grandfatherly concern about her future happiness. In 1991, in his eightieth year he sent a cheque for £100 for her nineteenth birthday and he wrote, "It does not seem 19 years since we were celebrating your arrival with some very fine wines – and little did I know, that I would be alive at the very end of your teens. It has been fascinating to watch you grow up and see the characteristics which were so marked in you as a little girl grow and develop. I hope that I shall live long enough to see you settled with someone who will make you happy, year after year, and decade after decade."

However fiercely he mocked marriage and conventional family life, there can be no doubt that he cherished the surrogate children and grandchildren that he selected for himself. He treated them with extraordinary generosity and affection.

As with the rest of his life, it would seem that within his "family" the young still brought out the best in Jack. With them he was still generous and loving and warmly involved, with none of the bitterness that seemed to taint his relationships with his older friends, whom he felt no longer needed his help or encouragement or support.

There were, of course, a few old friends who still inspired affectionate regard, and one measure of those who meant most to him can be judged by the dispositions of his will. He not unreasonably felt that his friends had all done quite well enough in life to no longer require significant financial help from him. As he aged and as they prospered, the amounts to be left to them went pretty steadily down. Some of the excessively generous dispositions of his early wills were dramatically axed in his late eighties, but he still left modestly handsome sums (£5,000 to £10,000 or their equivalents, such as cancellations of outstanding debts) to the physicist Leslie Green, the lawyer Dante Campailla, the historians Neil McKendrick, William Noblett, Joachim Whaley, and Simon Smith, the journalist Peter Oborne, and the barrister David Evans. Another measure of the depth of his friendship is offered by the portraits of his friends, which he had painted by Steven Hubbard and then presented to their wives – these included portraits of Leslie Green, Dante Campailla, Neil McKendrick, William Noblett and Joachim Whaley. He also had Melveena McKendrick painted by John Ward.

To judge from his comments in later life, the relationship that left the deepest scars was his friendship with Graham Wright. It ended, after a spectacular row, with Jack stopping his car and ordering Graham to get out. The cause of the row was said to be the admission by Graham that he had been sleeping with Marjorie Howard with whom, to judge by their correspondence, Jack had himself been conducting an impassioned affair. He always used to say that the worst moment in his life was when Bert Howard, almost casually, later informed him of Graham's subsequent suicide. The sense of profound regret, doubtless intensified by guilt and remorse, never really left him. When he referred at one of his eightieth birthday celebrations to "a marriage (or the closest I came to it) followed by suicide", his older friends were somewhat bemused but decided that he could only be describing his relationship with Graham in the 1930s.

There were, of course, many other friends and close colleagues in Cambridge, such as Sidney Grose, Christopher Morris, Rupert Hall, John Kenyon, Barry Supple, John Burrow, Quentin Skinner, Roy Porter and more recently Paul Readman and Bill Fitzgerald (who was exceptionally kind to him in the last year of his life), but they never quite made the inner circle – by which I mean they were never invited to join Jack on his summer holidays, their wives and children never became part of his extended family, and they never figured in any versions of his will.

That almost all of these English friends were male is partly a reflection of the predominantly male world that Plumb spent most of his professional life in, but it should not be forgotten that (often after an initial reluctance) he became friends (in some cases very close friends) of many of their wives – such as Pamela Hansford Johnson, Helen Morris, Terry Green, Valerie Winterton, Joyce Williams, Selina Morrison, Jan Campailla, Melveena McKendrick, Virginia Papaioannou, Patricia Skinner, Lesley Noblett, Alice Whaley and Caroline Evans.

There were other geographically more distant friends who obviously meant a lot to him at different stages of his life – American friends such as Pat and Liz Moynihan, Dick and Beattie Hofstadter, Ben Sonnenberg, Bob Pirie, Jane Wrightsman, Brooke Astor, Leon Levy and Shelby White. Jack was always willing to play the part of distinguished academic Englishman for the American grandees who took him up, in much the same way that he was willing to play a grand form of court jester to the English Royals. He always enjoyed the company of the rich and powerful and he was proud to number them amongst his friends. Some of them liked in turn to pamper and spoil and flatter him. He always found such attentions wholly acceptable and boasted how these grand friends insisted on seeing him and entertaining him in their great houses. He could be a wonderfully entertaining guest and, when he set out to do so, could be remarkably charming. Alas, as with his less grand friends, the charm diminished with age and rumours started to drift across the Atlantic of less than ecstatic hosts awaiting first with anxiety and later with dread the annual visits from Jack. It has to be admitted that (especially in his later years) he could be as difficult and as demanding a guest as he had once been such an entertaining and charming one.

Pat Moynihan was a friend of very long-standing and as their respective careers prospered they both grew to admire the other more and more. Jack also had a great capacity for making new friends and exciting long-lasting admiration – Ben Sonnenberg, for example, took him up very enthusiastically and did much to promote his journalistic career in America; Brooke Astor extended hugely generous hospitality to him in her house on the Hudson River and the Levys were even more generous in a whole host of ways – not least in making available the apartment in the Carlyle. By many members of the Rothschild clan he was regarded as "family" and he always enjoyed "family rates" when they acted for him professionally. Sybil Cholmondeley remained a firm friend right up to her death. In later life to judge from his correspondence, he numbered new friends such as Princess Margaret, Johnnie and Raine Spencer and Colin and Anne Glenconner amongst his intimate social circle – according to Colin Tennant's biographer, Lord Glenconnor improbably boasted that he was convinced that Jack was in love with him. Those he regularly entertained would massively extend this list.

Such socially grand friends show how far he had moved socially and financially. As an exercise in social mobility it was striking by almost any standards, but it is important to recognise that he never ceased to give his time, attention and if necessary his finances to encourage and promote the humblest undergraduate. Even in his late eighties, he was still befriending and inspiring young Christ's historians as he had been doing for the previous half century.

32. PLUMB'S POSTHUMOUS SALE IN 2002

The sale of Jack's remaining possessions on 14 May 2002 showed that many of his friends had returned his generosity with a handsome array of gifts to him. I experienced the curious experience of buying for a second time (and at hugely inflated prices) many of the presents that my family and I had given to him over the years.

Admittedly none compared with the wonderful present given to him by G. M. Trevelyan of Macaulay's beautiful leather-bound edition of Dean Swift's collected works with Macaulay's marginal notes. This gift was inscribed by Trevelyan with the words: "given to J.H. Plumb by G.M. Trevelyan, Christmas 1955, because of his admiration for Macaulay, his kindness to Macaulay's grand-nephew GMT, and his profound studies in the period of Swift's life". It seems a great pity that these volumes, given by Macaulay to Trevelyan and then by Trevelyan to Plumb, should not have been passed on by Plumb to Schama, who came closest to keeping alive and improving on the tradition that Plumb had championed and pioneered. By doing so, he would have refreshed the happy tradition of passing the baton on to a significant historical scholar who shared his aims as an historian.

It seemed very sad to me that the splendid Macaulay-Trevelyan-Plumb sequence was not maintained. There were ample candidates within the Plumb stable for appropriate additions to that distinguished sequence. If not Sir Simon Schama, then why not Sir David Cannadine or Niall Ferguson who are almost equally high-profiled historians. If not them, then why not Quentin Skinner, perhaps the most academically distinguished of the Christ's colleagues of Plumb's, or Sir John Elliott, perhaps the most distinguished of the non-Christ's colleagues who Plumb so much admired. Both Skinner and Elliott have received more than twice as many honorary degrees as Plumb, both have received the Wolfson Prize and both have received the Balzan prize (one of the world's most prestigious academic awards), both have held Regius Professorships and both would have been highly appropriate recipients of Macaulay's collected works of Swift.

Of less historiographical significance, but greater aesthetic interest, were the presents given to him by some of his grander friends such as the gifts from Houghton. These spanned three generations from the Dowager Marchioness of Cholmondeley to her grandson the 7th Marquess of Cholmondeley. Once again any suggestion that his friendship with the great and the grand was not fully reciprocated is firmly squashed by these hugely generous gifts, which he received throughout his life. The range of gifts from many of his personal friends (most of whom enjoyed resources light years away from those of the Cholmondeleys or the Rothschilds) provides further supportive evidence of the generous affection he was held in by so many of them.

The sale of the contents of his rooms excited a great deal of interest. One newspaper report referred to his rooms as "a collector's paradise"; a headline spoke of the "Astonishing legacy of the History Man"; and all the broadsheets ran highly coloured stories of what was on offer. Considering that they were little more than the dregs left after his burglary and his major sales in the 1990s, they raised a not inconsiderable sum. The total for the day's sale was well over three quarters of a million pounds, but more interesting than the total were the details of the auction. They confirmed what I had always suspected – that Jack was genuinely knowledgeable about his porcelain, his wine, his manuscripts and his silver, but far less so when it came to furniture and paintings. His furniture was frankly disappointing (even when one allows for how much had been stolen from The Old Rectory at Westhorpe), his paintings fetched much less than he had led one to believe that they would, and of all his possessions they probably proved to be his worst investment. The charming Cuyp of the little girl holding her dog's lead in one hand and a pretzel in the other fetched only £32,000 (not the quarter of a million that Jack had improbably boasted that it was worth when I had tried to buy it from him), the portrait of Sir Robert Walpole by Charles Jervas fetched only £38,000 and many of his other paintings showed only a very modest increase on the prices he had paid over twenty years earlier.

Other things did very well indeed and I watched with a mixture of pleasure and chagrin charming little gifts which I had bought for him for less than twenty pounds fetch many thousands each in response to fevered bidding. The Matthew Boulton candelabra, bearing the double star mark for 1784 fetched £6,500. I had bought them from Peter Stockbridge on Kings Parade (admittedly in the mid-1960s) for £175. They are currently on sale in London for £11,500.

Curiously Jack left almost no individual objects to close friends. Many would have treasured a modest keepsake but hardly any were forthcoming. "If they want them, they can buy them" was his bleak response when I urged him to leave some modest memento to many who I knew would cherish such a sign of affectionate regard. But every little teacup and every saucer must, he said, be sold along with everything else.

Every tie, shirt, suit and shoe had to be disposed of in the sale. This led to some comic items at the auction. The auctioneer's announcement of Lot 142 – a quantity of Sir John's shoes, "mainly size 6" amused the buyers. They were understandably intrigued at the thought that he might have had other sizes for special occasions. His friends smiled rather wryly at the thought that his designer-labelled clothes (Lot 141, "a Quantity of ties and dress shirts", Lot 143, "a Quantity of Tailored Suits", Lot 144, "a College gown and other clothing") were like everything else to be ruthlessly turned into cash. These characteristic and much-cherished items of clothing fetched only very modest amounts of cash. It was in such stark contrast to his attitude to money in his earlier years – when he loved spending it and giving it away, arguing that one "should never be under over-drawn" and mocking the "quiet rich who are so busy counting their money that they fail to enjoy it".

His close friends were especially surprised – and some of them hurt – by the seemingly heartless completeness of his sale. But he was in a way proved right. If they really wanted something they could always buy it, and most of them did.

It was rather touching that so many really did want mementos and they proved it by buying them. As a result many of his possessions will stay within the confines of what he often called his adopted family. My daughters were fiercely determined to buy some keepsakes from amongst the possessions of their surrogate grandfather. My younger daughter proudly displays "Jack's Chippendale mirror" above her fireplace and his opera glasses in her drawing room, whilst my elder daughter is able to speak with great authority about the role of Bletchley in the Second World War as a result of buying Jack's "Bletchleyana", including even the pencils and notepads used by those unglamorous and for too long un-sung, but hugely important code-breakers.

Other old friends staggered away heavily laden with silver, porcelain and furniture, and, as is only appropriate, Simon Schama now has a fine seventeenth-century Dutch painting from the Plumb collection adorning his wonderful home in up-state New York. It would be a source of great posthumous satisfaction to Jack to think of his possessions filtering down through the generations of his adopted family.

33. PLUMB'S SECRET DAUGHTER AND HIS ATTITUDE TO MARRIAGE AND CHILDREN

All Jack's close friends tended in turn to become permanent members of his ever-growing surrogate family. His friends' children became his surrogate grandchildren and were often treated with particular generosity – those currently in favour (including my own) were financially supported to varying degrees in their trips round the world and given substantial gifts with which to launch their adult lives (as was the young Thomas Noblett, William Noblett's son). He made no apology for his choice of, and the ruthless changes in, his favourites.

Parents, he said, had no option but to stick with and by their families, whereas he was in the happy position of being completely free to choose whom to favour, whom to drop and whom to take up again. The length of time that photographs of his friends' children remained on his desk in Christ's always signalled pretty clearly who was in favour and who was most definitely out. He never ceased to argue in favour of "self-selection, subject to frequent revision and change", in preference to "genetic chance which you were stuck with for life", as the most successful route towards the acquisition of a suitable "family".

Jack frequently claimed to have fathered a daughter but, when asked why he did not acknowledge her, he said he seemed "to have fathered a dud", who was best left in the care of the husband of her mother. Alas, he said, she had neither looks nor intelligence nor talent. He preferred, he said, to choose as his "family" those who had at least some of those virtues, preferably all three. How much truth, if any, there is in the story of the unacknowledged daughter I do not know. There was often an element of fantasy in the stories that Jack liked to tell about himself, and the appalling frankness of his chilling assessment of his offspring has a ring of Plumbian bravado about it. It reeks of a provocative brand of cynicism, which he would know that I, as a most devoted father of daughters, would find very shocking.

When I had previously asked him whether he cared about passing on his genes, he said that it would not be worth it if it meant that his life would be interrupted by child-rearing. He argued that family life was not really consistent with a successful professional academic career. It would at best interrupt it; it would certainly prevent one maximizing one's abilities; and it might well thwart it altogether. He felt that it proved his point when he reminded one that so many of the well-known late twentieth century historians in Cambridge were childless. Joseph Needham, Philip Grierson, Sir Geoffrey Elton, Sir Moses Finley, Kitson Clark, David Knowles, Maurice Cowling, Hugh Trevor-Roper, Jack Gallagher, Anil Seal, Roy Porter, David Joslin, Sir Christopher Bayly, Sir John Elliott, Sir David Cannadine, Linda Colley, Sir Noel Malcolm and Joachim Whaley were he said (as far as he knew) making no contribution to the Cambridge academic gene pool. If Jack Plumb had inadvertently done so with his unintended and unidentified daughter, he preferred that fact to remain anonymous and unacknowledged, and so it did.

When I pointed out that he did not need to go beyond the evidence of the star historians at Christ's such as Quentin Skinner (two children), Norman Stone (three children) and Simon Schama (two children) to show that fathering children was quite consistent with spectacular academic success; and if he was willing to go as far afield as Sidney Sussex and Selwyn, then he could add Asa Briggs (four children), Owen Chadwick (four children) and John Morrill (four children) to challenge his anti-family arguments. Needless to say he was not convinced. He brushed aside these examples, saying (quite reasonably) that such families would certainly not have suited his life-style or his historical career.

As for Plumb's belief that marriage alone would be a barrier to success and distinction for Cambridge historians, one only has to list Richard Overy (four wives and many children), John Dunn (four wives) and Roy Porter (five wives) to see that that is a highly questionable view. The two-wife club would be too long to list.

He remained a fervent atheist and cast himself (whether they liked it or not) as a ferocious "anti-God father" to all the children and grandchildren of his extended family. Any friend who married in church or who had his children christened could be certain to attract, at best, Jack's sustained mockery and, at worst, his prolonged denunciation. Any justification on the grounds of a wife's genuine beliefs or the potential faith of their children cut no ice at all with Jack. Even when he did agree to stand as a Godfather, as he did, for instance, for Dante Campailla's son, Nicholas, he still felt free immediately afterwards to mock without mercy the hypocritical motives of his parents. How glad some of those old friends, who had cowered under the lash of Plumbian mockery and disapproval, might have been to know that Jack had once been a confirmed Anglican, and for the hardly creditable reasons of trying to fake his way into a place at Selwyn as an undergraduate. I hope that, for that piece of information alone, this memoir may prove its worth to them.

To the very end of his life he was a firm non-believer and religion was to play no part in his funeral or his memorial. Although he did choose to be buried in an Anglican churchyard, belief played no part in that decision. His burial plot was within a few feet of the front door of his country home in Suffolk in which I believe he spent the happiest and most productive years of his life.

34. PLUMB'S 90TH BIRTHDAY: A SYMBOL OF OLD AGE AND THE BLACK YEARS

Jack's death was not, alas, a serene and untroubled one. He certainly did not go gently into that good night. Instead he raged – raged against the dying of the light. His last few days in Addenbrooke's after suffering a severe stroke were as miserable for his close friends as they seemed terrifying for him. With his right side paralysed and his speech all but destroyed, he lay on his back like a trapped animal. He seemed desperate to communicate. His still mobile left arm shot out like a lobster claw and with his left hand he grabbed at my wrist and implored me to stay with him. He seemed like a drowning man reaching out desperately for a rescuing rock. The only words I could make out through his garbled screams were "Save me" and "Help me", repeated over and over again. Alas no one could do either. He died alone in the night, but on the evidence of those who saw him during his last forty-eight hours of his life, he died in a frightened and profoundly miserable state of mind.

Indeed, the last years of Jack's life seemed to be increasingly troubled and often deeply unhappy ones. His unhappiness expressed itself all too often in anger and bitterness. He seemed to grow to hate almost everyone. He became deeply suspicious about even his oldest friends – doubting their loyalty and finding the evidence of their friendship sadly insufficient. We were almost all found wanting. Too many of us, he felt, failed his admittedly demanding tests of generosity, hospitality and devotion. Indeed, sadly, the closer his friends were to him the more he seemed to want to reject them. Those who cynically think that no good deed goes unpunished would have found plenty of evidence to sustain their view in Jack's last years in Christ's. Of his close friends, Jo Whaley, Bill Noblett and I were his most assiduous visitors and so were the most denounced when we were not free to visit. The college which had given him refuge and succour for so many years was reviled, the Master and the Fellows were bitterly denounced as greedy ingrates who wanted nothing but his money, his elderly secretary was treated abominably (frequently reduced to tears by his rudeness), and his most loyal friends were blackguarded behind their backs in the most disgraceful way.

I fear that my very last letter to him, written after his ninetieth birthday celebration which I had organised for him (as indeed I had organised his fiftieth, sixtieth, seventieth, and one of his eightieth birthdays and most of those in between), was written in words of sad reproach that over fifty years of friendship and loyalty should be treated so shabbily and so unworthily.

The story of his reactions to the way in which he hoped that his ninetieth birthday should have been celebrated might serve as a revealing diagnosis of his state of mind in the last year of his life. It symbolised his final black years in miniature.

When plans for the celebration were first mooted by me, he dismissed them as quite unnecessary. His college would surely organise a feast in his honour, his grand friends would surely organise something splendid in London, his rich friends in New York would surely summon him over the Atlantic to celebrate in true generous warm-hearted American style, his pupils would surely loyally get together to pay their respects as they had done for his eightieth, and he would take care of his old close friends by hiring the whole of Le Château at Montreuil in France for a weekend of festivities. My puny efforts would be irrelevant, but I would, of course, he added consolingly, be invited to join him in France.

Such bombast, such optimistic expectations and such *folie de grandeur* alas all came to nothing. He had so offended the Fellows of Christ's that they, perhaps understandably, were less than enthusiastic about arranging a feast. His grand friends in London, no longer the recipients of jollies in Cambridge at his expense, were less than keen to entertain someone whose reputation for choleric anti-social behaviour was spreading. New York remained silent. His American friends, as with is his former pupils, probably felt that they had done enough or simply had had enough. Le Château at Montreuil, as I had warned him it would inevitably be, was (only too predictably) fully booked for the summer.

In early August 2001, with only weeks to go before his ninetieth, a somewhat chastened but also very angry Jack complained bitterly to me that no one was doing anything about his birthday. Even his old friends were planning nothing and all the college was doing, he said (quite wrongly), was to offer him a cup of tea on his birthday. I reminded him that I had offered to arrange an appropriately large and lavish dinner in Caius for him, but at this late stage, with the college kitchens now closed for the summer, and many old friends already away on holiday, my options would inevitably be more limited than I would have wanted. Nevertheless, if he so wished, I was sure that something could be done. I could provide some of his favourite wines, Melveena could cook some of his favourite dishes and a modest number of his favourite old friends could probably by rounded up to fill the limited number of bedrooms we had in the Master's Lodge.

224

Giving the clear impression that he felt that this was probably better than nothing, he rather grumpily agreed to come. Alas, it was something of a disaster.

He arrived in a very bad mood on a very warm evening. He refused to remove his trademark headgear throughout the dinner, refused to cheer up and refused to find anything to like in the excellent food, the superb wine or the congenial company, all united in their efforts to make it a happily memorable celebratory evening for him. It certainly proved to be a memorable occasion but most certainly not a happy one.

Having no 1911 wines in my cellar with which to mark his 90th, I decided (in what I foolishly thought would be a pleasing conceit) to choose wines that would mark the end of his 80s and the beginning of his 90s. So we began the evening with Pol Roger 1990 and ended it with Château Lafite 1990 and Château Climens 1990. During the meal, we drank two 1990 premier cru white burgundies – a Chassagne-Montrachet and a Puligny Montrachet – and two 1989 clarets – Château Léoville Barton and Château Pichon Longueville Lalande. There was even a Château Coutet 1988 in reserve for dessert but we never got that far.

Having painfully insulted all of his old friends throughout the meal, having accused Melveena of trying to give him "mad cow's disease" by serving fillet of beef, having dismissed my wine as a characteristic display of profligacy on my part, and launched a particularly hurtful final attack on his closest friends, he declared halfway through the meal that he was leaving.

Charitably, one would like to believe that it was forgivable old age and understandable fatigue which led him to announce that he could "stand it no more" and then insist that I walk him back to Christ's before the planned celebratory speeches had been delivered, but the venom with which the attacks were delivered to all and sundry made it very difficult to be charitable. So my final letter to him (written on the 26th of August) included the menu for the evening and began with words, "I thought that you might like this record of the 90th Birthday Celebration which you half attended and enjoyed to an even lesser degree", and ended with the words, "I do not know who or what has poisoned your mind against your old friends but I am sure that it is a very unworthy response to over 50 years of friendship and loyalty". In response, I received some days later a scribbled barely legible note, which read: "I will try to explain my problem with you and my old friends". Alas he died before any such explanation could be delivered.

On reflection I very much regret that my last letter to him was one of sad recrimination, but, as Bill Noblett said, "In the circumstances it was a pretty mild rebuke", and "a very forgivable one" especially if compared with what Jack's response would have been if our roles had been reversed.

On further reflection, I suspect that he found the sight of his old friends and pupils, (all with highly successful careers, all happily married, all with children, all with the prospect of grandchildren, all with a future to look forward to, all obviously contented with their lot in life) an unbearably painful reminder that his nineties offered no such enticing prospects and no such warm family consolations. Such a vivid reminder that he might have made the wrong choice in dismissing the rewards that can come with a committed long term relationship may well have been the cause of the explosive rage and resentment that we witnessed that night.

It cannot be denied that in the last black period of his life, he offended many of his oldest friends. By this I mean much more than the professional quarrels and changing allegiances that mark and sometimes disfigure many scholars' lives. I can think of at least four of his favourite and most visited households that came to regard Jack as *persona non grata* in the final year of his life. The wives of life-long friends finally sadly said that they could take no more. Elaborate plans were hatched to conceal from Jack such celebratory occasions as Dante Campailla's 75th birthday at which once he would have expected to be an honoured guest. He was not invited to Quentin Skinner's 60th birthday, nor to Melveena's 60th in 2001. There had been simply too many ruined dinner parties, too many insulted guests, too much rejected food, too many offended cooks, too many wines disdainfully dismissed as inferior or declared to be far too good for the other guests – the litany of social offences started to mount alarmingly. Too often he simply refused to go home – plonking himself in the bedroom of his choice and simply refusing to budge, which could be a trifle awkward when the bedroom he chose was already amply occupied by other guests.

Conscious of my own great debt of gratitude to him, I tried to maintain the old traditions of friendship which reached back over fifty years. I visited him several times a week and telephoned even more often. He came frequently to lunch on Sundays and he always came to us for Christmas Day and always went to the Nobletts on Christmas Eve and to the Whaleys on Boxing Day. Indeed when it was just my family who were involved (who were well versed in Jack's flagrant flouting of even major social taboos, not to mention his casual dismissal of the normal social niceties), he continued to attend all our rites of passage, but when others of more delicate sensibilities were present, it became too big a risk to have Jack there. Sadly the reason he was not invited to Melveena's 60th birthday celebrations was because too many of the 60 invited guests said that they would not come if he were to be there, and even more said that they would not sit by, or even near, him. Many will doubtless think that in view of Jack's age we should have been more forgiving. Many of us doubtless feel guilty that we were not more tolerant. All one can say is that the provocation was often intense and the hurts sometimes too difficult to bear. It has to be admitted that he could be very cruel in his bitter old age. He never lost his intuitive insight into his friends' vulnerabilities and sensitivities. I have known old friends actually burst into tears when faced with a wholly unexpected and wholly undeserved barrage of insults.

Some of the extreme rudeness, which so many people complained about, may well, my medical friends tell me, stem from a not uncommon feature of great old age – that is, degeneration of the frontal lobes of the brain. If these areas, which control learned behaviour-patterns, degenerate, then courtesy, good manners and the acceptance of social taboos often disappear with them. As a result, octogenarians suddenly speak with the unconsidered directness of small children. Jack, in old age, often spoke like a two year old with Tourette's syndrome. It could be very disconcerting.

Some of Jack's rudeness was certainly childishly simple – "My God you're fat" (to a close female friend) or "Why do you dye your hair? It looks horrible" (to a close male colleague in Christ's) or "Why are you so mean?" (to very many old friends) or "You should have that dog put down, it's too old and ugly and smelly to keep" (to almost all dog owners) – but, when venomously delivered, it could often be surprisingly hurtful to those so addressed.

Sometimes it was difficult not to laugh at his brutal directness. He once greeted his godson, Nicholas Campailla, after not seeing him for a few years, with the words "What are you now – about 22 or 23?" When Nicholas replied, "Alas, no Jack. You flatter me – I'm in my thirties now", he received the tart and wholly unjustified put down "not your age, you fool, your weight! Twenty three stones, I meant, twenty three stones not twenty three years!" It does Nicholas great credit that he tells this story himself with great good humour, brilliantly mimicking Jack's voice and intonation.

Others were less forgiving. I recall one old friend who he told not to try to go through his door because she was too fat. When she replied sweetly (through gritted teeth), "Oh don't worry Jack I will slip through side-ways", he responded with the bleak follow-up, "That won't help, you are just as fat side-ways as you are front-ways". On that occasion, I feared that she might justifiably have hit him with the tea tray she was carrying.

Alas such examples were not rare aberrations. They happened all too often. Few events were safe from sudden hurtful salvos from Jack. Few friends were immune from them. I can vividly recall David and Caroline Evans's wedding when Melveena arrived in a new, much cherished and very much admired outfit designed by Jean Muir, only to be greeted by Jack with the words "For God's sake Melveena, when are you going to get changed? You can't turn up to a wedding dressed like that".

I can also recall the occasion when he opened a conversation with another particularly kind and particularly sweet-natured female friend with the words "I have always thought your eyes were too close together. But I'm not a bit surprised, it's a sure sign of a criminal character, you know". I feared that she might burst into tears at this wholly unexpected and wholly unjustified frontal assault on both her appearance and her character.

He had always been brusque. Geoffrey Parker tells the story of J. Steven Watson (the Principal at St Andrews) describing being introduced to Jack: "Jack came up to me and said 'Watson? Watson??? Good God: I thought you were dead'. Hard though I tried, my conversation never entirely recovered from his opening salvo". But with age what could once be laughed off as brusque had now often evolved into what could only be regarded as offensive.

He could be rude to places and institutions as well as individuals. When he was interviewed for the *Leicester Mercury* he said that he had always regarded the city of his birth as little more than "a city of Philistines". Little wonder that the *Mercury* headed his interview with the title "Waspish views of leading historian". Indeed the adjective "waspish" recurs over and over again.

Alas there are many other such stories – many too embarrassing to recount. All too often it was the brutal directness or the stinging venom with which the words were delivered which made them so hurtful. Those on the receiving end were often as much shocked by the crude way the normal social niceties were being flouted and customary social taboos were being ravished as they were by the words themselves.

One of the last Christmas parties that Jack spent with us at home at Caius was not exactly enhanced by such opening remarks to a succession of my guests as "When did you lose your virginity and with whom?" (this abrupt opening question was addressed to one of my daughters, in front of her unmarried aunt and uncle, who were visibly startled by the question); "You must have the most boring voice in the world – I really can't bear to listen to you" (addressed to one of my, not surprisingly, much-offended brothers); "I don't know why Neil wastes good wines on people like you" (addressed to one of my startled wine-loving friends); "My God, you look so old – you're really not wearing very well, are you" (addressed to my youthful-looking sister); "Get away from me you disgusting creature" (addressed to my sister's dog); "You are giving us far too much wine. You mistake profligacy for generosity. It's like pouring good Bordeaux down the drain giving Latour and Climens to this ignorant lot" (addressed to me and all my family); "Oh, God, not goose again!" (addressed to my wife, who had just expertly cooked two geese and was bearing them triumphantly to the table). Since all these observations (all wholly unjustified) were offered loudly to the whole table, it did not make for the jolliest Christmas dinner I can remember.

At the end of the dinner when it was customary for the male guests to accompany Jack safely back to Christ's, he declared that he was not prepared to leave. "I'm staying here", he announced. The announcement was blunt and non-negotiable. I explained that as he had turned down the offer of a bed for the night, we no longer had any free rooms. "Well send someone else home", he said. He then proceeded to inspect all the bedrooms in the Master's Lodge, stomping round from room to room and pushing open the doors with his walking stick (whether they were occupied or not), until he found one that met his exacting specifications. He chose an en suite bedroom, which he quite reasonably said that at his age he needed, but it was also the largest twin-bedded room. We explained that moving him in, and our other guests out, would require some complicated adjustments (people and luggage and clothes would have to be moved and beds remade), but he obstinately refused to move. And so he got his way.

Next morning he said that the room was far too hot, the windows far too draughty, and my pyjamas, which he had borrowed for the night, far too big. He added that the deserted and wholly silent college was far too noisy. And did we not know that he liked his breakfast tea delivered to him in bed by seven. And why weren't we dressed by breakfast to drive him to his next social appointment, where, he added lugubriously, the food was likely to be even worse than he had had with us.

Most of us tried to ignore these absurd examples of rudeness and almost infantile ingratitude. We tried to laugh them off as regrettable if increasingly typical Plumbian eccentricities, but as they mounted up, they grew more and more difficult for old friends to forgive and more and more difficult for others to tolerate.

"On reflection, I think that his many of his friends were remarkably tolerant of the eccentricities of his old age. They certainly received few thanks for either putting up with him or putting him up. Many could more than match my experiences – indeed swapping stories of Jack's latest social infelicities became something of a consoling game for many of his old friends. Sadly it has to be said that his behaviour declined even further with the passing years. Social misdemeanours were replaced with social outrages. On more than one occasion, we were relieved that acts of particularly blatant public misbehaviour did not make the public prints – one that I witnessed, involving a black schoolgirl from Brixton, who was visiting Christ's on an Admissions Open Day, risked an accusation of racial harassment and sexual harassment as well as justified offence at his extreme rudeness.

Such behaviour could be socially and publicly destructive as well as merely personally disconcerting. Quentin Skinner said that in Jack's case, the childishness was such that it was like sharing a college with an impossibly badly behaved two year old, but, if infantilism was the cause of Jack's worst excesses, one would have to add that his took a very extreme form. We have all known relatives who grew to be difficult and obsessive (and rather childish) in old age, but Jack was in a class of his own. It was claimed by many Fellows that he had single-handedly destroyed High Table dining in Christ's and after he died, *The Guardian* actually printed a letter deploring the appalling public manifestations of his rudeness. The catalogue of unforgivable outbursts (many too embarrassing to recount) was legion. What some of us found especially distressing was not only that wholly innocent bystanders such as tourists and students and even visiting sixth-formers might (and often did) attract his ill-concealed ire, but also that so much of the bile was directed at those he knew best. Joyce Williams, the widow of the historian E.N. (Taffy) Williams and one of his oldest friends, was so upset by his paranoid tirades when he visited her that she declared that she felt that she had been visited by the Devil himself.

I think that Joyce finally forgave Jack, but others found it too much to ask. Cornelia, my younger daughter, wept for him on his death and rebuked her elder sister for not being able to do so. But I suspect that Olivia felt that if old people render themselves absolutely unlovable, then it is not easily within the power of the young to love them, however much they try. As she grew ever more successful, Olivia treatment at the hands of her former patron and admirer changed very markedly. As her income as a partner at Linklaters soared above anything Jack had ever received, he understandably felt that she no longer needed his help or support, so she too became the target of very unfair criticism. She found it intolerable, too, when she was expected to sit silently listening to Jack running down her parents and "slagging off" his and her oldest friends. When endlessly asked questions such as "Why does your mother dress so badly?" and "Why is your father too mean to buy her anything decent?" she not unreasonably asked, "Why should I be expected to respond to such absurdly untrue and such absurdly unkind accusations?" So she simply stayed away – as did so many others.

Cornelia continued to write to him, but as he became increasingly difficult (and increasingly demonised by others), she too visited him less and less. When she did visit him, she certainly cheered him up. He in return was markedly less critical of her than of most. I think that this was because she always stood up to him and never allowed him to browbeat her into submission. He declared her to be a free spirit. He felt that he still had the power to help her. He felt that she still confided in him, that she still in some sense needed him. Even so, the demands of a busy professional life as a corporate lawyer in London increasingly kept her away. So to Jack it seemed that even his favourites were deserting him. That they were doing so was largely his responsibility.

He once perceptively wrote of the effects on those around him of A.L. Rowse's anger and contempt. His "contempt for the world, for people, for critics, welled out of him like lava, scorching everything and everyone, making a desert around him". Who would ever have thought that the once life-enhancing Jack would in his great old age achieve much same effect?

I suspect that much of the anger and unhappiness came from loneliness, but the more he expressed his anger the lonelier and unhappier he became. He drove people away and then brooded on their absence. Sitting alone in his room for days on end, he brewed venom against those who did not ring, those did not write and those did not visit.

They increasingly did none of these things because they increasingly feared the response. It required a thick skin and a powerful sense of loyalty and compassion to climb the stairs of O staircase in the First Court of Christ's in his last years. Admittedly his face would light up when one arrived but usually his mood would soon darken and his obsessive hatred of his two successors in the Master's Lodge would erupt into the most improbable and most paranoid fantasies. I would often come away vowing not to return. On one occasion, eighteen months before he died, I told him that his bile had become unbearable. Listening for hours to tirades against his and my old friends and colleagues was simply too much to bear. I said that there was no point in my coming to see him simply to listen to outpourings of such bitterness and such hate. I stayed away for three weeks or so and received scribbled notes imploring me to return. Needless to say I did so. I suspect that most people did not.

His deafness made his sense of being abandoned even stronger. In his eighties, this became more and more of a handicap. Amongst his friends, only Jo Whaley seemed able to make his hearing aids work and one often had conversations at crazy cross-purposes. This doubtless added further to his frustration and irritation. Since he could not hear, he decided to do what many deaf people do, that is to talk non-stop himself. It made it more and more difficult to divert him from his black obsessions on to more cheering subjects. For such an avid conversationalist, it must have been maddening not to be able to join in. It not only made him more than ever what many have called "a High Table hazard best avoided at all costs", but it also led to an ever-increasing sense of isolation. His threat that the Fellows would never get their hands on his money came surprisingly close to being true. Christ's was not mentioned in his will; it was not even mentioned in the Glenfield Trust into which all that he owned was to be tipped. He thereby succeeded in ensuring that Christ's would never get their hands on his capital. Even getting their hands on the interest from it would be dependent on the goodwill of his four trustees – of whom I am one.

When trying to understand Jack's ambivalent relationship with Christ's and indeed with Cambridge at large, and when trying to understand why in his later years the hatred seemed so comfortably to outweigh the love, one needs to remember that neither his college nor his university had been over generous to him. It was all too easy for those who saw Jack in his pomp to forget his early struggles and setbacks.

When I was foolish enough to chide him for his denunciation of Christ's and Cambridge, his fierce response was very revealing. "It's easy for you to think like that", he exploded, "you have been given everything on a plate by Cambridge – an open scholarship when you were seventeen, a First when you were nineteen, a starred First when you were twenty, a Fellowship at your own college when you were twenty-two and a tenured Fellowship at another when you were twenty-three, not to mention a University Lectureship when you were twenty-four and being asked to Chair the Faculty whilst still in your forties". I pointed out that things had slowed down quite a bit after that, but he snapped back, "You were made Master of a really major Cambridge College much younger than I got a lesser one! Unlike you I had to wait for everything. Whatever I was given was given grudgingly and too late to give me any real pleasure. I was turned down by St John's, not kept on by King's, only allowed a full Fellowship at Christ's when I was thirty-five, turned down for all the established Cambridge Chairs I really wanted, and only given the Mastership of Christ's as an after-thought when I was past the university age of retirement".

For someone twenty-four years younger, who had always seen Jack as a securely established and unquestioned success story and as a scholar of internationally recognised stature, it came as a shock to me to be forced to suddenly see his career from such a very different perspective. It was rather like a father suddenly revealing his vulnerabilities to a son who had never seriously questioned the outstanding achievements and the psychological security of the father figure. I was astonished that a man of such impressive achievements and such seemingly well-established authority should reveal such hurts and insecurities. I was amazed that he should compare his career unfavourably with the career of someone so obviously junior and subordinate and inferior to him.

It may well have been a failure of both insight and sympathy on my part not to have foreseen that such distant snubs still had the power to give pain, but I had assumed that later major triumphs would have completely and sweetly obliterated such ancient hurts. Clearly not so, for he went on to say, "No wonder you love Cambridge so much", he added, "Cambridge has given you all you wanted from it. I have given it my life and most of my money, and they still hate me. Why should I pretend to like my colleagues when so clearly they don't like me. They have never appreciated what I have done for this college. They only tolerate me because they want my money!" Given such an interpretation, it is not difficult to see why he grew to hate so powerfully the institutions to which he had devoted his life. The sense of rejection, the sense of generosity not properly appreciated, the sense of friendship and fellowship not fully reciprocated grew stronger and stronger with advancing age. By the end, they dominated his thoughts and drowned out the very real affections and attachments he had once so readily recognised.

35. PLUMB AND HIS MASTERSHIP OF CHRIST'S IN CONTEXT

Jack was all too well aware, when he finally succeeded in being elected to the Mastership of Christ's, that the then Master, the then Senior Bursar and the then Senior Tutor were all bitterly opposed to his election. The depth of their hostility to him fully matched his to them. The venom of Gorley Putt, the Senior Tutor, was not alas atypical when he envisaged Plumb's Mastership as "a reign of venomous and vengeful partiality which would make Christ's an uncomfortable home for any but his cronies and creatures". Ironically, Gorley Putt was himself to fall out so badly with Sir Hans Kornberg, Plumb's immediate successor, that on his deathbed he allegedly cancelled his million pound legacy to the college. Changing alliances and allegiances are all part of Cambridge college life, and Jack Plumb had had decades of experience in manipulating them himself, but it certainly greatly reduced his enjoyment of his Mastership to know how much some of his colleagues hated him. That his financial generosity to Christ's won him, at best he thought, such grudging acknowledgment from the Fellowship was a source of profound disappointment in his later life.

It is important, however, that the hostility to Jack's Mastership is not exaggerated. Put in the context of many Cambridge college headships, his relatively short period in office was in many ways a great success and was recognised as such. His success in raising significant sums of money for Christ's, his insistence on the highest standards in the recruitment of both dons and undergraduates, and his attraction of the rich and famous to the college undoubtedly raised its profile. As so often in his career, he was much more popular with the young than with his contemporaries and he had some warm young admirers who recognised his achievements as Master. As Sir David Cannadine concluded in his judgement on the Plumb Mastership: "although it was brief, his Mastership was undeniably brilliant".

Many Masters of other Cambridge colleges suffered far greater problems with their fractious and rebellious fellowships. Corpus Christi once got through four Masters in less than two years; Hugh Trevor-Roper at times faced open warfare from the Fellows of Peterhouse, being once chased across the road to seek sanctuary in the Master's Lodge whilst pursued by a furious Dean;

and the rebellious Fellows of my own college provoked the early resignation of two hugely distinguished Masters in succession (Sir James Chadwick, C.H., FRS, and Nobel Prize winner; and Sir Nevill Mott, C.H., FRS, and Nobel Prize winner); and the threatened early resignation of their successor (Joseph Needham, C.H, FRS and FBA). Extreme distinction did not save them from what was called the Peasants' Revolt in Chadwick's case and an often poisonous political atmosphere in his successors' case. Chadwick's daughters never forgave the college history for describing their father as a Master of "surpassing gaucheness"; Mott once summoned me to the Master's Lodge to ask "why do all the Fellows hate me?"; and Needham precariously secured his renewal as Master after his first two years by only a single vote.

Richard Hofstadter, the distinguished American historian, who became a Fellow of Caius along with me in 1958, said that he had never before encountered such vicious personal criticism of the head of an academic institution as he witnessed in Caius. The political manoeuvrings of the Mafia or the Mob were tame, he said, in comparison with the ejection of one Master (Sir James Chadwick) and the election of his successor (Sir Nevill Mott). He and I, as newcomers to the Fellowship, listened in amazement to the character assassinations of the departing Master and the incoming Master, along with the dissection of the merits and morals of any other aspirants for the post of Master. Tammany Hall politics, he said, were kindly by comparison.

My first college may have laboured under the fictional reputation of being highly politicised as a result of Snow's *The Masters*, but when I left Christ's for Caius, I soon learned that I was joining a college factually famous for political infighting between Masters and Fellows right back to Dr Caius himself in the sixteenth century.

The college history written by that kindly historian Christopher Brooke, who was passionately devoted to Caius, could not deny the hostility that our second founder inspired amongst the Fellowship. Before dealing with "the catastrophe" of Dr Caius, Professor Brooke reminds us that "we must contemplate the sad and heroic vision of the aging Dr Caius, ceaselessly generous in the care and resources he poured into the building and endowment of his College, ceaselessly at variance with many of his younger colleagues". The tone of the disagreements between Master and Fellows can be judged by the anonymous "Articles concerning the preposterous government of Dr Caius, and his wicked abuses in Gonville and Caius College" and the trashing of his rooms "burning what could be burnt, smashing what could not be burnt".

John Caius was a difficult character and had certainly done much to provoke the younger fellows, presiding over them in what they not unreasonably regarded as a dictatorial manner, but his fate shows all too clearly that Plumb was not unique in feeling that extreme generosity to one's college does not always earn one the gratitude one expects and deserves.

No Master left a more indelible personal imprint on his college than John Caius. His three famous Renaissance gates – the Gate of Humility, the Gate of Wisdom and the Gate of Honour – which symbolised the route through college of every member from admission to graduation, are still what Caius is best known for architecturally. His tomb with the words "Fui Caius" ("I was Caius") is a triumphant assertion of his posthumous status that brooks no challenge or contradiction. His funerary epitaph "Vivit post funera virtus" ("Virtue lives on after death" cocks an immortal snook at those rebellious fellows who made the end of his life so miserable.

Dr Caius's place in history is secure. His huge contribution to the college that bears his name is unquestionable. I quote his example to show that however towering a Master's achievements are, they do not necessarily save him from vicious criticism in his lifetime. His treatment at the hands of the younger Fellows was abominable, however much those Fellows were provoked by their irascible Master. Their behaviour puts into context how transient their concerns now seem when measured against the lasting fame of the target of their abuse. Dr Caius's place in history is assured. So should Jack Plumb's be. His legacy was not an architectural, it was the human legacy of presiding over a college as a dominant personality for over sixty years and leaving the further human legacy of an unrivalled band of brilliant young historians to carry on his influence long after his death.

Examples such as those of Dr Caius and Dr Plumb are all too typical of Cambridge's rich history of internecine battles between Fellows and Masters over the centuries. Too much should not be made of these quarrels however vicious they were at the time. They may cast interesting light on the character of those who provoked them. They may mar the lives of those they abused but they do not cancel out their lasting achievements. They often cast a significant shadow on them but they rarely obliterate them completely. The place in history of John Caius is as assured as is the place of Sir John Plumb. One is secured as the founder of a college, the other is secured as the founder of a college of historians.

The dislike that Plumb provoked, and the snide denunciations he evoked, and the enemies he certainly earned, all need to be recognised but not exaggerated. They pale into insignificance compared with what many Cambridge Masters experienced. They help to explain his problems but they should not be used to eclipse his very real merits as Master. They certainly do not compare in viciousness with what I have learned from the history of my own college and indeed witnessed in it in my own lifetime, although, thankfully, very rarely in my own spell as Master.

Compared with these and many other examples, Jack had a relatively easy ride, but, in his own eyes, his achievements as Master did not receive the recognition he deserved. What might have been the successful culmination to his fifty years in Christ's was clouded by self-doubt and disappointment and by bitterness and recrimination. When they recognised the success of his fund raising by naming the new auditorium after him, it merely reminded him that whilst he had had a mere room named after him, Lord Todd had had a whole building bearing his name. Even worse, in his eyes, the Plumb Auditorium nestled inside the Todd Building as if to advertise its subordinate status.

36. PLUMB AND PUBLIC RECOGNITION: THE FILM *"IF"* AND *DESERT ISLAND DISCS*

It seems especially sad that a man who had deservedly won so much recognition in his lifetime should have died in such an unhappy and disappointed state of mind. In the sixties and seventies, he had earned the reputation of being the most widely read living historian, and his name popped up in the most unlikely places. In "If", the highly successful and highly subversive film on the English public school system, Dr J.H. Plumb was the real-life historian they chose to cite; on the race track, a horse named "'Professor Plumb" raced to victory; and a fellow historian, Clive Trebilcock, even named his dog "Plumb" – much to Jack's fury. Some of his pupils have even claimed that the "Professor Plumb", who was one of the suspects in the board game Cluedo, was named for Jack, and surmised that the well-known brand of "Dr Plumb pipes" were named for a younger pre-professorial Plumb. There were times when such claims seemed plausible, but the more prosaic truth is that they both substantially predated Plumb's modest public prominence. Equally unconvincing is the suggestion by his enemies that the use of the word "plumb" as an intensifier, in phrases such as "he was plumb crazy", owes anything to Jack's behaviour patterns.

Sadly he often felt that even these modest signs of name recognition served only to attract academic malice and that his modest celebrity inspired little more than envy and jealousy. He sometimes felt that attracting twelve million viewers for the *Royal Heritage* series was used simply as a stick to beat him with.

Jack's pupil, Sir Simon Schama, now carries the title of the most widely read and most widely viewed living historian and has been declared a "National Treasure" by *The Sunday Times*, but even he has not wholly avoided the envy and jealousy that such success seems inevitably to bring. Fortunately Schama seems to have learned to rise above the academic malice that huge popular success seems so often to engender. Jack found it harder to take. The fact that Schama receives even more well deserved eulogies than his mentor did at his peak of popular publications must help. As a result Schama's natural vivacity seems to survive pretty well unscathed. In sharp contrast Jack more and more took both his pleasures and his publicity rather gloomily. It would have been highly improbable that he would ever have been described, as Schama has been, as "the thinking woman's crumpet", but, if he had been so labelled, it seems unlikely that he would been able either to laugh it off or simply to enjoy it as Schama's natural exuberance seems to allow him to do.

It has to be admitted that, in his younger days, Jack had quite enjoyed some mild celebrity. He certainly enjoyed being asked to publicly pontificate on the merits of *Lady Chatterley's Lover* in the infamous trial in 1960 and, characteristically, said that he took especial pleasure in contributing to what Philip Larkin called "the birth of sex in England" as a direct consequence of the verdict in Penguin's favour.

He initially was delighted at the reference to him in Lindsay Anderson's film "If" which appeared in 1968. When it was shown in Cambridge the undergraduate historians in the audience all cheered at the following exchange:

"Mr Stewart (the history teacher): "George III was a mollusc who never found his rock": who said that?"

Mick (pupil): "Plumb? J.H.Plumb."

Later he wondered if he was being publicly mocked, because he was all too well aware that the elegant phrase attributed to him was, in fact, a slight misquotation from Sir Lewis Namier, who had written "George III was a mollusc who never left his shell". He could be surprisingly sensitive on such matters.

Other public recognition was more obviously to his liking. He greatly enjoyed being invited onto *Desert Island Discs* in 1978, and took great delight in the opportunity to choose as his first disc Handel's triumphalist "Zadok the Priest", the theme music that had introduced *Royal Heritage*, his hugely successful television series. But many who listened to the interview with Roy Plumley commented on the extent to which Plumb had reinvented himself for public consumption. As my wife remarked, "that is Jack in full chameleon mode". To be fair, he had often commented that "we're all authors of our own life stories and it is only sensible to produce the best possible and most interesting version that you can".

Nevertheless, many of his friends were quite taken aback to listen to a voice, that they could not recognise, give a most unexpected interview. In a measured, rather affected upper-class drawl, Jack managed to avoid mentioning any member of his family, any one of his famous pupils, any one of his friends, any one of his backers such as Howard or Snow or any one of his colleagues. The only historian he mentioned was G.M. Trevelyan but he did manage to let drop such Plumbian gems as "the three quarter of a million copies I sold of my first book helps me to run my car" when speaking of his Penguin history; or "my first best seller" when referring to *The First Four Georges*; or "another of my best sellers" when referring to *Royal Heritage*. His current concern, he said, was a book entitled *The Pursuit of Happiness* – something, which in later life, he was singularly unsuccessful in capturing.

Once again, he seemed to take pleasure in irritating the Fellows of his own college by stressing that he would have hated being purely a don with no means of frequent escape from Christ's. He also seemed to enjoy annoying his fellow historians by stressing that he would have hated being "a pure historian" without business interests outside academia, but he mainly succeeded in puzzling his friends with his version of his musical tastes.

Most of us were interested to be told that he tried to learn to play the piano for seven years in his childhood (something I had never heard mention of before), but gave up when he encountered a Bach fugue and realised that he would never be a successful piano player. More of us, however, were surprised to be told that he never let a day go by without listening to classical music, and even more surprised to be told that he could not bear "not regularly to listen to Beethoven". It was not a version that those who knew him best (especially my wife and I who had shared a house with him for many decades) could easily recognise. More convincing was his talk of his "great passion for jazz" between the ages of 15 and 25, but there were not many who knew him then who were still about to question or confirm it.

However he ended the interview at his truthful best, characteristically and effortlessly negotiating one of the finest luxuries I have ever heard on *Desert Island Discs*. He also made one of the best choices in his selection of "the book" he was allowed to take in addition to the complete works of Shakespeare and the Bible. For "the book", he asked if he could have correspondence, and, when told that he could, he chose Voltaire's letters, casually warning Roy Plumley that they amounted to 118 volumes. As for the luxury, he said that if he had been asked a week earlier he would have chosen Château Lafite '45, but since then he had drunk a bottle of Château Latour '61 in magnum and would now prefer to have that. He first asked for a case but negotiated that up to a dozen cases – a quite remarkably impressive and valuable luxury.

In his final choices he had triumphantly succeeded in being both a characteristically smart negotiator and a characteristically self-indulgent one.

And he must surely have been pleased to learn that he had followed on a week after his soon-to-be new hero Margaret Thatcher had appeared on the programme, and been even more pleased that he matched her in the popularity stakes measured by the recorded number of listeners. Neither one of them was in the David Attenborough or Spike Milligan league of mega popularity, but they were both in the top few per cent.

Alas such modest bits of celebrity and public recognition did nothing to soothe the ache within. Sadly, neither his knighthood and his academic honours, nor the trivial signs of populist name recognition seemed to give much solace to the real life Professor Plumb. Indeed such demotic recognition seemed often merely to annoy him. Instead of being mildly amused and mildly flattered, he found them irritating and rather demeaning. They did very little to cheer him up in his mature years.

What he always valued were the star pupils he taught. As Geoffrey Parker wrote: "Jack loved to count 'his' FBAs, a metric that he really valued – and with reason. I don't think anyone else, in any field, could match his total. He would also have been proud to know that so many of his advisees have been elected honorary fellows of Christ's." Parker is quite correct, they do constitute two unmatchable lists. If I do not list them here it is because their names are those of the "usual suspects" who have been so ubiquitously listed already in this memoir.

In his later years such causes of good cheer seemed all too rare. As he said at the eightieth birthday given by his pupils, "You may be surprised to learn that I am not a happy man". Many of us, alas, were no longer surprised.

37. PLUMB'S CHANGING ATTITUDE TO HIS PUPILS

There were flashes of the old Jack even in the last dark months of his life. I can vividly remember trying to interrupt and divert him from an angry monologue on the wickedness of the Master of Christ's and the folly of the Fellows and the greed of both. He stubbornly refused to be diverted. Indeed he expanded his denunciation to all academics. In his later years he became bizarrely convinced that all academics were overpaid and under-worked. Even worse, he became convinced that they were all criminally delinquent in carrying out what he regarded as their very undemanding duties. They were all idle and second-rate. Surely, I asked, he did not think this of his own pupils of whom he was surely legitimately proud.

"Which pupils?" he barked. "Well what about Quentin Skinner – after all he is the Regius Professor?" I murmured. "I don't count Skinner", he replied, "he is not really a historian at all any more. Anyway he is really one of yours. He's a Caian! I never even taught him. Norman Stone is another one of yours and I am certainly not counting him even if he did get the Modern Chair at Oxford!" "Well what about Simon Schama and Roy Porter, then. They are both products of Christ's and your own teaching? Surely they have done exactly what you would have most wished of your pupils – Roy is one of the most productive and versatile professional historians alive today, and Simon has brilliantly kept alive the Plumbian tradition of writing history as literature which appeals to a mass audience. Both are accomplished journalists as well as scholars. Both use radio and television to great effect. Neither of them has allowed themselves to be trapped into the narrow scholarly specialisms that you always despised. They have both written major works that command both respect and wide readership. They constitute a legacy of which any mentor could be proud and of which you in particular should take delight". "Yes", he said rather grudgingly, "they have done well, but they have so much free time. They don't seriously teach any more as I always continued to do. At least you still teach. You at least still have pupils". Then, suddenly warming to his theme, his face brightened and he declared that perhaps a combination of Porter's prodigious professional productivity, Schama popularising brilliance and my teaching record might in aggregate just about equal what he had achieved alone.

Taking heart from this return of his old ebullience and his old combativeness, I gently suggested that some might think that, admittedly in their own more limited ways, some of his pupils might even have surpassed him. At this he grinned and said "But even if I concede that you were a more successful teacher, and Roy a more productive scholar and Simon a more hugely successful writer, you would each still individually be less than half the man I was". Since I for one would very happily accept that assessment, I decided to quit the field whilst I was ahead. So I left contentedly clutching his generous "not one of you is even half a Plumb" verdict on behalf of all his pupils.

In happier times I am sure that I could successfully have made cases for much more generous assessments of not only Simon Schama and Roy Porter but also Rupert Hall, Quentin Skinner, John Burrow, Barry Supple, John Kenyon, David Cannadine, Norman Stone, Geoffrey Parker, Linda Colley, John Brewer, Niall Ferguson, Keith Wrightson, David Reynolds, John Vincent, Jo Whaley and many others. In happier times he might well have accepted my arguments. But in his final years one learned not to push one's luck. So I gave in leaving him for once chuckling happily at the outcome of our conversation. Such cheerful breaks in the gloom and paranoia of the last years of his life, alas, grew increasingly intermittent.

Some see Jack's "black period" as the result of a particular form of envy – the envy of youth and vigour induced by his own loneliness and loss of energy. For a man who had for most of his life enjoyed enormous reserves of energy and a life packed full of activity, it was galling to hear of how the diaries of his friends and pupils were still brimming over with exciting and interesting things to do. Jack longed still to have things to do. He longed still to be able to do them. He always said that he would never become like Snow, who in old age glared with implacable envy and hatred at the young and the active. Alas, he did not live up to his promise. Some undergraduates whom he tried to cultivate in old age received vitriolic letters castigating them for their ingratitude and their failure to visit him. The trouble was that their lives were as full as Jack's was now empty.

Boredom only served to intensify the sense of deprivation. "I scream with boredom in this terrible prison" was his description of a day spent alone in his rooms in Christ's. The trouble was the bile led to loneliness, the loneliness led to boredom and the boredom led to more bile. It was a vicious circle that few could break. Lord knows, some of us tried.

Some see his changed response to his older pupils (which for most of his life was exaggeratedly generous to the point of hyperbolic support) as the result of his loss of control. Physical weakness was difficult for Jack to accept but he bore wretched health and humiliating discomfort with remarkable stoicism for many years. Other forms of weakness he found more difficult to bear. Loss of power over others, a weakening sense of patronage, a diminishing ability to dominate, to advise, to instruct and to order the lives of his friends and pupils upset the nature of many of his relationships. I think what he found very hard to bear was an increasing sense that his pupils and his protégés no longer needed him or his support. They were increasingly beyond his control.

Quentin Skinner once said to me that if Jack had died the day before he (Quentin) got the Regius Chair in 1996 and the day before I became Master of Caius in 1996, our relationships with Jack would never have undergone the changes which so depressed us both. We would still remember them as being as warm, as mutually supportive and as invigorating as they had been for so many decades. Quentin felt that we had stepped out of his shadow, ceased to need his support and patronage – in effect had escaped from his control. Because we no longer needed his support, we were to receive the opposite. Because we no longer needed his patronage, we had to be punished for our presumption. We had presumed to rise above our station, so we had to be belittled and derided. He was particularly enraged when told that Quentin had turned down the offer of a knighthood. Matching his own highest public honour was bad enough, but the presumption to reject it was unforgiveable in Plumb's eyes. Coming after years of excessively generous support, it was a disturbing and unsettling reaction.

Looking back on the life of the younger Plumb, the evidence of a certain control freakery was always there. We just could not see it so clearly until it developed into its full caricatured force in old age. When the opportunities to exercise it had largely gone, frustration led it to take on a more and more unattractive form.

To be fair, I had thought that some escaped the malign effect of his censorious old age. I think that distance may have helped but I could not recall him ever including Simon Schama in his diatribes to me and no one can doubt that Simon had clearly escaped the need for Jack's patronage and support. Others, however, have informed me that unbeknown to me even Schama did not escape the repercussions of Plumb's outbursts of anger and denunciation.

In a very revealingly letter after reading a first draft of this memoir, John Brewer wrote à propos Jack and Simon: "I was used to dealing with someone who could be astonishingly generous and full of life as well as being nasty and mean-spirited. I didn't (and it certainly seems fortunately) have any contact with Jack in his last years, so I didn't witness the transformation that you describe – I think that you got the tone of hurt and disappointment spot on – understated but palpable. But I have always thought of Jack as a Jekyll and Hyde figure. I remember very well a dinner party that Simon gave for him at his house when we were both at Harvard. George and Zara Steiner were also present. I don't know why but Jack really had it in for George and was incredibly rude and nasty. Simon and Ginny (his wife) were distraught; the whole evening left a nasty taste. Next day we were at the American Academy of Arts and Sciences and he could not have been nicer: funny, magnanimous, the old Jack we so admired. But clearly the balance shifted over the years. You say that Simon alone seems to have escaped Jack's venom, but the dinner in Christ's for Simon's departure to Oxford ended up with a rare Schama bashing session which left Simon close to tears. It all started with Simon's tentative title for his Dutch book, the infelicitous "Breaking of the Dykes", but ended with general denunciation of those who were deserting him and Cambridge. But I should not just dwell on the dark side. I always greatly admired the way he nurtured and was never threatened by the bright and the young, he could be so generous, his lectures had such brio and brilliance, and he had a nose for a historical subject that made him the bloodhound of historians."

Like most us, John Brewer chose to forgive the darker side of Plumb in favour of the more important and more enduring positives. No one could have been more forgiving or more generous in his tributes than Simon Schama.

Simon visited him within weeks of his death and his account of his visit in *The New Yorker* shows that he could still bring out the best in Jack. It helped of course that Simon shared and practised Jack's belief that "history since Herodotus had been a public art, which somehow had become unnaturally imprisoned in the academy; unless it got out – at least for short breaks on parole – it would deservedly rot". It helped that few have done more to prevent it rotting than Simon and, of course, his mentor. It helped that he could respond as sympathetically to Plumb the entrepreneur as he could to Plumb the historian – after all he once called him "half Edward Gibbon, half Max Bialystock". (It is, perhaps, revealing that many of the Cambridge historians who have read this piece felt the need to ask "Who is Max Bialystock?"). It helped, too, that Schama (although his youthful charm and bubbly personality made him almost irresistibly liked and admired in a way that Plumb had never really enjoyed) had also experienced at first hand the coruscating envy that popular success can inspire amongst many academics. Whatever the reasons, his description of his last visit to Jack's rooms in Cambridge on 26 September 2001(within three weeks of Jack's death) is both generous and affectionate and shows that, in the right company, Jack could still be stimulated into an approximation of the Plumb of old. He could rise above his melancholia if not entirely shed it: "Illness had shrunk him quite a bit", wrote Schama, "so that he now not only sounded like the elderly Voltaire but looked like him too. Like Voltaire, Plumb held up a historical mirror that had become quite dark in old age. He was not sanguine about our chances of survival, and he likened modern America to the late Roman Empire, circa 300: impossibly over extended, beleaguered by barbarians, aware that all its glories of law and engineering might yet be demolished by incomparably less sophisticated peoples for whom destruction is a vocation and life is expendable." "Still, as the evening drew in, he wanted to know how we were faring after September 11th, and when I told him that on a recent Sunday night Times Square had been packed and the theatres humming, the old roguish twinkle came back for a moment and he recalled an evening not so long ago when we stood in his apartment at the Carlyle, hoisted glasses of Krug, and watched the lights go on down Madison Avenue, and he pronounced the whole scene "urban champagne". He would not have wanted us to lose our fizz."

Clearly he had not entirely lost his fizz, but there were very few of his friends who could any longer uncork it.

Few any longer had Schama's ability to re-ignite that happy combination of a scholar's insight and a *bon viveur's* unashamed love of the good things of life – a combination that was so characteristic of Jack Plumb in his prime.

Few of the current generation saw much of that old life-enhancing flamboyant mixture. He continued to be generous and attentive to a few undergraduates, he continued to support his young and still vulnerable protégés who still had their way to make, but the bitter, curmudgeonly side of his nature grew to be increasingly dominant with his older colleagues and alas his friends. They saw all too little of Plumb who "radiated warmth, buoyancy, optimism and hope". They saw all too much of the Plumb who "was consumed by doubt, loneliness, envy and disappointment". Alas this descent into darkness will be the only side of him that many saw during the late 1980s and 1990s.

38. PLUMB: THE END OF LIFE, HIS DEATH, HIS BURIAL AND A MEMORIAL DINNER

Nothing more vividly (or more darkly) exemplifies Jack's final state of mind than the instructions for his burial. His will instructed his solicitors that he was to be buried alone – no announcement of his burial was to be made, no-one but the undertakers should attend. There were to be no mourners, no friends, no family, no ceremony and no music. There were to be no words. There was not even to be a coffin. He was to be buried in a body bag. If he had wished to shock and to hurt even at the end, he succeeded.

One needs to remember that the arrangements for his death had been a favourite preoccupation of his for the last quarter of a century or more. I remember my younger daughter at the age of eight replying indignantly (when Jack said that children had nothing interesting to say and should not be allowed to join in adult conversation) by protesting that she and her sister had very interesting conversations with their parents whilst "all you talk about is death and restaurants". There was more than a little truth in that impertinent rebuke.

Jack loved to fantasize about the manner of his passing and the rituals that would accompany it. Jessye Norman was to sing, concerts were to be held, Fauré's requiem was to be played, those friends currently in favour were to attend. Later he decided to have a Jewish-style funeral and be buried within twenty-four hours in the presence of a very select group of friends. But with the passing years the list of those who would be allowed to attend started to shrink. The list of those who most definitely must be kept away started to grow. No announcement of the funeral should be allowed to occur in case the uninvited chose to gate crash his burial rites. It was a very far cry from the flamboyant funeral he had once planned for himself.

His final wishes were in one respect frustrated. Body bags are not bio-degradable and the church authorities insisted on a shroud, which somehow seemed more fitting. In his shroud, he was lowered on a piece of stiff cardboard into what seemed to be an entirely admirable plot, which he had negotiated for himself at St Margaret's Church in Westhorpe. It is almost by his old front door in the Old Rectory. By giving some land and by offering a generous subscription to the repair of the thirteenth-century church tower, he had managed to get what he thought would be a prime and spacious spot in the ancient and already over-crowded churchyard.

He had successfully negotiated an agreement that he should be buried on a plot on the path which led from the church tower to the Old Rectory where he spent some of the happiest and most productive years of his life. Only Jack would have had the cheek to ask for, and the persistence to get, such an apparently appropriate spot. To mark the grave, the outstandingly brilliant stone carver, Lida Cardoza Kindersley, was asked to produce a simple slate headstone bearing the words "J.H. Plumb – Historian – 1911-2001". Anything more was thought by a majority of his executors to be out of keeping with his last wishes.

Alas, on recently revisiting St Margaret's Church, I was dismayed to find the whole churchyard depressingly decayed and neglected. I had always much admired the church and always felt that it was very appropriate for a historian to live next door to a church which had been the local church for Mary Tudor. She was the daughter of a king (Henry VII), the sister of a king (Henry VIII) and the grandmother of a queen (the ill-fated "nine day queen of England", Lady Jane Grey) and, of course, as wife of the king of France, she had been a queen herself. She had lived in Westhorpe Hall, with her second husband, Charles Brandon, Duke of Suffolk until her death there aged only 37. Now, alas, there was no hint of any such royal or ducal connections. Now, with its bat-infested interior and its untended graves and its un-mown grass, it looked distinctly unloved and its churchyard embarrassingly uncared for.

This was the first time I had actually seen the Plumb headstone and was taken aback to see a rather modest round-topped gravestone more than half-covered in straggly uncut grass and weeds. To make it even more depressing, Jack had forgotten that the majestic lime trees which still line the boundary between the Old Rectory and the fine 13th century church were the kind that drip a sticky glue-like deposit every summer and his uncharacteristically understated headstone and its very restrained inscription (without his much treasured title) were completely obscured with dirty green moss which had happily fed on the lime trees' adhesive dripping. The deposit, which had built up on the unattended and unwashed headstone over the seventeen years since his death, made it virtually impossible to identify who had been buried there. As William Young, the American former World-Banker turned historian, and his Dutch wife, Angela who were accompanying us, said: "It looks like the modest headstone to one of one's favourite old dogs. The kind that one might find tucked away in the forgotten corner of a neglected English garden". It was very definitely not the handsomely simple headstone to a celebrated historian, lovingly preserved in a much-treasured spot that I had fondly imagined, and many of his pupils might have hoped for. As my wife said: "Even his worst enemy would have thought that he deserved more than that murky little memorial, left to lurk unseen and untended in that seemingly friendless graveyard". What made it worse was that the current owners of the Old Rectory had erected a huge wooden fence between their property and the church, so that instead of Jack's gravestone appearing aptly and picturesquely silhouetted against his old front door, it now lurked inconspicuously in the deepest shade of the exceptionally high fence.

Ironically the man, who had for so much of his life lovingly anticipated a spectacular funeral and a celebrated death, had achieved almost total obscurity.

As so often in his life, much of this was his own fault – the result of his misguided decision about the secretive and clandestine nature off his burial rites and his insistence on consulting nobody about them. If he had asked anyone who knew anything about trees, he would have avoided the fate of being buried under *Tilia x vulgaris* (the common lime) which is so prone to infestations by aphids. The lime is one of my favourite trees. Its soaring trunks and its summer flowers – so beloved by bees and so famed for their sweet fragrance – make it a handsome and memorable ornament for all parks and substantial gardens, but as all tree lovers know so well and as all garden books so earnestly warn one "never park your car under one". These limes produce all enveloping amounts of "sticky, sooty exudations" of the kind that have all but obliterated Jack's headstone.

I confess that I found my visit to his graveside profoundly depressing. I found it less than cheering to think that the two people who had played the major role in steering me towards a career as a historian – H.E. Howard and J.H. Plumb – had managed, largely due to their own folly, to have achieved such obscure endings to their lives and such invisible markers to their final resting places – one in an unmarked grave and one in a scarcely decipherable one..

If one Googles Westhorpe Church, one can read that the gravestone of the historian "J.H. Plum" can be found there – significantly twenty per cent of his surname had already been hidden from sight when that digital record was written. When I visited the site in 2018, it was a struggle even to decipher that much. Admittedly, if the gravestone received an annual autumnal clean, it could be restored to its modestly dignified original state, but that seems to be a highly unlikely outcome given the obscure rural setting he has chosen for his final resting spot. With the passage of time and the death of friends, the chances of such an annual clean will grow less and less likely.

In sharp contrast, where Plumb consigned his body and his gravestone to deep rural obscurity, his direct contemporary the distinguished historian Eric Hobsbawn left detailed instructions for his passing and chose that his ashes would be buried in Highgate Cemetery, mischievously "just to the right of

Karl Marx", and thereby ensured that they would remain immaculately tended and easily visited forever. The headstones of these two historians, once old friends, are remarkably similar but the faces they present to the world could hardly offer a greater contrast: one is crisp and clean and looks beautifully presented, the other is hardly readable.

This belated discovery made me especially grateful that we had at least toasted Jack's memory in a memorial dinner in his honour in 2002, because fortunately, although he insisted that there should be no memorial service in Christ's, he had made generous provision in his will for an occasion to be held in his honour within a year of his death. The occasion was "to be in accordance with the wishes expressed in his life-time".

Typically, Jack expressed different wishes to different people. Fortunately, the majority vote was for a dinner for his friends and pupils. We hoped that with suitable speeches, fitting food and appropriate wine, and the animated conversation that he so loved, his old friends and pupils would be able to give him the send-off he deserved. We could at least be sure what the main topic of conversation would be.

The dinner could not, alas, live up to Jack's published plans for the hundredth birthday that he never achieved. In *House and Garden* in 1987, he published his generous scheme for such an improbable occasion. "For my friends", he wrote, "I have made ample provision for my centennial in 2011, because I now collect only large bottles – for that fiesta, *imperiales* (eight bottle bottles). They are building up nicely: Lafite '75, Palmer '82 and Mouton Rothschild '82, Haut-Brion '79 perhaps to start them off. I only hope that half a dozen friends will be able to be there and take part".

It is just as well that this happy fantasy could never take place. First, it could not happen as he had envisaged because Jack would obviously not be present. Secondly, it could not happen with the wines he listed because the Mouton '82 was drunk at my sixtieth birthday at Waddesdon in 1995. I thought that it was wonderfully generous of Jack to present it in the wholly appropriate setting of a Rothschild wine cellar and I feel no guilt at all in having helped to consume one of the great clarets of the century (Parker gave it the perfect score of 100, and Michael Broadbent called it "a Churchill of a wine"). Thirdly, it could not happen because, of the other three *imperiales*, which Jack had planned as mere starters, there was no sign in his cellar when he died. Possibly Jack generously gave them away to friends before he died. More probably, they were simply part of a future fantasy that never became reality. If so it is just as well. Four *imperiales* (that is, thirty two bottles) for half a dozen friends might well have killed us.

Even without first growth imperials, it turned out to be possible for us to lay on an appropriate celebration of his life as he stipulated in his will. My cellar was able to produce wines of a suitable standard and we were able to drink to his memory in the vintages that he most admired and from the châteaux that he loved the most. In the buzz of memory and nostalgia, which such an occasion engendered, we were able to console ourselves that, in David Cannadine's words, "his darker side dies with him: the rages, the rudeness, the resentment, the regrets, the life so often lived at odds with his own nature – and with other people's too. But his happier, sunnier, warmer, more creative, more exuberant, more expansive side lives on – in his books, which still captivate with their high-spirited prose and unexpected insights; in his students and protégés, who will never forget his unique brand of inspirational magic; and most lastingly in Christ's College, which will be both a poorer and a richer place without him".

Surrounded by Jack's friends and his pupils, it was easy for us to recall what an unforgettable experience it was to be taught by him, easy for us to give thanks for the huge generosity from which so many of us have benefited, easy for us to recollect all those wonderful dinners he hosted, easy to invoke those great wines he shared with us, easy for us to relive those many summer holidays over which he presided so genially and so dictatorially in villas of ever increasing size and grandeur, easy to recapture the buzz of excitement which his lectures once created, easy to repeat his characteristic praise (and his equally characteristic put-downs), easy to think back to his delight in his latest purchases of porcelain and paintings and silver, easy to quote from his memorable prose. And – most important of all – it was even easier for us to remember that it was one of our life's greatest privileges to have been numbered amongst his friends. We had all been the beneficiaries of someone who had been for most of his life the most generous of men.

It is the recognition of just how privileged that friendship was, which makes his decline so unbearably sad. It is the recognition of just how much he enriched so many people's lives that makes it so painful to admit that he ended by impoverishing his own life and those of many around him. Let us hope that we shall all increasingly forget the black years and increasingly remember the good ones when, as C.P. Snow wrote of him in the 1960s, "he was one of the tonic spirits of our day".

We should never forget that there were more than enough of the good years to constitute a splendid legacy of which all his old friends and pupils can be legitimately proud. It is after all no small thing to have been the friend and professional colleague of a historian whose influence has been so pervasive and so profound. Arguably the message he taught and the values he disseminated and the pupils he launched on their careers have been, and will continue to be, of as great importance to his profession as the books he actually wrote himself. For as Simon Schama, the pupil who in my view best encapsulated the values he taught, has written, "If boldly conceived, thoughtfully researched and elegantly written popular history is once again enjoying an extraordinary flowering in Britain, it was Sir John Plumb who planted the seeds, and tended the garden, while himself producing some of its most dazzling blooms. From the beginning of his career to its end he never wavered from the view that history's vocation might begin in the academy, but it should not end there; that as an illumination of the human condition, the 'interpreter of its destiny', it was too important to be confined to the intra-mural disputes of the professionals ... Should history somehow survive as the great art it has been; as Macaulay promised, one part philosophy, one part poetry; should it somehow keep a place in the indispensable archive of our beaten-up world, it will be because Jack Plumb wrote and taught and lived as he did."

If "history is the new black", as many now assert, then Plumb and his pupils and protégés can take much of the credit.

Rather bizarrely but in some ways quite fittingly, Jack said he would like the end of his posthumous celebratory proceedings to be marked by the sounding of the last post by a solitary trumpeter. Perhaps after all he might have found the right way to signal the end of an era and the closing of a chapter in all of our lives, but in the event it was felt that the evening should end with the affection and nostalgia of Dante Campailla's speech rather than with the Grand Guignol theatricality envisaged by our old friend in his gloom-ridden final days. He had after all already made abundantly clear by his funeral arrangements his sense that we all die alone and that he in particular would be buried in lonely isolation. To underline that feeling with the mournful elegy of a sole trumpeter was felt to be out of keeping with the warmth and friendship and very real sense of gratitude that dominated his memorial dinner.

The dinner was unanimously declared to be a great success. Held in the Master's Lodge and the three great Combination Rooms of Caius, it consisted of old friends representing all aspects of Jack's life and career (ranging from historical scholarship to claret). It also encompassed a range of ages (from the late teens in the form of Thomas Noblett to the late eighties in the form of Joyce Williams), which was so characteristic of Jack's parties. As Hugh Johnson wrote afterwards, "Nothing, but nothing, compares with your suite of reception rooms in Caius: indeed to have Soane fix up an apartment simply for taking water between dinner and dessert could be mistaken for conspicuous consumption but how Jack would have loved it. He was, I thought, observing closely on Saturday night, and was probably frustrated not to find a single thing to cavil at." As many others wrote "it was the kind of party that Jack in his prime would have been proud to give".

Other *post mortem* reactions to his death were less celebratory. Some historians raised significant questions about his reputation and what it should be based on.

Professor Jeremy Black, for instance, asked, with reference to the responses to Jack Plumb's death and the assessments of his life, "Should historical reputation simply rest on assessments of scholarship alone?" In my view that is clearly a question demanding the answer "No". My reasons for thinking so are probably rather different from those that led Professor Black to ask it. Professor Black felt very strongly that Jack's obituaries had been too kind to him – indeed, too eulogistic. They had not dwelt sufficiently on Jack's malign personality. "None", he wrote, "captured the animosity inspired by a man spoken of as evil by Richard Cobb, Jack Gallagher and many other major scholars of their and Plumb's vintage." "It suggests to me," he wrote, quite rightly in my opinion, "that the rivalry between Plumb and Elton discussed by the obituarists should be placed as much in personal as in professional terms, and that his personality may have prevented Plumb from gaining the position and prestige he pursued, not least the Regius chair at Cambridge and a peerage".

Although I was very surprised to be told that Jack Gallagher regarded Jack Plumb as being "evil" (a view which Gallagher's closest friend and colleague, Dr Anil Seal, thought "was so highly improbable as to beggar belief'; and which Norman Stone, who knew both Cobb and Gallagher very well, dismissed as absurd), I nevertheless agree with Professor Black's argument that assessments based simply on published work, with little or no reference to the personalities that produced those works, are not only one dimensional but are a denial of what historians quite properly spend so much of their professional work doing – namely examining and assessing the character and personality of historical figures and analysing and explaining the consequences of those personality traits. I think that Professor Black is less than generous to some of the obituaries – some of which seemed to me to be admirably balanced and often far from flatteringly bland – but it is true that few of them had the space in which to do even superficial justice to a complex and driven character such as Sir John Plumb.

This memoir was designed to redress the balance of those obituaries that were thought to be too cosy, and also to complement those professional bibliographical assessments that were thought to be too arid. Partly it was inspired by the uncomplicated desire to place on record a portrait of a colourful and interesting character who so entertained and so enraged so many of his contemporaries. It was also designed to concentrate on the man, the better to understand the published work and the public career. There will be those who may find this book too painfully intimate at times and too based on my own conversations and experiences but those at least I can vouch for. There is plenty of colourful anecdotage, much of it alas mythical, for those who want to repeat such stories, but I have preferred to cite mainly those events of which my family and I had direct personal experience. They will have the advantage not only of being true, but also of being new.

There will probably be those who would prefer more time to be spent on his work and less on his life, but there have been ample dissections of his professional contributions to scholarship – notably the day-long historical conference organised by David Reynolds in Christ's and by the excellent assessment of his scholarship by David Cannadine in *The Proceedings of the British Academy* and in *History Today*. There are plenty of historians of the eighteenth century more than well qualified to assess his work (many of them now far better qualified than I am), but there are very few, if any, who knew him for so long and so well as I did, and very few, if any, better qualified than I am to assess the man, his life and his personality.

39. PLUMB AND HIS LEGACY: HISTORIAN AND TEACHER OF HISTORIANS

Several people, having read first drafts of this memoir, have asked me why the last years of Jack Plumb's life were so angry and so bitter and so miserable. As one distinguished colleague asked, "Why the constant rage? Why was he always so angry?" "Did he doubt the survival and longevity of his legacy at the end of his life?"

I think the answers lie partly in the realisation that rage always played a large part in his life; in drink his characteristic robust banter very often descended into barely controlled fury. Angry denunciations of what he regarded as his friends' and his colleagues' manifold and manifest deficiencies were a part of his late night drinking for as long as I can remember. I recall being taken aback even in my mid-teens when I was loudly and publicly denounced by Jack for my many shortcomings (mainly my lack of ambition) in the most violent and unforgiving language. At the time, I charitably put the violence of the language mainly down to drink and partly down to the tradition of plain speaking that prevailed in the provincial group dominated by the Howard brothers and Gordon Winterton. This group was used to denouncing governments and political parties and above all politicians in the most violent language. The Church, the aristocracy and the Royal Family were all denounced with a dismissive scorn, often viciously laced with vitriol. Contempt poured from them at the best of times – when over-excited by alcohol the members sounded like an orchestra of subversives all playing uninhibitedly in the fortissimo range.

As radical idealists they had improbably high expectations of social change. As committed teachers they had improbably high but also admirably high expectations of what their pupils could reasonably hope to achieve. Since I found the possibilities dangled before me immensely encouraging, I was quite prepared to put up with the violent language used to denounce anyone who failed to aim high and to work hard. I put the intentions of the personal denunciations down to a probably accurate recognition of my need to recognise what could be achieved and how much effort would be needed to do so. Who was I to expect to be more politely chastised than the whole Tory party, the Crown or the bench of Bishops? Youth probably made me more accepting: when a fatherless fourteen or fifteen year old was being denounced by a Cambridge don in his forties the effect of seniority could be both powerful and compelling. I suspect that many of us just got used to the bullying manner.

Others were less forgiving and many of his friendships apparently ended as a result of explosions of unforgivable rage. Important early relationships such as that with Graham Wright certainly ended in rage-induced verbal violence.

The bitterness was more largely a product of old age. It was fuelled by loneliness, ill health and a conviction that he was cruelly un-appreciated. Some of this was certainly justified. Not everyone treated him generously; not all of his friends or all of his beneficiaries recognised how generously he had treated them; not all were as forgiving as they might have been.

The misery came partly I think from a growing realisation that he might have made the wrong life choices – as a ninety-year old bachelor, who had outlived most of his close friends and driven away many of the survivors, he had no wife or partner or children or grandchildren to support and sustain him in his declining years. He had largely long broken his links with his birth family.

More of the misery came, I think, from a growing feeling that he had failed to achieve his lifetime's ambitions. In extreme old age he increasingly felt that his professional work was heading for a serious critical downgrading if not for complete dismissal. Professional as well as personal oblivion beckoned discomfortingly closer. "Was all that work worth it?" he would increasingly ask himself. "Has my life really made a difference? Will any of my work survive?" I often tried to reassure him. I reminded him that he had left a mini-masterpiece of historical biography in *Chatham*. I reminded him that *The First Four Georges* was being reprinted again so that its vivid evocation of Georgian monarchy would entertain and inform a new generation of readers. I reminded him that there were plans to re-publish *The Death of the Past,* which has recently been described by Niall Ferguson as another "minor masterpiece". I reminded him of the long-standing influence of the Penguin *History of England in the Eighteenth Century.* I reminded him of the scholarly standing of *The Growth of Political Stability* and the reputation of the two Walpole volumes – *The Making of a Statesman* and *The King's Minister.* He was partially reassured but he was nothing if not a realist. He knew that most historical scholarship has a relatively short shelf life and he felt that many of his professional enemies and his influential detractors would be eager to deflate, if not yet to destroy, his reputation. Some he felt would be happy to consign him to oblivion. He knew that really major figures can transcend personal animus, but he doubted that he was sufficiently significant to do so. He had already lived long enough to see some of his work being superseded and some of it was already being forgotten. "Not much of it", he said bleakly, "will live on".

Many of his academic contemporaries have certainly seen their work systematically superseded. The work of his great rival, Geoffrey Elton, has been spectacularly overthrown – not least by his own pupils. Two of the most brilliant and most highly-profiled of them, David Starkey and Diarmaid MacCulloch, have devastatingly picked apart Elton's portrait of Thomas Cromwell as the architect of what he famously called a "Tudor Revolution in government", the mastermind behind the creation of a modern bureaucracy. This is not the verdict on Thomas Cromwell that emerges from either the outstanding academic work of Starkey and MacCulloch or the hugely influential and popular fictional work of Hilary Mantel.

It would have given Jack great pleasure to witness the fall from grace of this part of Elton's work. It would have given him even more delight that the dominant thesis that my generation of Cambridge students dared to question at our peril has been so influentially undermined by a brilliant prize-winning novelist whose work has been made available to millions of readers and viewers. Elton was always particularly enraged by popular versions of Tudor history – the film version of *A Man for All Seasons* was a famous *bête noire* of his – and the thought of the once all-prevailing certainties of the Eltonian thesis being questioned by "a mere novelist" would run counter to all of his most dearly held beliefs.

Jack's work on Sir Robert Walpole and his thesis on the growth of political stability in early eighteenth century England has not yet suffered a whole scale revision of this scholarly magnitude and this level of publicity, but he was probably right to fear the eroding effects of future scholarly revision.

He certainly did not suffer critical revision at the hands of his own pupils in the way that Elton has. He was very relaxed at his former colleague Linda Colley's attempt to revise his work on the early eighteenth century. Indeed he was personally encouraging to Professor Colley. And he would, I hope, have been modestly gratified by my recent attempts to add to and consolidate his work on "The Commercialisation of Leisure" in the latest revised and much enlarged edition of *The Birth of a Consumer Society* published by John Spiers at EER Publishers in 2018. How he would have reacted to the detailed and, I hope, reasonably balanced reassessment of his character and personality and achievements in this memoir is quite a different matter.

In my view, he was excessively pessimistic about how much of his work would survive, but he may of course be right. The jury is inevitably still out on that, but I am confident that he made too little allowance for the surviving influence of his view of history and the influence of his pupils. His kind of history and his kind of pupils are his best hope of immortality. They I think are his true legacy. On reflection, to mark his burial spot we should probably have had carved on a rather larger headstone the words:

Sir John Plumb
Historian and teacher of Historians
1911 – 2001

That is how he should probably best be remembered. That is how he should have wanted to be remembered.

Other historians have concurred in this judgement. Sir David Cannadine wrote of Jack's later life: "his own career ... in a manner that was both indirect and ironic ... was now reaching its supreme culmination – not so much because of anything he himself was still doing, but rather through the endeavours and accomplishments of his most outstanding and illustrious protégées: among them Roy Porter, who was writing even more prolifically than Plumb was during the 1950s and 1960s; Simon Schama, whose best-selling books, television series and New York fame eclipsed anything Plumb had ever achieved; Quentin Skinner, who was appointed to the Regius Professorship of Modern History that Plumb had vainly coveted; and Neil McKendrick, whose long tenure of the Master-ship at Gonville and Caius College made him a college proconsul in ways that Plumb at Christ's had never quite been. At one level, this gave Plumb enormous pleasure, triumphing over his enemies at one remove, and ensuring that his influence would live on. But he also became deeply resentful of his most successful students, who had once been his clients, but had subsequently gone on to achieve more than he had."

Cannadine was too modest to include his own name in that list of those who carried the flame of Plumb's achievements into the future, but justice demands that it most certainly should be. He comfortably surpassed his mentor by becoming President of the British Academy, he was knighted earlier than Plumb, he has become an even more prolific journalist and broadcaster, his academic productivity shows no sign of slowing down, and he is now one of the most highly profiled historians in the world.

Once one includes the names of protégées such as Cannadine who were never actually taught by Plumb, but who were part of the Christ's fellowship chosen by Plumb, part of the Christ's history team dominated by Plumb, and part of the profession who escaped the confines of pure academe to flourish in ways that Plumb had done, then the names of David Cannadine, Niall Ferguson, David Reynolds, Linda Colley, John Brewer, Quentin Skinner and Norman Stone would most assuredly have to join the names of those he did teach as undergraduates – such as Rupert Hall, Eric Stokes, Simon Schama, Roy Porter, John Burrow, John Vincent, Geoffrey Parker, Joachim Whaley, William Noblett and myself. Many others could arguably be added to those two lists to confirm the depth and range of Plumb's influence – such as Frank Spooner, Barry Supple, John Kenyon, Jonathan Steinberg, Simon Smith, Bob

Robson, Michael Bush, John Thompson, David Blackburn, Dominic Lieven, David Nokes, Peter Musgrave, Derek Hirst, Clive Holmes, Geoffrey Baldwin, John Miller, John Beattie, John Money, Brian Hayes, Brian Hill, Paul Fritz, and Ester Moir.

There can be no doubt that, in this aspect of academic influence, Jack comprehensively outgunned all his main rivals. Neither Owen Chadwick nor Geoffrey Elton in Cambridge came close. Neither Trevor Roper nor A.J.P. Taylor in Oxford was in the same league. When it came to the massed ranks of Jack's pupils or the more select group of those of them who achieved international eminence, the big historical guns of late twentieth-century historians lagged way behind. Some of them (such as Lord Dacre) may have played the English Honours system more adroitly, but none of them matched the international impact of Plumb and his grandest and most celebrated pupils. Niall Ferguson has recently described himself as "*homo atlanticus*", as his life oscillates between New York and London and shuttles between Boston, New York and Washington. Other protégées, such as Simon Schama and David Cannadine and John Brewer, could justifiably claim to be leading members of the same international genus, as could Roy Porter have done before his untimely death, but they, and others of the same ilk, were merely following in the footsteps of their mentor who had joined that tribe some fifty years earlier, when he flitted back and forth from London to New York, preferably on Concorde, and criss-crossed the States on richly remunerated lecture tours.

It is then without question that one can justifiably cite his influence as a teacher as a major part of his legacy, but it is important that one does not suggest that that is not all he left us to remember him by.

Asa Briggs once reacted rather differently when he saw three portraits of historians, belonging to me and hanging together in the Master's Lodge in Caius. The portraits were of a pencil drawing of Joseph Needham by Michael Ayrton, a watercolour of Jack Plumb by John Ward and a preliminary sketch of me by Michael Noakes. "What a fascinating collection of Cambridge academic historians", he said, "Needham, the greatest historical scholar of the twentieth century; Plumb, the greatest historical communicator of the twentieth century; and McKendrick, the greatest teacher of historians of the twentieth century". I quote Briggs not to advertise the excessive generosity of his comments about me but to advertise that, in his immediate and instinctive judgement of Jack, he thought first of him, as did Schama, as an academic historian who opened up a whole new world of popular history written for mass audiences by an established scholar. It was an important corrective judgement that in our recognition of Jack's legacy as a teacher we do not forget his legacy as a writer who reached out to millions of readers. He pioneered the route to respectable popularisation.

In some critics' eyes this was his greatest contribution.

As a pure scholar he never matched the intellectual eminence of Quentin Skinner, the cleverest of all my many pupils and the most distinguished academic from the Plumb school; as a writer he never mastered the range of European languages that Norman Stone, the best and most versatile linguist from the Caius/Christ's school of historians, had at his command; as a professional academic he was not as prolific as Roy Porter; as a public communicator he was comfortably surpassed by Simon Schama. But he served another very important pioneering service for our profession.

He, first among Cambridge historians and together with historians such as A.J.P. Taylor at Oxford and Eric Hobsbawn in London, changed the direction of travel of leading academic historians in that they no longer wrote primarily for their academic peers and secondarily for those they were employed to teach. He, like Taylor, was only too happy to use the mass media, and pioneered the use of television in a way that none of his Cambridge colleagues had succeeded in doing before him.

He has almost inevitably been surpassed by many of those he mentored. He never mastered the use of the radio in the way that some of those who followed him at Christ's, such as David Reynolds and David Cannadine and Linda Colley, have done; he never mastered the use of television in the way that Simon Schama has done; he never mastered the use of the printed media to the extent that Niall Ferguson has done; but most of these would acknowledge that he lead the way. They, and other Cambridge historians such as David Starkey and Mary Beard, have become household names in a way that he never quite did, but they were following a route march that he had laid down before them. And none of them equalled the combination of a distinguished scholar, a pre-eminent teacher, an inspiring supporter and promoter of youthful careers, a sparkling prose writer, a prolific editor, a pioneering populariser of serious history, a successful Master of a Cambridge college and a most memorable character whose colourful life-style intrigued so many distinguished novelists.

Some of his gifts which made him memorable have already been well recognised. Many for instance have paid tribute to Jack's prose. Even those who he felt were hostile to him such as Sir Herbert Butterfield conceded that he had exceptional literary gifts: "he could pile up a beautiful paragraph, add colour to a scene, provide thumbnail sketches of individuals". Those more admiring judges such as Sir David Cannadine paid less restrained tribute to his "buoyant and colourful prose" with which "he could capture a character in a phrase or a sentence, and he was unrivalled in his capacity to set a scene and evoke an atmosphere". Of his early books written in the 1950s, Sir David was even more admiring: "All these books were written with a verve, brio, zest and élan that were unusual among university lecturers and professional historians, they abounded in broad panoramas and memorable vignettes, they showed real insight into people and places, they brought the past vividly alive, and they sold in considerable quantities throughout the English-speaking world and also in foreign translations. They were, in short, the very antithesis of Namier's 'technical' history, and owed much more to the Trevelyan templates of national narrative histories and sympathetic biographies. But the insight into character was all Plumb's own, and so was the scintillating style." Others such as Geoffrey Parker simply referred to his "fabulous natural style".

Many others sang the praises of Jack's "sparkling", "vivid" and (once again) "scintillating" prose. Even those, who found fault with other aspects of his work, often conceded that Jack Plumb was "a historian who could really write", "a born communicator who effortlessly brings life and excitement to the pages of history". The steady flow of royalties still arriving long after his death from his books such as *The First Four Georges* suggest that those literary gifts will long keep his name alive amongst new readers, just as it lives on amongst those millions of readers who bought his books in his lifetime. Those literary gifts and the much-read books that they embellished are a vital and central part of his legacy and should not easily be forgotten.

Jack should also be remembered as a richly colourful character. The variety of adjectives used to describe him (in a single brilliantly perceptive assessment by Sir David Cannadine in *The Proceedings of the British Academy*) gives one some impression of the many different sides to his complex Marmite personality. They offer an instructive and illuminating guide to his contradictory character and career:

"rude', "tight-lipped", "memorable", "ample wealth", "irrepressible vitality", "unabashed delight in the good things of life", "impassioned radical", "militant Thatcherite', "sparkling style", "unrivalled skills", "commanding figure", "a great enabler, patron, fixer and entrepreneur", "complicated, cross-grained and contradictory character", "vivid presence", "elusive personality", "warmth, buoyancy, optimism and hope", "doubt, loneliness, envy and disappointment|", "searing self-knowledge", "ignorant unconcern", "almost endearing", "difficult", "extraordinary activity", "torrential abundance", "more wealthy, more famous, more disappointed and more bad-tempered", "belligerence and combativeness", "provincial and proletarian", "humble origins", "loyal and grateful", "unusual gifts of curiosity and creativity", "eager, ardent and ambitious", "buoyant and colourful prose", "unrivalled", "unsure of himself", "difficult and troubled", "actively embracing Communism", "stimulated, intimidated and not-a-little confused", "depressed and dispirited", "eager to catch up", "short of stature and unprepossessing of appearance", "provincial inferiority", "bisexual", "wounding tongue", "determined pursuit of social acceptance, public fame and worldly success", "winning qualities", "learned how to charm and to captivate, to bully and to manipulate", "very odd", "loyal", "creative", "grateful", "acerbic tongue", "scornful agnosticism", "ferocious", "bitter", "visibly disconcerted", "star performer at the podium", "theatrical, witty, irreverent, iconoclastic", "small, unhappy and insecure", "abominably rude", "high academic standard", "fully informed by recent research", "arresting", "verve, brio and zest", "memorable vignettes", "fury", "rage", "anger, hatred and revenge", "a powerful sense of mission and a vivid sense of *audience*", "rattling narratives and vivid evocations", "covertly aspirational", "unprecedented success", "object of anecdote, gossip and speculation, in ways that few other historians were important or interesting enough to be", "sparkling and bullying", "more relaxed, more buoyant, more confident, more hopeful", "jaunty accessible style", "busy", "creative energy and intellectual curiosity at their peak", "a critical insight and an imaginative sympathy which remain unsurpassed", "flinging down the gauntlet", "more original and more profound", "most highly profiled historian in Cambridge", "tripped at the final hurdle", "ferocious", "undeniably brilliant", "crusty", "deaf, purple, snobbish, choleric and reactionary", "too bitter", "colourful and controversial, complex and conflicted", "wholly unique and genuinely original character", "sometimes splendid, generous and irresistible, sometimes maddening, outrageous and impossible", "a small man who in every other way was larger than life".

This extraordinary kaleidoscopic cascade of adjectival descriptions of his life and work brilliantly conveys the difficulties and contradictions involved in writing about Jack Plumb.

One close colleague summed up the problems of judging him rather more economically when he wrote: "To call Jack Plumb 'Janus faced' is to do him an injustice. He has far more faces than that. If you encountered the benign sides of this multifaceted character you would find a man who was generous, charming, learned, life-enhancing and even inspiring, if you met the malign sides of him you would find him to be quite impossible in whole host of ways".

In truth, his imperfections were as glaring as his gifts were undeniable. For every positive, it was easy to find a negative, and vice versa. The final judgment was almost inevitably a powerfully ambivalent one with the verdict depending heavily on the perspective of the jury. He had what his admirers regarded as forgivable peccadilloes and his enemies regarded as unforgivable character flaws.

To his admirers, his peccadilloes seem relatively insignificant when judged against his positive achievements – his prolific publications, his inspirational teaching of so many outstanding pupils, and his generous personal philanthropy, which, to this day, helps to support so many young research students and so many talented research fellows at Christ's. They understandably see him as a force for good.

To his detractors, his positive achievements will always be tainted and defaced by those personal flaws, which (especially in old age) were so difficult to overlook – his incandescent rage, his abominable rudeness and his ruthless pursuit of his personal goals.

As someone who knew Jack well for over fifty years and who owes him an abiding sense of personal gratitude for encouraging and promoting my career and being such a generous friend to me and my family, I place myself firmly among the admiring camp along with so many of his grateful pupils; but as a colleague of many years standing, who saw his stature amongst his fellow historians in Cambridge being damaged and undermined by his erratic behaviour in the later stages of his life, I cannot deny that he provided his detractors with ample ammunition for their personal dislike and professional hostility.

Jack was well aware of the character flaws of the historical characters he wrote about and well aware of his own. It is hardly surprising that he was attracted to write about and quick to empathise with those he felt shared his own flaws and imperfections, just as he was drawn to write about those in whom he could recognise his own strengths. He clearly identified with the strengths and weaknesses of Sir Robert Walpole, the subject he wrote about at greatest length. He could have been writing about himself when he wrote: "The more that I have come to know this great man, the stronger my admiration has grown. His imperfections were many and glaring. He loved money; he loved power; he enjoyed adulation and hated criticism. But in everything that he did, he was richly varied and intensely human".

The Fellows of Christ's could also well be forgiven for thinking that they were reading about Plumb the Master of Christ's when he wrote of Walpole: "He gloried in his power, spoke roughly if not ungenerously of others, and let the whole world know that he was master".

Cannadine has perceptively argued that Jack must have found it easy to identify with Walpole (and to sympathise with what many others disliked in him) because he must have recognised so much of what his critics had patronisingly identified in himself – "the conquest of provincial obscurity, a delight in politics, patronage and manipulation, a pleasure in food and wine, pictures and porcelain, and a certain parvenu vulgarity".

Jack always found it easy to sympathise with life's rich humanity. As Snow wrote of him: "Creative energy was one of Professor Plumb's most obvious gifts – another is his sense of reality. No other historian can convey so vividly the feeling for how men breathe, eat, breed, enjoy themselves, go about their business, hope, worry and die. He is not too fastidious, he has a brotherly sympathy for the lusts of the flesh and the pride of the eye. All his books are written in what the French used to call the odour of man".

His true friends recognised this in both his life and his writing. They were forgiving of his many imperfections, and admiring of his many gifts. Let us hope that posterity will recognise that the latter were far more important than the former.

We should not forget that he informed us as well as he irritated us, entertained us as well as he enraged us, and inspired us as well as he infuriated us, and above all educated us. Perhaps the rage and intensity of his reactions to his friends and pupils served a greater purpose. Maybe the ferocity was necessary to achieve the inspiration. Maybe his angry insistence that his pupils should aim so high explains the remarkably high success rate of those he taught and promoted. Maybe it was the intensity of his convictions that helped to make him so memorable.

So his memory should live on not simply as a professional historian and a teacher of professional historians but also as an often attractively memorable if always deeply conflicted character, which is why I have written this piece. It is the historian's duty to record the fascination of individual men and women. It is also a duty that includes trying to capture the lives of some of our more interesting colleagues. In the long run it may be of more interest and possibly of more importance than assessing the significance of their historical scholarship. In the short run it can also be far more diverting to most readers. And as John Aubrey so disarmingly said of his own hugely diverting *Brief Lives* (the character and tone of which always greatly appealed to my subject), "How these curiosities would be quite forgot, did not such idle fellows as I am put them down".

Quite how much one does "put down" about the private life of a public figure is always a sensitive matter.

Painfully intimate revelations about Mozart's at-times childish vulgarity and almost infantile silliness (as revealed so vividly in Peter Shaffer's play and film *Amadeus*) jarred unacceptably with those who understandably wished simply to cherish the sublime music he wrote; the even more painful revelations about Picasso's brutal treatment of the women in his life jarred with those who wished simply to acknowledge his artistic genius; the sexual antics of David Lloyd George, when revealed in their full priapic excesses, seemed to some an unnecessary blight on his undoubted record of political achievement; the revelations about the habitual drunkenness of William Pitt ("a three bottle of port a day man") were to some an unwanted intrusion into the life of our youngest-ever Prime Minster; justifiably conscious of his epic achievements and his inspiring rhetoric, not everyone wished to be reminded of the heavy drinking of Winston Churchill or of his preoccupation with the

"Soft underbelly of Europe" which led to his spectacular mistakes at Gallipoli in the First World War and in the Dodecanese in the Second World War; at a much lesser level, many felt that it was unnecessary to reveal that the charming and charismatic Jeremy Thorpe took such alarming sexual and legal risks when his political career seemed to be riding so high; and recounting the extreme violence of the private lives of artistic geniuses such as Bernini and Caravaggio is also felt by some to be an un-necessary revelation of their human failings and an unwanted corrective intrusion of historical fact in the face of their towering achievements. Similarly, not everyone wishes to be reminded that Ben Jonson was a murderer, even fewer wish to be informed that Charles Dickens was a racist who also treated his wife appallingly.

On all such matters, Jack Plumb was always in favour of full disclosure, when death and discretion and the passage of time allowed it.

When discussing twentieth century historians, for instance, not all admirers of Eric Hobsbawm, who rivalled Plumb in his lifetime as one of the most widely read living historians, like to be reminded of the fact that to his critics he was an apologist for mass murder because of his belief that the death of twenty million people would be justified by the hope of a new communist world order. Not all admirers of Roy Porter, who wrote and edited over a hundred books before the age of fifty, are interested in the fact that he was married five times as some if not all of his obituaries claimed. Not all admirers of the great Joseph Needham welcomed the revelation that he lived for many decades in what amounted to a *ménage à trois* with his wife Dophi and his mistress Lu Gwei Chen. Not all admirers of the apparently faultless Owen Chadwick wished to be reminded that as an undergraduate he had trashed a railway carriage in an outburst of drunken vandalism. Not all admirers of the intimidating quality of mind of Hugh Trevor-Roper wished to be reminded of his spectacular error of judgement with regard to the "Hitler Diaries".

Plumb was always full of interest in such details and such revelations. In history as in life, he was always fascinated by how people lived their lives.

In his view, to write about Dylan Thomas without dealing with his drinking would be to falsify history, to write about Jack Kennedy or Bill Clinton without dealing with their sexual infidelities would be to misrepresent their characters.

Indeed Jack Plumb always argued that he was as interested in what manner of man he was studying as he was in their well-known achievements. He was always as interested in Robert Walpole the man, as he was in Walpole the politician – to him they were indivisible. On all such matters, Jack always took the view that it was the historian's duty to present a "warts and all" portrait. Certainly in his own work, he never hesitated to present both the light and the dark sides of the historical characters he described. I hope that those who read this piece will accept that I have tried to follow his lead.

Few would claim that Jack Plumb was an exemplary character, but even fewer would deny that he could be an especially interesting one who lived an unusually full and diverting life. Even now, eighteen years after his death he continues to evoke discussion and controversy. As Bill Noblett said (as he delved ever further into the Plumb archives) "In death, as in life, he never ceases to surprise us".

In revealing many of those surprises, I hope that I will have helped to preserve aspects of his life that have remained so securely hidden, but which deserve to be remembered.

One of the favourite places he chose to be photographed in was in front of the Master's Lodge in Christ's. Revealingly he stood there under the Christ's founder's motto of "Souvent me Souvient", the old French for "Remember me Often". If this memoir helps Christ's alumni and Cambridge historians to recall and remember the manner of man that Jack Plumb was, it will have served its purpose. If it reaches readers who knew nothing of the character and personality of this great historian who provoked so much fevered interest and frustrated speculation in his lifetime, it will have done even better.

40.
ACKNOWLEDGEMENTS

I am very grateful for all the help and advice I have received in writing this memoir. My greatest debt of gratitude I owe to my family – who I feel were in a particularly privileged position to help since they have seen at close quarters the best and the worst of Jack Plumb, often on a daily basis, over the last three or four decades of his life. One daughter laughed out loud as she read this piece; one wept. Both, as professional lawyers, read the piece with the utmost rigour, ruthlessly cutting out anything that they thought might be libellous (quite a bit in the first draft) or too revealing (rather more in the first draft). My wife confined herself to meticulous proof reading and to offering corrective judgments when she thought I was being too generous – which, in her view, was quite often.

To my elder daughter Olivia, I owe especial gratitude, because, when I managed to wipe out completely the first 80,000 words on my computer, she spent many hours putting together most of the original script from scanned earlier paper versions.

I am very grateful, too, for help from many of Jack's friends – old friends, new friends, ex-friends, fond friends and those understandably ambivalent friends like Joyce Williams, who often hailed him as the devil incarnate ("Here comes Il Diabolo, the impossible old bugger") but usually managed to do so in an obviously affectionate manner. Jack always seemed to elicit strong reactions and excite strong and mixed emotions. They covered the whole spectrum from uncritical hero-worship to those who saw him as the incarnation of evil. I suspect that the majority response was a rather intense form of ambivalence. It really was very difficult not to recognise his very real virtues and it was almost impossible (especially in later life) to overlook his glaring vices.

I have been fortunate too in being able to benefit from the help and advice of many who knew him well both personally and professionally. Two Regius Professors (Sir John Elliott and Quentin Skinner) have read early versions of this memoir and made very helpful and encouraging comments.

Sir Keith Thomas reviewed very appreciatively and constructively the 1974 tribute, much of which is incorporated in this much longer piece. His final paragraph in the *Times Higher Educational Supplement* read: "Most remarkable of all is the piece with which the book opens. This is a personal tribute by the editor (Neil McKendrick) to J.H. Plumb himself, originally delivered at a valedictory dinner in Cambridge. Candid, witty and affectionate, it is a *tour de force* in a most difficult genre. No one with any interest in other people can fail to be gripped by this unforgettable picture of creative exuberance". Such a generous reaction to that early portrait of Plumb encouraged me to attempt this more substantial and more nuanced depiction of the man.

Other historians who read various versions of this memoir include Professor Asa Briggs, Professor Philip Grierson, Professor Sir Simon Schama, Professor Sir David Cannadine, Professor Niall Ferguson, Professor Vic Gatrell, Professor Joachim Whaley, Dr Brian Outhwaite, Professor Peter Mandler, Professor John Brewer, Professor James Raven, Professor Norman Stone, Professor Geoffrey Parker, William Noblett, Peter Fullerton, William Young and many others. Many of them saved me from error.

Most helpful by far in terms of the archival evidence was Bill Noblett, who Jack always ranked as the most efficient of those who acted as one of his youthful research assistants. He has an unrivalled knowledge of the Plumb archive in the Cambridge University Library, having, for instance, already read nearly ten thousand of the 18,000 Plumb letters housed there. His help has been invaluable, and many aspects of Plumb's private life would have remained completely hidden without his brilliant detective work. Without his work on Plumb's editorial work for Penguin and for American Heritage, another important aspect of his career would have remained under appreciated. I owe him a great debt of gratitude.

Bill Noblett (photographs of Plumb), June McKendrick(Plumb's birth certificate and photograph of his birthplace), Catherine Twilley of the Christ's College Development Office (portraits of Plumb and Snow) and Dame Rosie Winterton (photographs of Plumb sailing with the Green Wyvern Yachting Club) all helped in proving potential illustrations for this memoir, and I am very grateful to them, even though not all of their suggestions made the final cut.

This memoir is currently being read by others who will be fully acknowledged in due time when and if they respond. It is always especially encouraging when those who have known him best for the longest periods of their lives, who have shared a house with him, shared holidays with him and regarded him as part of the family, recognise the man they knew best in this memoir. So I was especially pleased when my eldest daughter wrote, after reading this piece: "An extraordinary personal memoir of an extraordinary man. Funny, sad, moving, sensitive, engaging and intimate. Jack's complexities shine through every page – brilliant and entertaining, infuriating and exasperating. I recognise every part of him. Jack lives on indeed." (Olivia McKendrick, my biased daughter).

It was also very reassuring when distinguished historians of the calibre of Professor John Brewer and Professor James Raven and Professor Norman Stone, found this memoir "a riveting read", "an astonishing read", "a compelling read" and "an unstoppable read", and urged me to publish it. The adjectives most commonly used by those who have read it were "revelatory" and "almost alarmingly enlightening".

Even more encouraging was the response of Professor Geoffrey Parker, who wrote to say "double surgery has left me unable to work, stand or travel. But I can still read, and last night I read your memoir of Jack at a single sitting. I couldn't put it down: what a wonderful pen portrait you provide of a man who had such an immense impact on both of us. Thank you again for bringing Jack back to life like this." In addition he sent three pages of comment and correction for which I am deeply grateful.

I am also indebted to Dante Campailla (now in his nineties), who knew Jack Plumb very well for an even longer period than I did, for his helpful and supportive reading. I am also indebted to his son, Nicholas Campailla for his encouraging response to this portrait of his godfather.

Since the above list contains friends and historians who could not bear Jack, and some who remained firm admirers, I hope that I have chosen a balanced set of readers. I am, in any case, indebted to them all, but none of them is responsible for any errors of fact or judgement. They are my sole responsibility.

Even some of Jack's closest friends and colleagues who have read earlier versions of the memoir were genuinely astonished by some of the facts that it contains. Professor Philip Grierson wrote "I find it hard to believe that we were near neighbours for so many years and that I knew so little about him and nothing at all about his life outside Cambridge"; Lord Briggs wrote "What a fascinating study. I read it avidly in two long sittings, very surprised that I found so much out that I did not know before, including the details of Jack's early life and of his experiences with women. I knew something of the Leicester background and I knew of his prurient interest in other people's women. But a whole side of Jack's extraordinary life about which I knew nothing was revealed"; Professor Quentin Skinner wrote "Your account includes information (lots of information) that will cause amazement even to people like myself who may have supposed that they knew him fairly well. I had never really known about the family background, and insofar as I ever heard him speak of it, I now see that I was hearing some of the fantasies he wove around the life as he would have liked it to be. I never even knew that there had been a brother, and found your account of that relationship very painful. But what struck me most of all was the number of facts about his later life that left me astonished, The whole story of his war years; the fact that he may have been a father; that he nearly published a novel; that he tried his hand at fiction again in old age. And some of the detail too: about his antics as a destroyer of cars; about his portrait as Master; about the sheer opulence of those holidays. All news to me! I was greatly struck, however, by your emphasis on the extent to which severe and continuous ill health must have played a part in the decline and fall of his personality. Practically everything you say on this score – the effects of the botched prostate operation, the falsely diagnosed cancer, to say nothing of the strokes – was also new to me, and shows that he really did meet those disasters with genuine stoicism. Nor is it in the least surprising, as you rightly stress, that in the face of these mounting disasters he should have slowed down just a little bit in his academic production."

I learned a lot from their responses to my first draft just as I learned even more from the replies to my invitation to attend the celebratory dinner in Jack's memory. Not all of the responses or the replies were mistily nostalgic. One response finished with the unforgiving words "I'll be sorry to miss such lavish hospitality, especially paid for by such a curmudgeon, though I don't think that the "old times" you mention are ones I would care to relive!" Another wrote "In his old age he was as corrupt and as offensive as an over-ripe Stilton and very much not to my taste". Another said "I'm glad that I won't be alive when the diary is published. He lived his life rather like Thomas Creevey wrote. He abused and reviled everyone behind their backs and mocked and chivvied everyone to their faces. In the privacy of his diary he would have been free to give his malevolent side free rein. I shudder to think what his prurient imagination would have dreamt up to record, but one can be sure it would be highly coloured and very unfair. Alas it would probably be as readable as it would be paranoid. He could be memorably malign". Another (a Caian colleague of mine) simply wrote, "I could not bear the man".

I have, I hope, been reasonably frank about Jack's life and character. Close friends and colleagues may well think that there is still much that I have left out. They would, of course, be quite right. I certainly have not said all that I could and, some may argue, should have said, but I have been constrained by my duties as an executor of his will and the restrictions that Jack placed on the use of his archive. To ignore those restraints and flout those restrictions would be illegal as well as indiscreet. I have also been careful to impose my own restraints by not identifying any living lovers of either sex. So the complete picture will have to wait until those embargoes on various parts of his life are successively lifted. Then, and only then, will the full story of Jack Plumb be told in all its arresting and colourful detail. Only then will the full social and sexual range of his life be fully revealed.

It is entirely possible that when the embargoed parts of the Plumb archive are finally lifted, the verdict on the last decades of his writing life may be significantly revised. Rather than the dramatic decline in literary productivity, which some commentators have identified and stressed, we may find that Jack's decision to switch from professional historian to enthusiastic diarist is fully vindicated. He may not have enjoyed the health and the stamina to undertake major historical research, but he did enjoy the delight of exploring a whole new social world, and enjoyed to an even greater extent recording the secrets which his characteristic fascination with other people's private lives revealed. It allowed him to do what he had always craved. It allowed him to write, like a novelist, without the need for archives.

So it is entirely possible that what he called his "posthumous productivity" will match and even surpass the deluge of words he published in his prime. He borrowed the phrase "posthumous productivity" from A.L. Rowse, who in turn had borrowed it from Goethe. Rowse had much in common with Jack. He was a poor working-class grammar school boy of uncertain sexuality who had flourished both professionally and financially from his widely read publications – especially in the States – and moved decisively from left to right in his political affiliations. He too lived a secretive private life and boasted towards the end of it of moving from what he rather quaintly called "homo" to "hetero". Arguably he rose higher than Plumb in terms of public recognition and public honours – a C.H. came his way, which trumped anything which Plumb received – but they shared a mutual recognition of being historians who published prolifically for huge audiences.

I well recall Rowse, when he was staying with Jack at the Old Rectory at Westhorpe, quoting Goethe's dictum that "the true sign of genius was posthumous productivity" and urging Jack to amass and cherish his archive in the way that he had done with his own papers to intrigue future historians. Jack certainly followed his advice and his personal papers in the University Library in Cambridge more than match the Rowse papers in the University of Exeter. The big difference was that Jack, in the last decades of his life, set himself to write a personal chronicle that was specifically designed to remain secret for a very long time. His quite exceptional gifts of extracting confessional autobiographies from unsuspecting confidantes were in his last years fully employed on members of the royal family and the surrounding members of the English aristocracy and the smart set they attracted to entertain them.

We can be certain that there will be no flood of distinguished historical works such as those that have so strikingly enhanced Trevor-Roper's posthumous reputation. Personally I very much doubt that Jack's ambition to be the "Chips" Channon of the late twentieth century will, as he hoped, leave a more lasting literary impact than the prolific professional history he produced in the third quarter of that century. He certainly went to considerable lengths to protect his unpublished diaries from prying eyes, and they will not be finally revealed until very late in this century.

When it does finally emerge it will reveal a great deal more about the private life of Sir John Plumb.

By then I shall long be dead, but, if this memoir provides a useful starting point for my successors, then its preliminary and eyewitness character will have served its purpose.

Neil McKendrick

Lightning Source UK Ltd.
Milton Keynes UK
UKHW021003101019
351299UK00002B/18/P

9 781911 454830